Mastering Management Education

Mastering Management Education

Innovations in Teaching Effectiveness

edited by

Charles M. Vance

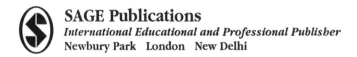
SAGE Publications
International Educational and Professional Publisher
Newbury Park   London   New Delhi

For information address:

SAGE Publications, Inc.
2455 Teller Road
Newbury Park, California 91320

SAGE Publications Ltd.
6 Bonhill Street
London EC2A 4PU
United Kingdom

SAGE Publications India Pvt. Ltd.
M-32 Market
Greater Kailash I
New Delhi 110 048 India

Printed in the United States of America

Library of Congress Cataloging-in-Publication Data

Main entry under title:

Mastering management education: Innovations in teaching
  effectiveness / edited by Charles M. Vance.
       p.   cm.
  Includes bibliographical references.
  ISBN 0-8039-4951-0.—ISBN 0-8039-4952-9 (pbk.)
  1. Management—Study and teaching.   I. Vance, Charles, 1952-
HD30.4.M374   1993
658'.007—dc20   93-14936

93 94 95 96 97 10 9 8 7 6 5 4 3 2 1

Sage Production Editor: Astrid Virding

Contents

Foreword

Major changes are occurring in the field of management and management education. Clearly, the first is the explosion in the generation of new knowledge and practice. Network structures, different types of strategic alliances (within and between organizations), new forms of "contracts" between employer and employee, and different approaches to influence and control are just some of the examples of how today's world is different from the past. This means that what we presently "know" will soon be replaced by even more advanced approaches. Thus what is taught in the classroom can have a distressingly short half-life.

The second major change is the shift in where this new knowledge is being generated. In the past, knowledge (be it in the physical or social sciences) frequently was born in university research labs. It was then the job of faculty (especially in professional schools) to disseminate this knowledge to the practitioner. But now, as much (if not more) knowledge is being generated in the field.

The third significant change is in what is being demanded of employees. A couple of decades ago, we wanted "a few chiefs and many Indians." Remember that the best-selling management book in the 1950s was Whyte's *The Organization Man,* with its emphasis on button-down collars and button-down minds. What was wanted was compliance. Now the focus is on initiative, empowerment, and acting in an innovative and entrepreneurial way.

These changes will force us to modify fundamentally not only what we teach but how we teach. In terms of the latter, the pattern in the past was the (knowledgeable) faculty imparting answers to the passive (ignorant) learners. Interesting, isn't it, how much that pattern paralleled the leadership style of the past decades! The leader was supposed to be all-knowing and put as much effort into controlling subordinates as we have put into controlling students.

But this pattern won't work for at least three reasons. First, the pattern will not function if we no longer have all the final, definitive answers, and if our students come with expertise of their own. We may need to teach about matrix, self-directed work teams, and TQM, but with increasing frequency our students will already have had direct experience in those areas. Both parties now come with their own expertise, which will demand more of a *partner* relationship between instructor and learner than has occurred in the past.

Second, if our "knowledge" will become quickly outdated (if it hasn't already), then we need to do more than teach the facts from research studies. Most important will be teaching learners how they can continue to learn. The *process* of learning how to problem solve may be more important than the specific answer itself. Furthermore, rather than their automatically accepting the validity of what we impart, students need knowledge in how to test the validity of new knowledge that they will soon have to face. Finally, they will increasingly need the ability to generate knowledge on their own.

Third, we need to make sure that we don't send the wrong metamessage. If organization members of the future (present?) need to take initiative and ownership for their own work, are we doing them a service by the tight control (and ensuing passivity) that we demand in most of our classrooms? What does it mean to have an empowered learner?

There are no definitive answers as to how management education will evolve in the next decade, but this book will stimulate teachers to begin to think in different ways. The range of articles not only provides the reader with new approaches but also forces the reader to challenge some basic assumptions about what can (and should) occur in the classroom. Whether or not you agree with the conclusions drawn by each author, you will be stimulated by this array of approaches and ideas.

Charles Vance has done an excellent job of culling through the *Journal of Management Education* (and under its previous names) and editing to produce this fine collection. But after you have finished this volume, don't stop here. There is much richness left in those past issues of the journal (for a sampling, refer to the Appendix). As we advise managers to keep experimenting with new ways of leading, it would benefit us as teachers to take the same advice.

David L. Bradford
Stanford University

Preface

There seems to be a frequent appearance these days of articles and editorials that cry out for an increased priority toward teaching effectiveness at the college level, including an enhanced relevance of the curriculum for meeting real-world professional needs. Change from within the academic community is typified by the recent work *Scholarship Reconsidered: Priorities of the Professoriate,* in which Ernest L. Boyer, president of the Carnegie Foundation for the Advancement of Teaching, persuasively redefines the meaning of scholarship to be much more inclusive of teaching. Forces of change from outside academe are even more persuasive regarding the appropriateness of increasing our focus on teaching effectiveness. Legislative bodies and diverse sources of public criticism have begun to build a clear mandate for greater accountability of educational institutions, including schools of business and management. This mandate is leading toward an increased emphasis on outcome measurement and assessment in higher education—with faculty teaching effectiveness increasingly viewed as an important link to institutional outputs in the form of enhanced student skills and performance capability.

There are also critical curricular implications attendant to the dramatic changes that we face with globalization, international competition, multiculturalism (both abroad and domestic), technological advancements, realignment and redefinition of political and economic systems, and corporate/organizational restructuring for survival and competitive advantage. Many have called for updates and revisions to make that which we teach about organizations and management much more responsive to these significant changes. As typified by the resulting brouhaha at the Harvard Business School over an ill-fitting approach to teaching about diversity, schools will face major problems if they believe they can continue effectively to pour these new potent wines of change into old curricular bottles of instructional content and method.[1]

This book begins to speak to this increasingly recognized need to improve curricular impact through our teaching about organizations, their effective management processes, and their myriad issues and interactions involving people. As the title suggests, this book is a collection of innovative works that contribute to teaching effectiveness. These articles have been taken from past volumes of an important professional publication of the Organizational Behavior Teaching Society, which for the past 20 years has been dedicated to the dissemination of knowledge about teaching effectiveness in the organization and management disciplines. This publication has been known over the years as first *Exchange: The Organizational Behavior Teaching Journal,* then *The Organizational Behavior Teaching Review,* and finally today as *The Journal of Management Education.* This journal and the annual Organizational Behavior Teaching Conference (known with affection by a rapidly growing number as simply OBTC) have been the two major channels of the Society for purveying helpful knowledge and experience on teaching effectiveness. The journal in its early years had a predominant focus on the organizational behavior curriculum but soon broadened its purview to a wider array of business, management, administration, and organizational studies curriculum contexts. The renaming of the journal to *Journal of Management Education* was consistent with the society's efforts to broaden its scope and help make its work more inclusive of other related disciplines.

In 1989 the board of the Organizational Behavior Teaching Society asked me to begin work on a collection of past valuable works from the journal that merit repackaging for broader exposure. It seemed a shame to allow such useful treasures from the past to rest in relative anonymity, especially in these days of an increasing outcry for added value in teaching. As I began to search the journal from its first edition, with helpful guidance and input from several Society members, I found many more gems for publication than could possibly fit into a single volume. The numerous fine, thoughtful articles I encountered dealt with critical issues and creative ideas surrounding broad thematic areas including (1) what should be taught in such topical areas as leadership, power, diversity, and organizational theory and how those particular topics could be taught effectively; (2) how to teach in particular academic disciplines, such as organizational behavior, human resource management, business ethics, strategy, and international management; (3) personal career concerns of faculty; and (4) general methods for effective teaching. With the help of several reviewers, I decided for the present volume to take up the fourth theme of general teaching methods, with hope that future volumes will follow to reintroduce and bring to broader exposure additional excellent works from this and other thematic areas. I have included references to many of these other works in the Appendix. Even if unavailable at your local library, they can likely be obtained through the interlibrary loan and copy services that most libraries provide.

Although the title of this book refers to management education, it reaches well beyond this specific context to the other organizational and administrative science disciplines, including organizational communication, sociology, and organizational psychology as well as health, education, and public administration. The articles included here also have great relevance to the nontraditional adult education contexts of corporate training, management development, and executive education. In most cases, the articles have been edited very little, with changes made primarily in language to reflect the broader scope beyond the organizational behavior curriculum.

This volume is organized into seven sections related to traditional and current teaching methodologies: class lecture and discussion; case method; simulations, video, and high-tech applications; experiential method; learning in groups; participative course management; and teaching about diversity within a diverse learner environment. Each section begins with a thoughtful introduction and recommended readings and resources by one or more recognized authorities on teaching who, by the way, are themselves exceptional teachers (find out for yourself by meeting them and observing them teach at the next Organizational Behavior Teaching Conference). Each section then continues with a selection of innovative articles related to the section's focus. I am impressed by how timeless and thought provoking these articles are. I do not exaggerate in saying that most have spurred a significant change for the better in the courses that I teach in human resource management.

Several individuals have provided helpful input and encouragement for this book: Kate Rogers, John Bigelow, Larry Levine, Richard Trainor, Cynthia Fukami, Peter Vaill, Allen Bluedorn, Peter Frost, Jim Stoner, Cathy Enz, Allan Cohen, Karl Weick, Lyman Porter, and Roy Lewicki. I am also appreciative to Kimberly Perrin, Mary Ann Reed, and Patricia Newkirk for their valuable assistance in preparing and organizing the many distinct parts of this book.

I am particularly pleased to have the past and present editors of the Organizational Behavior Teaching Society's journal—David Bradford, Craig Lundberg, and Larry Michaelsen— included among those providing section introductions. Each has had a significant influence on my personal career and thinking about teaching. Each has also given valuable input for this book. More fundamentally, each has had a significant influence on the nurturing of ideas, shaping of manuscripts, and polishing of articles represented in this book. Whatever contribution I am able to make with this edited volume pales beside their contribution. This book was only possible through their exceptional editorship.

Charles M. Vance
Loyola Marymount University

Note

1. See *The Wall Street Journal*, Oct. 30, 1992, sec. B, p. 1, col. 3.

Reference

Boyer, E. L., *Scholarship reconsidered: Priorities of the professoriate.* Lawrenceville, NJ: Princeton University Press, 1990.

From Lecture to Interactive Discussion

LARRY K. MICHAELSEN
University of Oklahoma

Lecture and *instruction* are nearly synonymous terms on university campuses today. Where I teach at the University of Oklahoma, many faculty members and most students refer to their classes as lectures, and only two types of classes are listed in the schedule bulletin. The vast majority are officially designated as lectures. (The remainder, primarily located in the physical sciences, are designated as labs.) Furthermore, most of our classrooms are designed so that students' attention will be focused on a single spot in the room where the instructor is expected to stand to deliver his or her lecture.

Lecture and discussion methods constitute the most common forms of classroom delivery in colleges today. In fact, many teachers probably consider their approach to be a lecture, although it also includes various levels of class discussion. At least in the United States, there are likely relatively few cases of *pure* lecture delivery (exclusively one-way) without opportunity for questioning and discussion. Still, there is likely too much straight lecturing, resulting in less than optimal learning. The purposes of this first introductory section are to recognize major strengths and limitations of the lecture method and then to provide useful information on how the class learning experience can be enhanced through approaches that promote interactive discussion.

The lecture method of instruction dates back at least to the Middle Ages, when it was used to overcome the extremely limited availability of written materials as a means of transmitting knowledge. During that period, lectures were virtually the only teaching method in use. By tradition, students stood next to their seats and waited so that they could compensate

1

their instructor by placing coins in the hood of his academic robe as he circulated around the room at the conclusion of his lecture.

Then as now, the primary strength of the lecture method is that it can be an efficient mechanism through which ideas can be transmitted from an instructor to his or her students. In addition, an enthusiastic lecturer can accomplish a variety of other significant educational objectives, including the following (see Chism, Jones, Macce, & Mountford, 1989):

1. Lectures are sometimes the only practical means to expose students to subject matter that would otherwise be unavailable (e.g., original research, current developments that have not yet been published in traditional textbooks, and personal insights and experiences of the instructor). Furthermore, information of this type (i.e., information about management issues or "declarative knowledge"; see Anderson 1982, 1983) is the foundation on which the management education process must be built.

2. A lecturer can be very effective at communicating the intrinsic interest of the subject matter. In this case, the value is not so much in what is taught at the time, but what is learned later through additional study and thought.

3. An effective lecture contains information about two important things. One is the subject being taught. The other is a thoughtful, scholarly role model for students to emulate as they conduct their own inquiry into other subjects and at other times.

4. Lectures can be very effective at tailoring material to meet the needs of a particular student audience. This can be done by doing such things as using examples that are familiar to students and injecting humor to maintain student interest and enthusiasm.

Given academic tradition alone, it is quite likely that the lecture method will remain popular for the foreseeable future. And given the above strengths, it is apparent that lectures are here to stay. The question isn't whether or not to use lectures, but what can we do to ensure that lectures are maximally effective when they are used?

Limitations of Lectures

The lecture method does, however, have its limitations with respect to the development of the kind of cognitive skills that students will need in their future jobs. In part, these are the result of limitations of the lecturers. As students will attest, even the most gifted lecturers have a difficult time maintaining student interest and enthusiasm over the entire class period, much less over an entire course. In addition, the lecture method is, by its very nature, subject to a number of problems caused by the capabilities of the learners and/or the nature of the learning process. These include limitations in students' attention spans and the inability of lectures to promote learning beyond the simple acquisition of facts.

STUDENTS' LIMITED ATTENTION SPANS

One of the most serious problems associated with the lecture approach is that lecturers typically speak at the rate of approximately 300 words a minute, whereas students are typically capable of processing two to four times that rate. As a result, unless a lecturer provides enough additional content-related information (gestures, voice modulation, visual aids, etc.), students will experience an attention gap, and their minds will inevitably fill this gap with thoughts about something else. As a result, it is only a matter of time before one of these "fillers" becomes more interesting than the lecture, and the student's mind wanders off in that direction. Although this distraction process typically takes place after about 10 minutes of straight lectures for students in typical college classes (see Penner, 1984), there is some indication from studies of medical school students (Stuart & Rutherford, 1978) that the student maturity and interest in the subject matter might delay the process for another 5 minutes or so.

Thus, even though the primary strength of the lecture method is its usefulness in transmitting information, straight lectures of any substantial length are rarely effective in accomplishing that goal. In fact, the majority of studies seem to indicate that the exclusive use of the lecture method constrains students' learning (Bonwell & Eison, 1991). As a result, even as a means of transmitting information, it is essential to supplement lectures with other types of activities, such as interactive class discussion, if they are to be effective.

HIGHER-LEVEL LEARNING AND PROBLEM-SOLVING SKILLS

Although teaching about the practice of management is an important part of our role as management educators, an aspect of our role that is equally important is developing student ability to use their knowledge in productive ways. Furthermore, educators (e.g., Bloom, 1956; Gagne, 1985; Gagne & Briggs, 1979; Serey & Verderber, 1991) and cognitive psychologists (e.g., Anderson, 1982, 1983) are in clear agreement that (1) learning about concepts and being able to use them are qualitatively different cognitive processes (e.g., Baldwin & Ford, 1988) and (2) developing students' higher level cognitive skills requires a different kind of teaching strategy. Hearing a lecture on how concepts apply to the workplace is likely to have little if any impact on students' ability to use the concepts in their future jobs (e.g., Burke & Day, 1986).

In general, developing the ability to use concepts involves much more of an active process than simply listening. As a result, one of our greatest challenges is creating teaching strategies that allow students to practice using the concepts we want them to understand (e.g., Bonwell & Eison, 1991; Wexley & Baldwin, 1986). Failing to do so would be somewhat like expecting students be able to ski after having watched the winter Olympics on television. Thus, to be effective, lectures must be supplemented with opportunities—such as interactive class discussions—for students to become actively involved with the concepts being presented.

Improving Lectures

The articles selected for this section provide a number of perspectives and practical ideas for increasing the effectiveness of instruction by building in opportunities for students to become more actively involved in the learning process. William Ewens offers the metaphor of the teacher and the students sitting astride a log in a comfortable, informal setting for learning and sharing; he suggests ways that discussions can create a parallel learning opportunity. In his article, Mark Kriger points out the importance of questions as a means of enhancing learning and provides both conceptual and practical ideas for increasing the effectiveness of the questioning process in leading class discussions. Dennis Gioia makes a distinction between participation (being actively involved) and contribution (increasing others' learning) and offers a number of ideas for ensuring that student involvement is focused in a way that promotes learning. Finally, Donald Bowen, Joseph Seltzer, and James Wilson examine an important area that is often neglected in the primary emphasis in lectures and class discussion on cognitive and rational processes. In their article, Bowen and colleagues look at different forms of emotional reactions that we may encounter in our students and in ourselves as a result of increased personal and active involvement in the learning process. They suggest how we might deal with these volatile situations in a way that leads to productive learning.

ADDITIONAL RESOURCES

Management educators are not the only ones who are concerned with increasing the ability to present material in ways that increase learning. In fact, we have a great deal to learn from other sources. One source that I strongly recommend is *Teaching Tips for the Beginning College Teacher,* by Wilbert McKeachie (1990). McKeachie provides ideas to improve lectures, ranging from course design issues to detailed and practical suggestions for adding spice and clarity to presentations. Another source is *Active Learning: Creating Excitement in the Classroom*, by Bonwell and Eison (1991). The strength of their book is that it contains numerous ideas for improving lectures and class discussions by increasing the extent to which students are actively involved in the learning process.

References

Anderson, J. R. (1982). Acquisitioning cognitive skill. *Psychological Review, 89,* 369-406.

Anderson, J. R. (1983). *The architecture of cognition.* Cambridge, MA: Harvard University Press.

Baldwin, T. T., & Ford, J. K. (1988). Transfer of training: A review and directions for future research. *Personnel Psychology, 41,* 63-105.

Bloom, B. S. (1956). *Taxonomy of educational objectives: Cognitive and affective domains.* New York: McKay.

Bonwell, C. C., & Eison, J. A. (1991). *Active learning: Creating excitement in the classroom* (ASHE-ERIC Higher Education Report No. 1). Washington, DC: ASHE-ERIC.

Burke, M. J., & Day, R. R. (1986). A cumulative study of the effectiveness of managerial training. *Journal of Applied Psychology, 71,* 232-245.

Chism, N., Jones, C., Macce, B., & Mountford, R. (1989). *Teaching at the Ohio State University: A handbook.* Columbus: Ohio State University Center for Teaching Excellence.

Gagne, R. M. (1985). *The conditions of learning and the theory of instruction* (4th ed.). New York: Holt, Rinehart, & Winston.

Gagne, R. M., & Briggs, L. R. (1979). *Principles of instructional design* (2nd ed.). New York: Holt, Rinehart, & Winston.

McKeachie, W. (1990). *Teaching tips for the beginning college teacher* (8th ed.). Boston: D. C. Heath.

Penner, J. G. (1984). *Why many college teachers cannot lecture.* Springfield, IL: Charles C Thomas.

Serey, T. T., & Verderber, K. S. (1991). Beyond the wall: Resolving issues of educational philosophy and pedagogy in the teaching of management competencies. In J. D. Bigelow (Ed.), *Managerial skills: Explorations in practical knowledge* (pp. 3-19). Newbury Park, CA: Sage.

Stuart, J., & Rutherford, R. J. D. (1978). Medical student concentration during lectures. *Lancet, 2,* 514-516.

Wexley, K. N., & Baldwin, T. T. (1986). Management development. *Journal of Management Development, 12,* 277-294.

Suggested Readings

Albanese, R. (1989). Competency-based management education. *Journal of Management Development, 8,* 66-76.

Hill, W. F. (1982). *Learning thru discussion: Guide for leaders and members of discussion groups* (2nd ed.). Beverly Hills, CA: Sage.

One
_____

Teaching Using Discussion

WILLIAM EWENS
Michigan State University

In the teaching literature, *discussion* usually refers to a diverse body of teaching techniques that emphasize participation, dialogue, and two-way communication. The discussion method is one in which the instructor and a group of students consider a topic, issue, or problem and exchange information, experiences, ideas, opinions, reactions, and conclusions with one another.

For many of us, our image of education involves more than the mere transfer of information. We want students to formulate applications of abstract principles, to gain practice in logic and thinking, to give us prompt feedback, and to develop the appetite for further learning. In short, our images of effective teaching involves the exchange of ideas between instructor and student—the Socratic model of "Mark Hopkins and a student at two ends of a log" (Goldsmid & Wilson, 1980).

Available research evidence also supports the general effectiveness of discussion techniques. Compared with the traditional lecture method, discussions elicit higher levels of reflective thinking and creative problem solving, including synthesis, application, and evaluation. There is also evidence that information learned through active discussion is generally retained better than material learned through lecture. Moreover, students often prefer to participate in discussions rather than be passive learners in a lecture (McKeachie, 1978).

Summarizing the advice of educational authorities (see the References and Suggested Readings), here are several strategies for teaching using

This chapter originally appeared in *Exchange: The Organizational Behavior Teaching Journal,* Volume 10, Issue 3.

discussion. Discussions vary widely across topics, cases, and instructors, and there are few general truths that apply to all teaching situations. With these qualifications in mind, however, here are some of the main points emphasized by experts on teaching.

Proper Discussion Techniques

If our primary purpose as teachers is to communicate specific information, perhaps the lecture would be more successful. And if we desire extensive participation by all members of our class, perhaps we should break the class into smaller groups (dyads, triads, or larger "buzz groups") for part of the period. Classroom discussions, as typically practiced, are a middle-of-the-road teaching technique for instructors wanting moderate levels of student participation (Zander, 1979).

Beginning Classroom Discussions

Discussion implies involvement. Ideally, the student and instructor collaborate to meet mutual goals. Here are some ideas for starting discussions:

- Start the discussion by posing a broad, open-ended question, one that has no obvious right or wrong answer but that will stimulate thought.
- Begin with a concrete, common experience, a newspaper story, a film, a slide, a demonstration, or a role-play.
- Analyze a specific problem. Ask students to identify all possible aspects of the topic or issue under consideration.
- Be benignly disruptive. Start the discussion with a controversy by either causing disagreement among students over an issue or by stating objectively both sides of a controversial topic (Goldsmid & Wilson, 1980; Berquist & Phillips, 1975).

Eighteen Discussion Suggestions

Listed below are some further suggestions for promoting useful classroom discussions:

1. *Discussion requires preparation.* For thought-provoking issues, allow students time to be prepared. Give the questions ahead of time or at least allow students time for reflection before they talk. Also remember to give yourself plenty of preparation time before the class begins.

2. *Break large problems into smaller, more specific problems.* Discussions often appear disorganized because different students are working on different parts of the problem and thus become frustrated by what seem irrelevant comments by other students. Thus the teacher should break the discussion problem into smaller parts, so that all students are working on the same part of the problem at the same time. The teacher then attempts to keep the students aware of the discussion problem that is the current focus. For many problems, typical steps might include formulating the problem, suggesting propositions or hypotheses, getting relevant data, and evaluating alternative solutions (Maier, 1963).

3. *Ask questions at different levels of abstraction.* Don't get stuck at some particular level of analysis, say at the factual level. Also ask questions that require analysis, application, synthesis, and evaluation.

4. *Provide encouragement and praise for correct answers and risk taking.* Be positive, nonjudgmental, and supportive. Encourage participation by at least a smile, a verbal or nonverbal acknowledgment, or a few words of encouragement. Avoid inappropriate moralizing, preaching, threatening, warning, judging, ridiculing, or blaming. Such practices tend to stifle effective discussion.

5. *Don't use unnecessary jargon.* Explain your terminology. Phrase your questions carefully so that they will not confuse students.

6. *Adopt the 10-second rule.* Learn to be patient and to tolerate silence. Silence, after all, can be a powerful motivator for speaking. Practice waiting as long as 8 to 10 seconds for responses to difficult, thought-provoking questions.

7. *Learn to paraphrase.* Paraphrasing, sometimes called *active listening,* involves interpreting what students say, reformulating it, and presenting your interpretation back to the student in your own words. It is a method of communicating understanding and involvement that, if practiced conscientiously, involves more than merely repeating or parroting the student's comment (Gordon, 1974).

8. *Allow students to answer.* Resist the temptation to answer your own questions.

9. *Learn students' names.* Learning their names displays your concern and lets students know you care about them as individuals. Although simple, it is one of the most important techniques to promote discussion. If you have trouble remembering, use devices such as assigned seating or name tags during the first 2 weeks to help you and the students learn each other's names.

10. *Seat students facing one another.* Seating students in rows may reduce discussion among them. Seat them in a circle to promote classroom interaction.

11. *Adopt the role of troubleshooter.* Reduce ambiguity by presenting facts or requesting necessary examples, by refocusing or redirecting the discussion, by summarizing, or by preventing premature closure of the discussion.

12. *Handle disagreements creatively.* List the pros and cons of an issue on the blackboard, allow representatives of differing points of view to debate, make people temporarily argue from a perspective opposite from their own, or employ other techniques to reduce destructive classroom conflict.

13. *Promote openness and honesty.* Try not to be defensive. Don't be afraid to admit ignorance, and learn to say, "I don't know." Use alternative views as teaching resources, and try to promote a friendly atmosphere in the classroom.

14. *Promote student self-help.* Help students learn to evaluate their own progress and to identify discussion problems and barriers that have developed. Encourage good student thought habits and help students identify their own mistakes.

15. *Encourage student interaction.* Encourage students not only to ask you questions but also to react to one another's ideas. Promote the idea of education as a democratic endeavor in which people learn together. Ask students to comment on each other's remarks and ask them to respond directly to one another.

16. *Be a positive role model.* Actions are often more important than words. Be careful to provide an example through your actions of your most important values.

17. *Draw on student skills.* Draw on the tremendous reservoir of existing skills and practical life experiences already present in the class. Get individual class members to contribute to problem areas for which they have special knowledge or experience.

18. *Summarize, summarize, summarize.* Periodically, and at the end of the class period, appraise the progress of the class by summarizing the main points of the discussion. Restate issues, point out diversions and barriers, and praise classroom successes.

References

Berquist, W., & Phillips, S. (1975). *A handbook for faculty development.* Washington, DC: Council of Small Colleges.

Goldsmid, C., & Wilson, E. (1980). Discussion. *Passing on sociology: The teaching of a discipline.* Belmont, CA: Wadsworth.

Gorden, T. (1974). *Teacher effectiveness training.* New York: Wyden.

McKeachie, W. (1978). Organizing effective discussion. *Teaching tips* (7th ed.). Lexington, MA: D. C. Heath.

Maier, N. (1963). *Problem-solving discussions and conferences: Leadership methods and skills.* New York: McGraw-Hill.

Zander, A. (1979). *The discussion period in a college classroom* (Memo to the Faculty, 62). Ann Arbor, MI: Center for Research on Learning and Teaching.

Suggested Readings

Eble, K. (1988). *The craft of teaching: A guide to mastering the professor's art* (2nd ed.). San Francisco, CA: Jossey-Bass.

Hill, W. (1982). *Learning thru discussion: Guide for leaders and members of discussion groups* (2nd ed.). Beverly Hills, CA: Sage.

Thompson, G. (1974). *Discussion groups in university courses: Introduction.* Unpublished manuscript, University of Cincinnati Faculty Resource Center, distributed by ASA Teaching Resources Center.

Two
_____

The Art and Power
of Asking Questions

MARK P. KRIGER
State University of New York at Albany

There comes a time when one asks even of Shakespeare, even of Beethoven, is this all? (Aldous Huxley)

The assumption behind this article is that the process of asking questions in the classroom can be one of the most powerful, if not *the* most powerful, tool available to an instructor or discussion leader. "What are the issues here?" "What options for action does X have?" "What should Y do in this situation?" "What business is this company in?" These and other questions, when asked at the appropriate moment and with the right intent, can set in motion a process of inquiry that can transform a student or an entire classroom into a state of aliveness and greater understanding, a feeling that something greater is being created in the classroom. What was simply case data or a set of dry theories becomes infused with new insight and experience. Why are questions powerful? How do questions transform experience and the process of understanding?

What Is a Question?

A question is an engagement of attention. It is defined by the *Oxford English Dictionary* as "the act of asking, investigating, or inquiring into some problem or doubtful matter. . . . To inquire [is] to seek for truth,

This chapter originally appeared in *The Organizational Behavior Teaching Review,* Volume 14, Issue 1.

knowledge, or information." Thus to ask a question is to engage in a process of which the end result is the acquisition or realization of truth and/or knowledge. The very asking of a question presupposes that the questioner is looking for a state of understanding, or a state of affairs, that is currently not present. Here lies the fundamental power of questions: They are the means by which we, both teachers and students, seek to transform our understanding of the world and ourselves.

Toward the aim of understanding the power and dynamics of question asking in the classroom, this article presents: (1) a hierarchy of questioning content, (2) a breakdown of the ingredients of the question-asking process for classroom discussion, and (3) a typology of kinds of questions as tools. The overall objective will be to provide for instructors who lead class discussions a deeper understanding of some of the complexity and diversity of elements that go into the construction of questioning dynamics.

Several assumptions and beliefs underlie this discussion. First, the ability to ask good questions, properly timed, is a critical teaching (and managerial) skill to be mastered by instructors in teaching (and by managers in managing). Second, instructors can use a question to teach, to control, to punish, to transform, or to help someone to learn to inquire. Given this multifaceted nature of questions, it is important for teachers (and managers) to understand and to explore the range of possibilities that questions present the skillful teacher or communicator. Finally, I believe that questions are often the most visible part of a much larger learning and inquiry process that is only partially undertaken in any given classroom setting because of a variety of constraints: the subject focus, the class needs, instructor biases and wishes, class sentiments, the abilities of individuals (including the teacher's), and time constraints. The use of questions in managerial settings has a number of correlates; however, this issue is beyond the scope and intent of the present article (see Fisher, 1987).

Kasulis (1982) notes that there are three primary dimensions to questioning: (1) what is asked (content), (2) how it is asked and when (process), and (3) to whom the question is asked. He states that "the discussion leader's primary tool is the question. For a question to be effective, it must ask about the right issue, at the right time, of the right person" (p. 42). The next three sections will expand on each of these three dimensions and examine the content, the process, and the tools of questioning.

Levels of Question-Asking Content

Questions serve a variety of purposes. On one level, they are a means for inquiry and focusing attention that allow one to probe into the nature

Figure 2.1. Levels of inquiry (questioning content).

of things, whether they be cash flows, individuals, organizations, or worldviews. There are several modes of question asking, which vary from more concrete to more abstract in content: (1) inquiry into what is the issue or problem at hand (having facts), (2) analysis of a case or situation in conjunction with relevant theories and models, (3) inquiry into what can or should be done (doing or action), (4) inquiry into what is or can be (being). The objects of these modes of inquiry can thus be organized into a series of levels with questions of *being* at one end and questions of *having* at the other (Fig. 2.1).

What is the utility of looking at things in this way? First of all, it provides a convenient way of separating different classes of question asking that can occur.[1] At the factual level, much of the process in class discussion is often initially spent trying to understand what we have in front of us in the way of factual information (i.e., having the same data) and what assumptions we have about the data. By asking questions at this level the instructor can (1) get agreement or disagreement on the factual data at hand and (2) probe the students' assumptions and perceptions of the people, organization systems, and situation at hand.

At the next level of abstraction—analysis—the students and instructor can engage in a process of analyzing and attempting to understand larger meanings from the data and information available. At this level the class is attempting to form higher order abstractions and generalizations from the case. The major question here is, "How are we to analyze the situation?" Relevant theories, models, and frameworks can be and often are brought to the analysis to help organize the data into coherent patterns of understanding.

The next level is that of action and prescription: for example, "What are the alternatives for action?" Here the mode of inquiry changes from data

TABLE 2.1
Twelve Modes of Question-Asking Content

Level	Past	Present	Future
Being	What could you (the organization) have been?	Who are you?	What should you be?
Doing (action alternatives)	What could you have done?	What are you doing?	What should you do?
Analyzing	Were other methods of analysis available?	What is our analysis of what is going on here and why?	How should we analyze the situation?
Having (resources, information, or data)	What could you have had or acquired?	What is the case here?	What should you have or acquire (as regards information or resources)?

and analysis to action. The normative version of this question is, "what should X do in this situation?" At this level, the class is visualizing and investigating the alternatives of what can and should be done from the vantage point of different key protagonists.

The final level deals with being. Appropriate questions at this level are, "What business(es) is this organization in?" "If you were Mr. Post, vice president of purchasing, what would you be feeling in the situation at the end of the case?" This level deals with why and how things are the way they are. Questions at this level need to be properly framed in a context because they can be highly abstract. For example, in a session on career development and job change, an instructor might ask students to address the question, "Who are you, in terms of your career?" or "What do you aspire to be?"

With the addition of time as a dimension, the preceding having-analyzing-doing-being hierarchy takes on an additional dimension of complexity by leading the questioning process into past, present, and future modes (Table 2.1). For example, the question, "What is X doing, in the role of general manager, to build an effective team?" has correlates in the past and future tenses. "What could X have done?" asks the class to be in the role of Monday-morning quarterback and "What should X be doing (to build an effective team)?" places the class in the role of trying to manage the future based on their assumptions, knowledge, and perceptions of the present.

Thus the instructor has the option of moving the class up and down a ladder of abstraction (i.e., ontological classes of having-analyzing-doing-being) and across a temporal dimension of past-present-future. How does this translate into the pragmatics of an effective classroom discussion?

The Process of Question Asking

There are at least nine ingredients to the process of question asking. The mix is determined by the instructor's objective, the task to be performed by the question, and the current situation in the classroom. These include

1. Why the question is being asked—intent
2. What is being asked—content
3. Length of question, length of response requested, and quickness of the question
4. Linkage to previous question(s), relation to previous discussion, and timing of the question (when it is asked)
5. To whom in the class the question is directed
6. Tools and resources available (e.g., availability of lecture material, types of questions, video material, addenda to a case, handouts)
7. Willingness of the instructor and the class to venture into the unknown or potentially hazardous areas of inquiry (e.g., explore male-female work relations, or political, religious, or racial issues)
8. Use of nonverbal behavior, which includes
   A. Paralanguage: the tone in which the question is asked (voice qualities, volume, speech rate, pitch, laughing, yawning)
   B. Gestures, body language, facial expression, and eye behavior
   C. Proxemics: movement of the instructor within the classroom and use of space (e.g., movement toward the class tends to either heighten intimacy or increase tension, depending on the accompanying gestures; movement away from the class creates an emotional distancing) (Fisher, 1981)
9. The interaction effects of all the preceding elements and management of them into an appropriate gestalt.

How does an instructor decide among the above ingredients to come up with a particular line of questioning at a particular time? In many ways it is a skill that is more an art than a science, because the variables are too numerous to decide in a linear fashion in the heat of the moment. The skilled instructor, in considering whether a question is a good one and what to do next, is constantly assessing implicitly or explicitly the above nine ingredients with a corresponding self-directed question (Table 2.2).

There is no one right answer to the set of questions in Table 2.2; however, the questions are important to consider and have in mind as the class

TABLE 2.2
Self-Directed Questions About Class Process

1. What are the *objectives, aims,* and *intent* of the class session? (to address the issue of why a particular question)
2. What are the *needs* of the class?
3. What is the *climate* and *tempo* of the class?
4. *Where are we* now in the process plan(s) for the class?
5. *Who should I call on* and what is the ability, experience, and personality of the individual I am considering calling on? (i.e., How will he or she likely respond to my question, given what I know of their experience, personality, and skills? Will they add to depth of the classroom-learning experience?)
6. What *other resources* are available? (e.g., the use of lecture material, video material, addenda to a case)
7. How far do I wish to move from *safety* into *unknown* or hazardous territory? (i.e., Is the question going to take us into a sensitive area such as male-female work relations?)
8. What *nonverbal behavior* (i.e., gestures; body language; tone, pitch, volume, and speed of speech; eye behavior; and movement within the classroom) should I use to accentuate or play down the question?
9. Does what I am about to do or ask feel right?

discussion unfolds. It is also clear that an instructor does not have the time to ask these questions sequentially in any given situation. The classroom process is a dynamically moving gestalt in which the appropriateness of the next step in the process is often intuitive and felt rather than deliberated on at length. There simply is not time to think out all or many of the alternatives.

A Typology of the Kinds of Questions as Tools

As mentioned earlier, questions are multifaceted. They can either cut to the heart of a discussion, skillfully probe the subject at hand, transform a student's self-understanding, or punish a student for a wrong approach. Questions of this latter kind are included in the typology because there are classroom situations in which recourse to punishment and control are necessary. For example, if a student continues to dominate a discussion, taking the class further and further away from the subject despite nonverbal signals from the instructor, then use of a question to stop the student from going further may be warranted. There are ways of asking questions that are both nonthreatening and threatening (Sudman & Bradburn, 1982, chaps. 2-3). However, the use of such punishing or threatening questions should generally be exercised sparingly or excessive polarization of the class may result in dysfunctional or unwanted conflict.[2]

Alternatively, question asking is an ancient technique for leading another person to a different or higher level of understanding. The method of questioning used by Socrates is a well-known example of this. On the one hand, Socrates sometimes used questions laced with sarcasm to chide or to goad the person being questioned. On the other hand, the eventual and implicit intent of Socrates was to lead a student toward the good, toward virtuous action, and toward true understanding. Implicit in the question asking of instructors is a transformed state of affairs for which the student cognizes and understands a set of issues from a broader or higher level of awareness and, subsequently, will be able to use this broader awareness to act more skillfully. However, the transformational step from knowing about (theory) to knowing how (skillful action) is not a simple or straightforward process.[3]

Given the above, 28 kinds of questions are offered as tools or resources for use in the class discussion process (Table 2.3). This list is not intended to be exhaustive.

To Question or Not to Question

Dillon (1981, 1983) found that a question-answer relationship between instructor and student can foster in the respondent dependency, passivity, and reactivity. Dillon discovered that if the pace of questions is too fast (i.e., too many questions per unit of time) then students have little time to think, explain, or explore their understanding. Dillon (1983, p. 12) points out that when a teacher uses questions there are several natural consequences:

1. When individuals are asked a question, they are socially constrained to respond to it
2. When asked a question, a person usually responds with only that information specified by the question
3. The questioner-teacher enjoys the right to speak again
4. Respondents (usually) address their remarks to the questioner, not to someone else.

These consequences raise the issue of the appropriate use of questions. An instructor has multiple roles corresponding to these four consequences. First, the instructor is socially constraining a student to respond. Many students feel uncomfortable when asked a question for fear of responding incorrectly or inappropriately. Second, the instructor needs to encourage and reward students for going beyond the immediate question to deeper levels of analysis and understanding. This process usually takes a number

TABLE 2.3

Examples of Questions for Use as Tools in the Classroom Discussion

A. Opening Questions

    1. General opener: "John, will you please lead off with an analysis of the situation?"

    1a. General opener with a specific assumption or from a specific point of view.

    2. Solicitation of issues or questions: "What are the issues in this situation?" or "What questions does the present problem situation raise?" (Instructor writes down an enumeration of issues or questions on the blackboard for further exploration.)

    3. Action question: "What would you do if you were James Edwards, at the end of the case?"

B. Analysis Questions

    4. Question asking for analysis: "What theories, models, or methods might we use to analyze the present problem or case?"

    5. Question asking for evaluation of and/or critique of what has been said: "Does anyone see another way of evaluating/analyzing what has been discussed so far?"

C. Action Questions

    6. Action question: "What would you do in this situation?"

    7. Action question from a specific vantage point: "What would you do in this situation as the vice president of marketing?"

    8. Change of assumption(s) and/or facts followed by asking, "Now what would you do?" (This is especially useful to change the class to an action focus.)

    9. Normative action question: "What should X do now?"

D. Questions That Redirect the Class Process

    10. Information followed by a question by which the instructor is looking for the next level of analysis: "Our calculations show that sales have been increasing by 50% per year. What impact will this have on the various functional areas over the next 5 years if this trend continues?"

    11. Open-endedness of the question: soliciting a yes-or-no response versus an open-ended response.

    12. Lengthy question that helps set the stage for the student, which is especially appropriate for students who are shy or are intimidated by classroom participation. (One caution: the lengthy question tends to give away the instructor's preferred vantage point and some of the answer.)

    13. General question that asks for disagreement: "Does anyone disagree?" (This type of question builds opposition and can be used to increase the level of creative tension in the classroom.)

    14. Question directed to a specific person asking for agreement or disagreement: "Bill, do you agree with the previous answer?"

    15. General query for other viewpoints: "Are there any other viewpoints?" (This type of question is useful when the class has been going down a perceived dead end or has been supporting only one position.)

    16. Specific question, which focuses discussion when the class has been excessively diffuse: "What now?"

    17. Role-playing: "Frank, will you play the role of the president?"

continued

TABLE 2.3
Continued

---

18. Factual question, or asking for more data or specific analysis concerning the case: "What is the debt/equity ratio for this company?"

19. Question asking for a lengthy and/or detailed answer: "Will you elaborate in more detail?"

20. Question that challenges and/or probes a particular student: "Sharon, do you really think that your solution will work in the long term?"

21. Sarcastic question, which puts the pressure on, tests the depth of conviction and the level of thinking.

22. The zinger, or the use of a series of questions to get a student to go out on a limb and then asking a question that recalls a previous piece of information that contradicts the position the student has just affirmed. (Essentially, one cuts the limb off after having forced the student to step onto it.)

23. Reopener: "Are there any further questions?"

24. Summation or closure question, for which the instructor asks for a student to summarize the major points of the discussion: "Margaret, if you had to choose two or three themes that were the most important findings in our discussion today, what would they be?"

E. Metaquestions (Questions About the Class Process or Content)

25. Opinion questions, which ask for the beliefs, opinions, or perceptions of the class concerning the case analysis or subject at hand: "John, what are your thoughts about the analysis so far?"

26. Feedback question; this is often used at a point in the class at which several directions may be taken: "Where should we go from here in our discussion?"

27. Process question: "Mary, are you aware of whether or not the class is listening to what you are saying?" or "How many of you wish to change the focus of our discussion?"

28. Question concerning previous discussion: "What did Bill (the person speaking 2 minutes ago) say?"

NOTE: Some of these questions may fit under several subheadings.

of class sessions to build supportive norms for mutual problem solving as well as to build norms for disagreement and conflict among students. Third, the instructor can always interrupt the class discussion with an observation, a question, or a direct command, because the instructor usually has multiple power bases (i.e., legitimate, referent, reward, coercive, and expert bases of power). Finally, the instructor is often trying to encourage respondents to address their remarks to each other rather than always to go through the teacher as an intermediary. When this student-to-student dialogue occurs, a class is often engaged in mutual problem solving rather than being highly dependent on the instructor for learning. This is one of the major advantages of case discussion (Christensen, 1981).

As a result, it can be just as important for an instructor to know when *not* to ask a question as to know when and how to question.

Dillon (1983) suggests that "a single, well-formulated question is sufficient for an hour's discussion. It will take the teacher some time, thought, and labor to prepare this question for class" (p. 22). This may be an extreme for many instructors, but should nonetheless be considered because the tendency to overquestion is strong.

There is also a vital distinction to be made between problem solving and problem finding. Mackworth (1965) notes that problem finding and formulating and stating new questions can be more important than problem solving. He posits that problem finders are much scarcer than problem solvers, in part because problem finding requires originality and creativity. Macworth (1965) states:

> The real mark of the basic researcher is that the unforeseen problem is a joy and not a curse . . . an uncharted hill is not an obstacle; it is a new height to be scaled because it provides a different viewpoint from which innumerable details can be seen in perspective. (p. 54)

The questioning process allows us to scale new hills by problem finding, whether we are basic researchers, students, or managers.

In the discussion of a particular problem situation case or applied concept the previously mentioned ontological levels of action and being have great importance. It is at these two levels that questions can have the greatest transformative power: Questions can be used to shift discussion up (and down) the ladder of abstraction—from having data to questions of being—as well as to shift discussion across temporal dimensions from the present into the future or the past. By skillfully timing and asking questions an instructor can potentially transform students at several levels:

1. The level of facts and their acquisition
2. The level of analytical ability
3. The level of action and doing
4. The level of being: coming to a deeper understanding of who we are

However, most of us (including instructors) are the products of years of involvement in primary-, secondary-, and college-level courses where questions have been used not to engage students at the higher ontological levels of action and being but to make sure that information and analytical problem-solving techniques are mastered. It is when we consider questions as transformative tools that question asking can become truly self-empowering. However, if an instructor asks too many questions, a unilateral class process tends to arise by which the instructor or discussion leader becomes the center of the exchange. By selectively asking questions, providing adequate space for response, and encouraging students to build on and respond to each others' comments, an instructor can foster a more collaborative and multilateral process. In the role of orchestrator of the discussion and problem-finding process, as opposed to being an imparter of information and factual knowledge, the discussion leader becomes a balancer and manager of several ongoing dynamics or key tensions, which can turn into false dichotomies if the instructor is not careful:

content	process
open-ended questioning	close-ended questioning
creativity	control
analysis	activity
rewarding	punishing

The skillful managing of these tensions by the discussion leader can be a further source of learning for students who will have to manage a similar set of dynamics and tensions in the workplace.[4]

Conclusion

Effective question asking, like conducting an orchestra, balances the situational needs of the moment. Not only is the content of the question important but so are process and timing integral to effective question asking. Ideally the participants come to feel that the class has engaged in a discussion that builds from the opening to the ending. In such a classroom, the inquiry into and exploration of subject matter becomes enlivening, relevant, and enlarges understanding of the subject matter and oneself.

A well-timed question is one of the major resources available to a discussion leader. Alternatively, there are few things as deadly in the classroom as a poorly timed question (i.e., a question that is at odds with the objectives, the needs of the class, or the present situation). Effective question asking can create a learning experience that not only is remembered for a long time by the participants but also changes one or more of the students in a fundamental way—to be more effective and skillful managers and/or better human beings.

The skillful instructor often teaches more through example than through what is said. The more sensitive a teacher is to the types of questions, their ingredients, and their intent, the more students come to feel that they, and not the instructor, have led the discussion. At this point, the discussion leader can leave the center stage and the students can begin asking questions of one another and on their own.

Notes

1. These levels are rarely looked at sequentially in a class discussion nor should they necessarily be.
2. See Bales et al. (1979) for an extensive discussion of dysfunctional polarization and conflict in groups.
3. See Roethlisberger (1968, 1977) for extensive discussion of this process.
4. See Roethlisberger (1968) for his discussion of false dichotomies.

References

Bales, R. F., Cohen, S. P., & Williamson, S. A. (1979). *SYMLOG: A system for the multiple level observation of groups.* New York: Free Press.

Christensen, C. R. (1981). *Teaching by the case method.* Boston: Harvard Business School, Division of Research.

Dillon, J. T. (1981). To question and not to question during discussion. I: Questioning and discussion. *Journal of Teacher Education, 32*(5), 51-55.

Dillon, J. T. (1983). *Teaching and the art of questioning.* Bloomington, IN: Phi Delta Kappa Educational Foundation.

Fisher, D. (1981). *Communication in organizations.* St. Paul, MN: West.

Fisher, D. (1987). Questioning and management. *Questioning Exchange, 1*(3), 171-176.

Kasulis, T. P. (1982). Questioning. In M. M. Morganroth (Ed.), *The art and craft of teaching* (pp. 38-48). Cambridge, MA: Harvard University Press.

Mackworth, N. H. (1965). Originality. *American Psychologist, 20,* 51-66.

Roethlisberger, F. J. (1968). *Man-in-organization.* Cambridge, MA: Harvard University Press.

Roethlisberger, F. J. (1977). *The elusive phenomena: An autobiographical account of the field of organizational behavior at Harvard Buisness School* (G. F. F. Lombard, Ed.). Boston: Harvard University, Graduate School of Business Administration, Division of Research.

Sudman, S., & Bradburn, N. M. (1982). *Asking questions.* San Francisco: Jossey-Bass.

Suggested Readings

Dillon, J. T. (1986). Questioning. In O. Hargie (Ed.), *A handbook of communication skills* (pp. 95-128). London: Croom Helm.

Hunkins, F. P. (Ed.) (1972). *Questioning strategies and techniques.* Boston: Allyn & Bacon.

Hyman, R. T. (1979). *Strategic questioning.* Englewood Cliffs, NJ: Prentice-Hall.

Payne, S. L. (1951). *The art of asking questions.* Princeton, NJ: Princeton University Press.

Three

Contribution!
Not Participation in Management Education

DENNIS A. GIOIA
The Pennsylvania State University

> We're scrapping classroom participation as a grading criterion in this course. (Introductory comment by the author to a skeptical management class)

If you could identify the 10 best teachers you know and ask them to distill their knowledge about effective teaching to the five most important factors, I would venture that *classroom participation* would show up on your and virtually everyone's list. In the process of reading various writings on how to conduct classes and talking to other well-reputed instructors, I hear a strong refrain that sings the praises of participation. Everyone knows that participation by the members of a learning group is good, right? Of course it is. But is it the most effective way to run a class? Maybe not. The notion of participation is so well entrenched in the collective mind of the teaching profession that I wonder if we have not unconsciously stopped considering what we are after when we work with a class.

It seems to me that what we are ultimately striving for in a class is thinking and thought. With that premise in mind, and at the risk of engaging in some minor level of anathema, I would suggest that we should not necessarily be encouraging participation in the class, but rather *contribution to* the class. Participation for its own sake is a fruitless enterprise.

This chapter originally appeared in *The Organizational Behavior Teaching Review,* Volume 11, Issue 4.

Participation must have purpose, and that purpose should revolve around thinking through concepts, issues, and practices for the benefit of self and others.

Most of us have engaged in attempts to draw more people into class discussion. And it really feels good to see a substantial portion of the class joining in. Indeed, success at achieving class participation is a seductive sort of accomplishment—so seductive that it often leads to a de facto presumption that the class is successful simply *because* so many people are more actively involved in it. With all the effort devoted to (and feeling rewarded for) getting people to speak up, however, a rather counterproductive value becomes instilled in the class: a value for talking instead of thinking.

When participation for its own sake happens, a special skill is required on the part of the instructor, a skill for managing equitable participation, rather than managing the production of on-site understanding by class members. In an insidious way, when an instructor is managing participation, he or she is cheating the students while trying to please the students. For that reason, I have stopped encouraging participation in class and started encouraging contribution to the class.

If we consider the conceptual distinction between participation and contribution, the strength of the foundation for classes based on contribution becomes more apparent. *Participation* connotes involvement, sharing, and simply taking part, all desirable attributes especially for the social dimensions of a class. *Contribution,* on the other hand, connotes not only social but also intellectual involvement and sharing of knowledge and knowledge construction. In addition, it also implies the willful intent to assist others in the forging of understanding. Contribution not only includes but also enlarges on the values represented by participation, because it rivets attention on the goal of generating usable knowledge.

Concentrating on contribution causes people to think about what they are going to say, instead of simply blurting out ill-considered opinions, superficial observations, and irrelevant personal examples. It also tends ultimately to focus the class on a shared goal of creating a learning setting in their own image.

The Contribution-Oriented Class

The overarching feature of a contribution-oriented class is an overt concern with the following litmus test question: "Does a student comment contribute to class process and peer understanding of the concept under discussion?" Facilitating contribution to the class, of course, requires a slightly different teaching philosophy and process on the part of the instructor. For that reason there are perhaps some initial costs associated with running a contribution-oriented class. Most of these, however, are associated simply with adopting a moderately different set of skills and considerations. For one thing, the instructor's role is somewhat more difficult initially because he or she is not just facilitating participation, but facilitating discussion that moves a class toward understanding a specific point. Just any commentary from the class simply will not suffice. That means that the instructor must be able to identify those individuals who are likely to make a contribution (based on personal knowledge of student work history or intellectual interests) *and* be able to integrate germane information into an evolving point for the benefit of others in the class. It also requires an ability to make quick judgments about whether a student's comment constitutes a contribution to the issue at hand and, if not, a subtle ability judiciously to take an alternative tack or solicit an observation from another student.

This process is somewhat delicate in the initial stages of a new class, because if people have to think through what they are going to say or believe they must say something profound, they are likely to be intimidated to the point of simply clamming up. Thus it is necessary to build a culture in which people *expect* to contribute to the class and do not fear embarrassment. That process is, however, a lot less difficult and time-consuming than one might suspect. One of the easiest ways to do it is simply to point out the rationales for why you are emphasizing contribution instead of participation. Every student can identify with the experience of sitting in class listening to the same five people repeatedly dominating discussions with their personal perspectives and, as a result, having class time degenerate into just talk. Or worse, a forum is created for relatively few students' opinions. Probably all of us have experienced that situation, and almost everyone, *especially* the other students in the class, wishes for some way to avoid the boredom associated with it.[1]

This problem is mitigated by stressing contribution, which in turn, is in some ways easier to manage than participation. If student comments seem to be drifting from a coherent observation, some pointed questions often can refocus the discussion and simultaneously reemphasize the value for contribution, for example, "How is your observation (example, story) furthering our understanding of this concept?" and "How are your experiences contributing to some general point we might make?"

Another effective way to orient the class toward contribution is to note the myriad ways that students can make contributions. Useful methods include (1) providing recapitulations and summaries, (2) making observations that integrate concepts and discussions, (3) citing relevant personal examples, (4) asking key questions that lead to revealing discussions, (5) engaging in devil's advocacy, and (6) disagreeing with the instructor, so that the difference of opinion serves as both counterpoint and a basis for exploring all sides of a concept, issue, or practice. With all these options available students soon see that there is some avenue for them to contribute.

Perhaps of most importance is training yourself to discriminate between participation and contribution. This skill requires that you not reward everything that is said but acknowledge those points that further a discussion or lead to ultimate understanding of a concept. It is apparent that contribution cannot be made without some level of participation but participation need not be excessive. One of the most useful contributions is sometimes made by an individual (the "strong, silent type") who will sit through almost an entire class without saying a word but who is obviously vicariously involved in the discussion. Then, near the end of the class, he or she comes forth with some pithy comment that captures the essence of the day's session. That is a highly valued function, and noting it publicly tends to encourage the many introverted or quiet students, who recognize that they do not have to go against their nature to feel like they can contribute. It sometimes helps to note, perhaps somewhat tongue-in-cheek, that extroversion and participation have not yet been correlated with intelligence. Thus normally reticent people can be more easily drawn into the class.

A focus on contribution tends to bring forth all the advantages of participation while helping avoid the disadvantages. Students who would normally participate will still participate, albeit in a way more systematically oriented toward contribution. *Overparticipation* is discouraged and thus solves one of the more nagging problems of discussion-based classes. Overparticipation, it can be noted overtly, is sometimes worse than no participation. Those students who might never participate, no matter how much they are exhorted to do so, soon become engaged as well, because contribution can be defined in their own terms.

Managing Class Contribution

As alluded to earlier, the success of a contribution-oriented class hinges on the establishment of a nonintimidating culture where everyone's contribution is expected. Typically, it requires several weeks of demonstration by example that the class is informal, laid-back, and nonthreatening but also aimed at serious thought. Those expectations soon turn into a self-fulfilling prophecy. It also helps if the instructor's own teaching agenda (whether lecture or experiential exercise) seldom takes up more than 50%

of the class. Students quickly learn that *they* must generate and sustain the remaining agenda (within the framework of the day's topic and the guidance of the instructor). "Hitchhiking" on the instructor's or class colleague's ideas can then set the stage for creative and useful contributions in the best traditions of brainstorming.

Several specific teaching techniques tend to encourage contribution and discourage mere participation. First, you can use *think breaks,* pointedly calling "time out!" for everyone to silently think through a comment just made to see if it makes sense or constitutes a worthwhile observation. Second, you can hand out some contrived, mythical awards during class discussions: one is a "Reader's Digest Award" to the person who most succinctly captures the gist of a discussion, another is a threatened "Monopoly Award" for rambling students (they don't want to get this one).[2] It takes a good-humored firmness to use a monopoly award, but it can be effective. Indeed, by midterm, monopoly awards can become transformed into "Gong Show" rejections as other students cheerily shout down long-winded or pointless discourses.

There are several other course/class features that can facilitate the orientation toward making contributions. For example, discussion leaders can be appointed who know well in advance that they are to be prepared to handle the class. Usually, the role of the discussion leader is to prepare a set of crucial questions that will influence others in the class to contribute ideas. This technique serves as a good means for making the important point that there are two sides to contribution: first (and most obvious), one can make a useful comment and, second (and often less obvious), one can elicit useful comments from others. Asking critical questions and eliciting ideas from others is a rare managerial skill that becomes well honed in a contribution-oriented class.

Other features are fairly straightforward. It is important to get to know everyone in class so that you can talk to them personally. It is also important to have classrooms with movable furniture. The most effective arrangement typically is the classic executive program "double *U,*" with the students arrayed around the perimeter of the room, two rows deep, with the discussion leader and the instructor sitting in the open end of the *U.* Such an arrangement allows everyone to see and verbally interact with everyone else. Having the instructor seated during the discussion furthers the notion that the class is a place of sharing as well as learning. I have taken to referring to this teaching style as "teaching by sitting down," in good-natured counterpoint to Peters and Waterman's (1982) notion of "management by walking around."

The instructor's role in a contribution-oriented class is multifaceted, and includes facilitator, resource, coach, cheerleader, iconoclast, questioner, integrator, supporter, referee, Socratic muser, occasional anarchist, and feigned dunce. Perhaps of greatest importance is the polishing of skill in identifying people experiencing the "tip of the tongue" phenomenon—on the verge of contributing but hesitant to speak up—and drawing them into the discussion.

Evaluation Issues

Naturally, if contribution rather than participation is to be emphasized the issue of grading must be dealt with. Contribution might be deemed harder to assess than participation, but that typically is an inaccurate perception. Participation grades are usually rendered impressionistically. Over time, one develops a strong impression about who is participating in discussions and who is not. In some cases, daily records are kept. Either way, the bottom line is a very suspect grade base—who talked the most.

Contribution grades are better and, in a sense, even easier to render. First, they are as easy to decide simply because a similar sort of impressionistic criterion applies. During a semester, one develops a good sense of who is contributing to the class. Second, contribution becomes a better grade base because there are more criteria available for judgment that suit the many different ways that people can contribute knowledge. (Witness the many possible ways of making contributions noted above.)

It is fairly important to have some systematic way to record contributions. For those who consistently contribute good ideas and relevant examples, or for those who seldom do so, the written record is not crucial. For those students who infrequently offer gems or make definitive observations, however, a written record is necessary. Otherwise, the foibles of human memory tends to undervalue their contributions at final grade time.

The standards I apply to class comments to assess contribution include the following questions: "Does this comment enlighten me or the class members?" "Does it provide a new angle on my presentation of a concept that makes grasping the point easier?" "Does an example provide a good demonstration of a concept and thus assist others to comprehend the way things work?" "Does someone consistently play the role of 'recapper' in a way that effectively paraphrases points?" "Is someone a constructive devil's advocate?" "Do students make key or even outrageous statements that galvanize the class to wrestle with an issue without my help?"

Focusing on contribution grades also permits some unusual criteria and evaluation sources to be used. For instance, you can enlist the aid of the students in class by conducting a poll of their votes on who most stimulated their thinking during the course. Such a process not only supplements your own impressions but might also lend more equity to a given student's grade for class contribution. Also, a factor such as "What did a student teach the instructor?" can be applied. Admittedly, that is a tough criterion for a student to meet, but it can be reserved for those special cases when a student says something that raises a point you had never considered and adds to your understanding (It happens!). Furthermore, you can use contribution grades to reward moxie or organizational smarts, which is often beneficial to those students (we've all seen them) who seem to understand organizations and management issues better than others in the class, yet never seem to do very well on exams based on book learning.

By almost any standard, then, an emphasis on contribution is a preferred alternative to an emphasis on participation. Contribution encompasses participation and goes several steps further. More than anything else, it tends to focus in on what we in the teaching profession are supposed to be all about—actively thinking and learning on site in the classroom.

Notes

1. As an aside, the shortcomings of using participation as a criterion often tend to be magnified with MBA classes. MBAs are people with a war chest full of organizational examples and experiences at the ready. These come spewing out at the slightest cue. If participation is an explicit part of the grade base, class time can easily become an object lesson in story telling.

2. Thanks to Dan Brass for the ideas for these two awards and their Madison Avenue labels.

Reference

Peters, T. J., & Waterman, R. H., Jr. (1982). *In search of excellence: Lessons from America's best-run companies.* New York: Harper & Row.

Four

Dealing With Emotions
in the Classroom

DONALD D. BOWEN
University of Tulsa

JOSEPH SELTZER
LaSalle University

JAMES A. WILSON
University of Pittsburgh

What is the role of emotion in the classroom? If a student expresses strong feelings, do we encourage insight and growth or is it an indication of an unpleasant intrusion into the orderly processes of teaching? Are emotions in the classroom constructive factors, perhaps to be stimulated by the instructor, or destructive forces to be avoided and discouraged? Are there situations or topics that are more likely than others to elicit strong feelings from students? What is the appropriate response by the teacher to emotional outbursts? Do the more common (but less spectacular) feelings of apathy, boredom, dependency, and so on also require our attention? What ethical, clinical, pedagogical, and professional issues are involved in dealing with student emotions?

Emotion is a *pervasive* aspect of human experience. Yet ironically, the topic of emotion is almost universally absent from the subject indexes of management and organizational behavior textbooks. Nevertheless we recognize the part that emotion plays in understanding the behavior of organizational participants, and our theories would be incomplete without such critical

This chapter originally appeared in *The Organizational Behavior Teaching Review,* Volume 12, Issue 2.

variables as job satisfaction, anger and distrust in organizational conflict, fear and insecurity of the powerless, and triumph following conflict or achievements.

Our thesis is that similar emotions pervade the classroom as well. There is little point in debating whether emotions have a place in the classroom, because they exist there as they must in any human endeavor. Students may be artful in hiding feelings of fear, dependency, resentment, or boredom from the instructor (and often from themselves), but they sometimes express curiosity, interest, elation, or amusement rather openly. Academic norms of rationality, impersonality and formality, however, militate against the free expression of even positive emotions in class. Is such a climate conducive to learning?

As Simon (1983) has noted,

> focusing attention is one of the principal functions of the processes we call emotion. One thing an emotion can do for and to you is to distract you from your current focus of thought, and call your attention to something else that presumably needs attention right now.

Moreover,

> most human beings are able to attend to issues longer, to think harder about them, to receive deeper impressions that last longer, if information is presented in a context of emotion—a sort of hot dressing—than if it is presented wholly without affect. (pp. 21, 32)

We agree that students will learn and internalize more when the material arouses their emotions. If emotions are inevitably present in the classroom, the issue for the instructor would seem to be how to take advantage of their presence to foster learning, while minimizing the obstacles that dysfunctional emotions can also create. Anxiety, boredom, or hostility in students or teachers can become a major barrier to communication and attention. We would also like to suggest that the emotions useful in learning are not always pleasant. They may include occasions experienced by students (at least in the short term) as negative, such as when they receive feedback or needed criticism or when their low self-esteem is acknowledged (which they thought was secret and unseen or which they themselves could not label). By the same token, although we do not advocate becoming overly protective of students, we do oppose, on ethical grounds, coercing students into experiences that they would not willingly choose if they knew what was coming beforehand. Similarly, we question stimulating student emotions to satisfy instructor needs to pry, punish, or manipulate.

Congenial emotions may seldom be a problem, but when student emotions become obstacles, the best teachers seem to possess the ability to convert negative to positive reactions in the service of teaching. However, some teachers are undoubtedly more comfortable in dealing with feelings (their own and those of students) than others. For the instructor to whom the entire connotation of emotions is negative, we suspect that any attempt to tamper with the emotional climate of the classroom is likely to do more harm than good. We will address instructors who seek to develop their abilities in management of classroom emotions; those who wish to: (1) minimize the triggering of dysfunctional emotions, (2) maximize the experience of feelings that foster learning, (3) rechannel inhibiting emotions so that they facilitate, rather than impede learning, and (4) maximize transference of emotional learning to career situations.

Sources of Affect in the Classroom

To address these issues, we will first consider factors that engender emotion in the classroom by investigating forces in the situation (structures, culture, norms, rules, and expectations), forces in the student, and forces in the instructor (Tannenbaum & Schmidt, 1959). In so doing, we have selected incidents that we have experienced in teaching both undergraduate and graduate students to illustrate important issues in dealing with classroom emotions.

THE SITUATION

Stimulating, challenging concepts and activities stir emotions. For example, experiential exercises that foster intergroup conflict often get the group going. Which is not to say that in choosing an activity, affect alone should be the criterion; learning requires a balance between safety and confrontation (Walter & Marks, 1981).

As an example of an overly threatening activity, Seltzer once assigned the widely used exercise the "Kidney Machine" to focus the class on group decision making (Phillips, 1974). The exercise requires participants to choose which of several fictional characters will be allowed access to the limited time available on a kidney machine and condemns the others to die. The exercise stimulated a lively discussion, but one student later told the class that it was difficult for her to participate because her sister was, in fact, only alive because of a kidney machine. The same learning points could have been made with an alternative value-clarification exercise that would not force students to deal with such life-threatening issues.

Although instructors clearly cannot assume responsibility for the rare idiosyncratic response when activities or topics represent real-world phenomena that students will encounter, there is still a need to select issues that minimize the likelihood of such an upsetting experience. Moreover, the Kidney Machine incident also points out the need to ensure that students have the option of *not* participating without damaging their grades or relationships with other students. Finally, whatever the activity assigned, a commitment must be made to provide adequate time and support for addressing the emotional issues that may arise.

Activities that are highly manipulative, those that mislead students, and those that create power differences or conflict may also create gratuitous emotions without adding to the learning. In some cases, the learning points may be lost and what students really learn is that it is permissible for authority figures (in this instance, the instructor) to play God if they have both sufficient power and adequate conviction that they know what is good for others. We are not suggesting that all activities with surprise endings (i.e., for which the outcome is not what students will expect) should be avoided. Being duped is not necessarily being exploited. Students will usually perceive benign intent if the results are benign.

By way of contrast, consider the "Interviewing Trios" exercise in which students rotate through three roles as interviewee, consultant, and observer (Hall, Bowen, Lewicki, & Hall, 1982, pp. 88-93). The interviewee talks about a problem and the consultant practices nondirective listening. The observer provides feedback to the consultant on the consultant's behavior while listening, and then the roles are rotated. There are two important differences that differentiate this exercise from the Kidney Machine in the areas of safety and support. First, the interviewee can choose the problem to be discussed and control the depth and extent of disclosure. Second, the exercise fosters trust, intimacy, and reciprocity, thereby creating a climate of support.

Challenging students' previously learned ideas and assumptions is essential to learning but often an emotion-stirring experience. Challenge requires confrontation as when the instructor as devil's advocate provides creative turbulence through discursive questioning. Similarly, in laboratory-training courses (another instance for which informed consent is essential), interpersonal confrontation is a key element of the learning process. However, other pedagogical approaches, such as films, experiential activities, role-plays, small-group discussions, psychodrama, and events in classroom interaction (domination of discussion, snubs, name calling, obscenities, etc.) also can and do elicit emotion.

When student groups work together, a common issue is the *free rider* who does not do an equal share of the work. It is frequently difficult for the group to deal directly with the culprit and negative feelings build. An opportunity for teaching constructive conflict resolution is lost if the instructor does not help the group clear the air. If group meetings occur outside the classroom, the instructor may have difficulty keeping abreast of developments in the group, unless special arrangements are made. One example of an early-warning system is Bowen's requirement that ongoing groups turn in a sociogram of the group at midterm (Hall et al., 1982, pp. 373-375).

Other characteristics of the classroom situation also affect the emotional tone of the class. There seems to be differences between large and small classes, graduate and undergraduate classes, required and elective courses, classes taught in Northern or Eastern schools (where students are more aggressive) versus Southern schools (where it is impolite to express directly negative emotions). The implicit assumptions of the pervading student culture vary substantially from campus to campus but need to be taken into account in interpreting student behavior and in adjusting one's teaching style.

Teaching in a business school can make encouraging the expression of feelings especially difficult. The norm of business organizations against the expression of emotions (especially for males) is also strong among business faculty and sometimes, even, among students who view the classroom climate as anticipatory socialization—an anteroom for their future roles. Do we do our students a disservice if we do not attempt to build these norms? (Ironically, our colleagues in arts and sciences characterize business school curricula as narrowly doctrinaire and as "industrial ROTC" programs.) Or are we adequately preparing them for the impersonality; bureaucracy; politics; and even authoritarianism, dehumanization, and unfettered ruthlessness they will inevitably encounter? Merely speaking to these issues can arouse emotions and defenses such as denial, rationalization, and suppression (as well as anger toward the instructor for being socialistic or antibusiness) or depression for the student who suddenly recognizes what lies ahead. Values, ideas, ideologies, and politics usually contain strong emotional components and elicit strong responses. Topics such as free enterprise (pro or con), sexism, homophobia, and racism often raise emotions to the boiling point on both sides of the issue.

As an example, several years ago Wilson was picked up bodily and moved from the lectern—gently—by six African American students who thought that his lecture on racism in corporations was correct enough but that they could do it better from experience. They proceeded to do so and were soon confronted by some white students who later joined them in the well of the amphitheater—peacefully—to discuss and debate the point for themselves and the now-riveted MBA class. ("It was the best class I never taught," Wilson observes).

On the other hand, our errors are often errors of omission. Business schools, purveyors of the middle-class mores of the corporate world, are likely to ignore or reject working-class values and issues. We tend to teach models, theories, and behaviors appropriate to an economic system that some students (and some instructors) find controversial or even reprehensible in its impact. Such objections seem legitimate fare for universities devoted to examining all sides of issues. But the objections may never be heard if we do not encourage students to voice and examine their initially emotional reactions.

We have now arrived at our essential point that instructors can be more effective to the extent that they can encourage, rather than discourage, the emotional reactions of students to controversial or challenging material. When strong feelings emerge, the first step should be to help the struggling student articulate his or her feelings. The teacher's problem at this point is to discourage their defensive reactions or those of other students, without implying that the strong feelings of others are not equally legitimate and worthy of expression. The process orchestrated must be one of focusing on the feelings of each speaker and encouraging everyone else to listen and understand the speaker's viewpoint without assuming that they must subscribe to it. Once feelings have been aired, the class will be able to turn its energy to analyzing and evaluating the position voiced. Other feelings—such as learning anxiety, interpersonal attraction, and intimidation—although less likely to be expressed, also have a major impact on the individual's experience.

All of this is a very tough act for the teacher who does not have substantial insight and awareness of how his or her own defenses and emotions operate—a topic we will return to in discussing what instructors can do.

THE STUDENTS

Occasionally, as we have seen, a classroom experience will stimulate strong feelings in an individual, a situation that the instructor could not anticipate. Seltzer recently had a student walk out in the middle of a negotiation exercise. Other students fantasized about what had happened to her, and the activity was substantially disrupted. About 45 minutes later, she returned and talked privately with Seltzer. With some encouragement, she explained that she had been overwhelmed by the conflict (which seemed rather tame to Seltzer) and by the instructor's intimidating presence as an observer. It would certainly appear that the problems were primarily issues of the student's self-consciousness and discomfort with conflict, rather than the responsibility of the instructor.

In a sensitivity training group (t-group) course, Bowen had a tearful student say, "I've never had a friend in my whole life!" The outburst followed some feedback to her, which she and the instructor perceived as expressions of caring (but which some participants viewed as negative— probably on the assumption that it must have been because her reaction was to cry).

In both of these examples, chronically low self-esteem seems to have been at the heart of the problem. Many people carry around stored-up anger. The anger may be the reflection of unconscious feelings of low self-worth and may surface as scapegoating, depression, apathy, or self-hatred. It may be seen in the behavior of the sleeping student, the drunk student, or the sneering you-can't-be-serious look of the student too frightened, superior, or cowed to confront.

Inevitably, we will encounter students whose life experiences have made them more vulnerable, some who are trying to cope with upsetting situations outside of class, and even a small number with real psychiatric disorders. An episode initiated by the latter student can be disruptive and even dangerous, although it may not happen more than once or twice in a 40-year career. Wilson, a licensed psychotherapist, has observed two instances of unconscious homosexual panic in the course of 20 years of teaching. It is often in behavioral classes that these individuals will act out their problems or that repressed material will surface—for reasons both obvious (reduced structure and control) and more subtle (panic of the primitive psyche). *Defensive projective identification* is a more common reaction signaled by the student who asks, "How come you know all about me and were talking about me in your lecture?" Table 4.1 lists some of the more common defenses and psychiatric disorders that the instructor may encounter, together with their primary symptoms.

Students who are particularly stressed or responding to happenings in their personal lives or for whom unconscious material has surfaced almost invariably react unexpectedly and are, therefore, a particular problem for the instructor. When such episodes occur in the classroom, students are intensely aware of the reactions of the professor and failure to cope effectively may elicit anger or fear in the rest of the class, which lingers as an obstacle in the teacher-student relationship. The ability to recognize abnormal behavior and to understand its symptomatic significance is a first step in developing a constructive response.

Scapegoating is an occasional classroom occurrence with strong emotional underpinnings. The scapegoat is often a student who is somehow different (e.g., a minority) or a student who manages to volunteer for the role. The difficulty is that one can misdiagnose the situation as a problem in the scapegoat's behavior rather than an example of the group's expressing collective emotions by blaming their frustrations on the scapegoat. Should scapegoating be detected, the most effective action for the instructor

TABLE 4.1
Common Psychoses and Defense Mechanisms

Type	Symptoms or Indicators
Psychopathologies	Maladaptive behavior to the point of impairment of functioning.
Depression	Depressed mood; weight loss or gain; insomnia (unipolar depression) or excessive need for sleep (bipolar depression); lethargic behavior (interspersed with bursts of energy in bipolars); loss of interest in activities; low self-esteem and feelings of worthlessness or guilt; difficulty in concentrating, remembering, or making decisions; circular thinking; recurrent thoughts of suicide or death.
Paranoia	Deeply suspicious of others, secretive, jealous, blames others for problems, argumentative and overly sensitive, tense, cold and lacking emotional response, humorless.
Schizoid	Few social relationships (a loner); appears dull, aloof, and without warm feelings for others; indifferent to reactions of others; daydreams excessively.
Borderline personality	Erratic and unstable relationships, moods, and self-esteem; argumentative, irritable, and sarcastic; impulsive; unclear sense of self and values; periodic bouts of depression; poor reality testing; tends to project own feelings to others and overly identify.
Dependent	Lacking in self-confidence and self-reliance, passive expectation that others will make decisions for them, unable to make demands on others, seeks protection, subordinates own needs to those of others; counterdependent variation is demanding, challenging, rebellious, suspicious, and hostile toward authority figures.
Passive-aggressive	Resists demands of others, stubborn, and ineffectual in fulfilling work responsibilities (habitually late, does not return phone calls, procrastinates, and forgets).
Defenses	Unconscious mechanisms that protect the person from anxiety or conflict.
Projection	Attributing one's own unacknowledged feelings or characteristics to others and blaming others for one's difficulties.
Acting out	Direct expression of unconscious wish or impulse to avoid being conscious of the feeling that accompanies it.
Intellectualization	Instinctual wishes and feelings dealt with in terms of ideas, concepts, theories, and so on to avoid acting on them.
Regression	"Forgetting" or not noticing potentially anxiety-arousing ideas, feelings, facts, and so forth.
Denial	Distorting or denying elements of external reality to avoid unpleasantness.
Dissociation	Temporary but drastic modification of one's character or sense of personal identity to avoid emotional distress—evident in sudden and exaggerated change in behavior—may appear not to listen, see, or be involved over some period of time.
Reaction formation	Preventing dangerous desires from being expressed by exaggerating opposite (acceptable) attitudes or behaviors.
Identification	Increasing feelings of self-worth by identifying with admired persons or institutions.

SOURCES: Davison and Neale (1986), Vaillant (1977), Lazarus (1963), and Allen and Allen (1984).

is probably to provide reflective behavioral feedback to the group (describe their behavior, but don't interpret it) and allow the group to examine its own behavior.

The instructor is also a marvelous candidate for scapegoating. If students are not doing well in a class, it can be safely predicted that a number of them are blaming the instructor who may first discover the problem from teacher evaluations—long after anything can be done about it (except when midterm teacher evaluations are employed as an early-warning system).

One strategy that usually does the trick in dealing with scapegoating is to ask the entire group to look at its behavior and feelings (you may need to give them some help in surfacing the feelings first). If real scapegoating is occurring, it is common for one of the more self-responsible students to confront the group with its behavior. "Why are we blaming the professor for this? Who is really responsible for our learning, anyway?"

THE INSTRUCTOR

Our own behavior has a particularly important impact on student feelings. We may encourage students' trust and affection with kindness and sensitivity or keep them at a distance and put them down with intellectual arrogance and superiority. Perhaps the most difficult situation for students is when we seem to bestow kindness and recognition on a few, but not all, students. Students find this situation particularly difficult, not only because they depend on us for our evaluations and grades but also because we are, for many, symbolic parents. Unresolved conflicts from relationships with one's parents are especially common among young people leaving adolescence and entering adulthood. The conflicts and their attendant (but often unconscious) feelings are likely to be projected onto authority figures such as teachers they encounter outside the home. A rejecting instructor may be taking the place of a rejecting parent for them, and this can be deeply terrifying and anger provoking to the student, especially if the student sees the teacher as *selectively* rejecting.

Because we are human, each of us inevitably has personal and developmental issues in our own lives ranging from simple exhaustion to midlife crises and neuroses. Consequently, we will occasionally make mistakes or unconsciously telegraph inappropriate needs to students. Some faculty even act these out, such as throwing chalk and verbal aggression. Probably more common is to deal with intense feelings, such as sexual attraction toward students, by denying their existence. We would expect such repressed attractions to be a major source of preferential treatment of students.

Students who depend on us for grades or as parental substitutes are particularly sensitive to our behavior and are hypersensitive to these cues. They may not be particularly good at interpreting the cues, however. Hence, the instructor who is particularly open to emotional responses may be seen as inviting intimacy. Conversely, teachers can also misinterpret student behavior. Positive identification by a student of the opposite sex can be perceived as seductiveness. Middle-aged males may be particularly vulnerable to younger women on this count.

As previously noted, some of us are more comfortable with emotions than others. Some can tolerate more equitably the sometimes disruptive or bizarre behavior that accompanies strong feelings. Most of us are more comfortable with certain types of emotional behavior (e.g., dependency or anger but not crying), or with certain types of students (women rather than men, younger students, etc.). Topics such as sexuality, alcoholism, mental illness, and death may be particularly difficult emotional issues for us. Strongly expressed emotion by a student inevitably triggers strong emotions for the instructor—which we may make a legitimate decision not to express, based on our own psychological integration, pedagogical ideology, or the realities of the institution. As long as the decision reflects a conscious weighing of realistic considerations, there is no problem. But when emotions make us uncomfortable, a common reaction is to attempt to exclude, deny (as in the denial of sexual attraction by faculty), or to control them. Denial or repression is an attempt to disregard reality; suppressing the expression of emotions by others may be a subtle form of censorship erected by our own defenses and rationalized by concerns about emotions disrupting the cognitive and intellectual work at hand. Could the conscious exclusion of relevant *cognitive* materials, a parallel form of intellectual censorship, be so easily rationalized?

Professors who teach in "soft" areas involving "people skills" are familiar with a phenomenon which may be a problem for any discipline which does not fit neatly into the expectations of others in business schools or other traditional curricula. Students may express anger because we do not teach them what they want to learn ("I don't see how I can use this stuff"), or because we are "different" from their other instructors, or because we resist becoming a mentor or "good mother" to them. Colleagues may become convinced that students should not, or possibly cannot, do exercises that have potential for personal or emotional exploration (*New York Magazine,* 1986). But business schools are increasingly challenged to accommodate disciplines and faculty who represent values other than the utilitarianism, materialism, positivism, and pragmatism of traditionally dominant ideology.

What We as Instructors Can Do

The following seem to us to be the most important steps that instructors should pursue to become more effective in dealing with emotions—their own and those of others.

SELF-AWARENESS

We can become more self-aware, with more knowledge of our own defenses, traits, tendencies, strengths, and weaknesses. Feedback from students and especially from peers can increase our awareness of the often unconscious ways we have an impact on others emotionally. Wilson has a pact with a colleague that permits either to enter the other's classes, unannounced, and later to provide feedback. Coteaching also provides extensive opportunities for reciprocal feedback. Taking a battery of psychological tests or entering therapy helps reduce the likelihood that one will lose control when taken by surprise. The t-group has been extremely useful for many in developing skills to deal with threatening situations. Similarly, training in group dynamics (e.g., the Tavistock method, etc.) can help one better understand what is occurring in the classroom.

SELF-MANAGEMENT

We need to monitor the emotions we express. Expressing all that is felt could flood students, and it is important not to confuse dumping with being open. Strong expression of anger or other emotions may be inappropriate. There is also a thin line between Socratic questioning and aggressive interrogation that causes embarrassment or reduced self-esteem. A helpful guideline in such situations is Bowen's definition of assertiveness: "Behavior that involves expressing one's ideas and feelings, and standing up for one's rights, *and doing so in a way that makes it easier for others to do the same*" (Hall et al., 1982, p. 114). As teachers, we need to be especially able to lead the way emotionally, to model, to support, and to take risks.

Bowen recalls several instances when expressing his anger to a class was a significant event in getting a class on track—and had the added benefit that students began to see him as a person rather than the mere occupant of the professor role. On the other hand, we can overcontrol our emotions. Seltzer once had a student tell him that he was "too soft and should let some people have it" when a large proportion of the class was consistently unprepared.

CREATE SAFETY

From the perspective of the student, the instructor is an extremely powerful person determining who passes and who fails, outcomes that can lead to important consequences in the student's life. The student peer group is another powerful force, because it is the source of social approval. Most students have learned that the most effective strategy for ingratiating themselves with both sources of power is to "get along by going along." This leads to a classroom norm of playing it safe. The risks of emotional expression will be avoided unless the instructor can encourage new norms that students willingly accept, because they recognize possibilities for their own growth in the change.

Teachers may be reluctant to challenge the dominant norms for fear that students may begin to take risks, leading to someone getting hurt. Although concern for students is laudable, such a conservative stance may represent an unconscious concern for his or her own safety on the part of the instructor. It may be more constructive to assume that both we and our students are much stronger and more resilient than we think. If we can reduce the impact of classroom norms for caution and reserve, we may enrich student learning substantially.

We can encourage safety for risk taking by (1) giving students choices about the level of issues and risks they will take, (2) encouraging reciprocity of disclosure and expression of emotions, (3) modeling openness and risk taking and by communicating respect and concern for the individual in the way that we respond to student comments and questions, and (4) encouraging the development of norms of both support and challenge. This implies a willingness to be open to experience rather than simply being comfortable with it.

ENLIST EMOTIONS FOR LEARNING

We should develop ways for emotional material to be expressed to enrich learning. Early in the course, the instructor can indicate the richness of behavioral data and create permission for the instructor and students to process what occurs. We can begin with our own self-disclosures and process our own behavior and feelings. Students can then be invited to follow suit by suggesting that emotions must have arisen as a result of the theory, exercise, or discussion, which might be worth discussing.

When students express emotions, capitalize on them as a teaching opportunity. Bowen once had a student who became so frustrated during a power simulation that he had to be physically restrained from hitting the instructor. Bowen ended the simulation at that point and began processing by saying, "I think you can now see what powerful emotions can be stirred up by power differences." The same tack can be taken when an exercise blows up—when students tear up the script and revolt, confront the instructor or each other, or sabotage the activity. In this case, the lesson learned may not be the lesson planned, but if the instructor begins by encouraging students to air their feelings about what is happening, the issues that emerge can always be dealt with as examples of problems that occur in organizations.

One problem for many of us is that students do not often express their emotions clearly and directly. If you ask a student how he or she *feels* about something, his or her response is likely to be an opinion or a perception, not a feeling. Similarly, students often ask a question when they want to make a statement. If a student takes a position on an issue, the impetus may be emotional, but his or her statement is likely to be couched in intellectual or moral terms. Ideas, values, feelings, and behaviors become inextricably intertwined in discussion, and the ability to listen for indirectly voiced emotions is a skill instructors should cultivate. For example, when students become antagonistic it often reflects emotional resistance to something they thought was proposed—but was not (emotions often cause distorted interpretations). Encourage the student to voice his or her objections fully and listen for signs of distortion. If there is no distortion to correct, listen for and reflect back (supportively) the feelings that seem to lurk beneath the intellectual facade ("You seem to feel very angry about that . . ." or "Is that idea kind of scary for you?"). When the student confirms the emotional reaction, it will probably be productive to explore what it is about the issue that the student (and often many of the others) find threatening or animating. The discussion will help even the uninvolved portion of the class more fully appreciate the validity or complexity of the topic.

As already suggested, we can also encourage group norms that support the expression of feelings. Bowen had a student share a personal experience that brought tears to her eyes. The group was highly supportive and in subsequent classes began to share emotions more freely. However, that can be too much of a good thing. Bowen had a t-group class that developed a norm of one person taking the hot seat each session and having a good cry. After half a dozen iterations, Bowen felt it was important to confront this behavior as interfering with the learning process.

Another valuable approach is to use student journals, which often reveal strong emotions otherwise not expressed. Journals operate as both interventions and controls by providing opportunities for student self-disclosure and for teacher-student interaction (although there is a risk of possible intrusiveness). Journals also give the instructor a chance to monitor what is happening with each student and to provide personal feedback to students.

AVOIDING THE THERAPIST ROLE

When emotions are expressed, there may be a need to counsel or to provide the opportunity for catharsis for the individual or the other students. In some cases it becomes obvious that therapeutic assistance is needed and referral to a clinician is advisable. Clinicians generally agree that it is a good rule *not* to do therapy with one's own students. In crisis situations, of course, we are ready to provide emotional first aid. For students with "normal" problems of life such as career-planning issues, we may grant a couple hours of office time. But for longer-term issues, we encourage the student to seek out the university counseling center.

One particularly troublesome issue, and one for which there is not complete agreement even among the present authors, is the question of whether one can simultaneously play the supportive role of counselor and subsequently grade the student, perhaps critically. The role is difficult for the instructor-counselor despite the fact that effective counseling requires a level of honesty that should make truthful feedback feasible, because one can never be sure that a low grade is really helping the student. Most important, however, the student may not be able to understand the "betrayal" of the supportive and caring counselor who has awarded a poor grade.

TEACH SELF-CONCEPT

Where possible (e.g., in management, organizational behavior, or human resource classes), include material on self-concept in the course and use activities, cases, and exercises that enhance self-esteem. If *self-concept* is a syllabus topic, it legitimizes dealing with the self as part of the course. An example of an excellent self-esteem-building activity is the "Me Tree" exercise for which students identify accomplishments they are proud of and verbally share them with a small group (Howe, 1977, pp. 98-100).

TAKE CARE OF YOURSELF

Ensure that you have adequate support for yourself. It helps a great deal to have a relationship with a colleague who is supportive of teaching and especially discussion of emotional issues. Seek out colleagues who enjoy sharing experiences to avoid becoming isolated. Avoid alienating potential sources of personal support by keeping lines of communication open with faculty in other areas. The experiential teacher can also attempt to educate traditional teachers to the value of experiential methods—not by attempting to sell the approach but by clarifying why experiential teaching may be particularly appropriate for what you teach (Bowen, 1980). This may help keep their responses more rational when they hear stories from students about what is going on in your classroom.

Conclusion

Behavioral classes in business schools are increasingly arenas in which emotional issues can arise in ways that either assist learning or inhibit it. Conflicts and confrontations can occur among students or across the lectern. As an instructor, the appropriate action is to monitor constantly and sensitively. Do not create or use emotional material that you cannot manage or deal with comfortably. Design experiences so that students maintain a level of control. Monitor yourself and be aware of rising defenses, feelings of anger, hostility, and so forth or aversions to certain students. Own up to mistakes as soon as possible and go on.

All of this prudence and caution should not deter risk taking on the side of growth, rich exercises and simulations, committed lecturing, and healthy confrontation. When emotions facilitate learning, help students to explore the important feeling issues. As usual, the middle way is best; do not avoid emotions or expunge them and do not encourage emotional nudism. Dramatics in the service of pedagogy is fine, but acting out is counterproductive for both students and teachers. Emotions remain central to human experience and cannot—*should not*—be ignored in our classrooms.

References

Allen, J. R., & Allen, B. A. (1984). *Psychiatry: A guide* (2nd ed.). New Hyde Park, NY: Medical Examination.

Bowen, D. D. (1980). Experiential and traditional teaching: A dubious distinction. *Exchange: The Organizational Behavior Teaching Journal, 5*(3), 7-12.

Davison, G. C. & Neale, J. M. (1986). *Abnormal psychology* (4th ed.). New York: Wiley.

Hall, D. T., Bowen, D. D., Lewicki, R. J., & Hall, F. S. (1982). *Experiences in management and organizational behavior* (2nd ed.). New York: Wiley.

Howe, L. W. (1977). *Taking charge of your life.* Niles, IL: Argus Communications.

Lazarus, R. S. (1963). *Personality and adjustment.* Englewood Cliffs, NJ: Prentice-Hall.

New York Magazine (1986, June 9). Bottom line mentality of MBA students.

Phillips, G. M. (1974). Kidney machine: Group decision making. In J. W. Pfeiffer & J. E. Jones (Eds.), *The 1974 annual handbook for group facilitators* (pp. 78-86). La Jolla, CA: University Associates.

Simon, H. A. (1983). *Reason in human affairs.* Palo Alto, CA: Standford University Press.

Tannenbaum, R., & Schmidt, W. H. (1959, March-April). How to choose a leadership pattern. *Harvard Business Review.* 95-101.

Vaillant, G. E. (1977). *Adaptation to life.* Boston: Little, Brown.
Walter, G. A., & Marks, S. E. (1981). *Experiential learning and change.* New York: Wiley.
Wilson, J. A. (1973). Curriculum reform: Some predictions. *MBA Magazine, 7*(4).

Suggested Readings

Aronson, J. (1977). *Mental health book guide.* New York: Aronson.
Bowlby, J. (1973). *Separation: Anxiety and anger.* New York: Basic.
Goffman, E. (1959). *The presentation of self in everyday life.* Garden City, NY: Doubleday, Anchor.
Horney, K. (1937). *The neurotic personality of our time.* New York: Norton.
Jongeward, D., & Seyer, P. (1978). *Choosing success: Transactional analysis on the job.* New York: Wiley.
Jourard, S. J. (1971). *The transparent self.* New York: Van Nostrand Reinhold.
Kovel, J. (1976). *A complete guide to therapy: From psychoanalysis to behavior modification.* New York: Pantheon.
Reichard, B. D., Siewers, C. M. F., & Rodenhauser, P. (1992). *The small group trainer's survival guide.* Newbury Park, CA: Sage.
Simeons, A. T. W. (1960). *Man's presumptuous brain.* New York: Dutton.
Steiner, C. M. (1974). *Scripts people live: Transactional analysis of life scripts.* New York: Bantam.
Suttie, I. D. (1963). *The origins of love and hate.* Harmondsworth, UK: Peregrine.

Case Method

CRAIG C. LUNDBERG
Cornell University

The case method is certainly one of the classic approaches of management instruction in that it has been used widely for a long time. Surprisingly, however, the origins and history of the case method as well as what constitutes a teaching case, its general use, and the several variations and issues of the case method are not widely known. This introductory note will, therefore, briefly discuss each of these aspects of the case method as a background against which to consider and perhaps better appreciate the selections that follow.

Where and How Did the Case Method Arise?

When the Harvard Business School was founded in 1908, Dean Gay and his maverick, almost antiacademic, small faculty of seven quickly agreed that business education was not the study of applied economics and that their purpose was "to give each individual student a practical and professional training suitable to the particular business he plans to enter" (Christensen, 1989, p. 22). The key words are *practical* and *professional*. This meant using a pedagogy that linked the classroom to the realities of business and engaged the student in a practice-oriented, problem-solving instructional mode. At the beginning, faculty were advised to use student discussion in addition to lectures. Executives soon were invited to come to class with a writeup of their own company problems and then lead class discussions focused on their situation. By 1921, with prodding from the new dean, Wallace B. Donham, the first book of written cases was published.

By 1924 the school's Bureau of Business Research had 20 MBA graduates at work preparing cases.

Behind the evolution of the case method is a philosophy of professional education that mates knowledge and action. This philosophy, in the words of Whitehead (1947), "rejects the doctrine that students should first learn passively, and then, having learned, should apply knowledge" (p. 218). Instead, the case method rests on principles elucidated by John Dewey, that is, education consists of the cumulative and unending acquisition, combination, and reordering of learning experiences. In Dewey's own words,

> Only by wrestling with the conditions of the problem at hand, seeking and finding his own way out, does he think. . . . If he cannot devise his own solution (not, of course, in isolation, but in correspondence with the teacher and other pupils) and find his own way out he will not learn, not even if he can recite some correct answer with one hundred percent accuracy. (quoted in Soltes, 1971, p. 81)

One of Harvard Business School's professors, Dewing (1931), reflecting on the essence of the case method, stated that because businesspeople must be able to meet in action the problems arising out of new situations in an ever-changing environment, proper business education, "would consist of acquiring facility to act in the presence of new experience. It asks not how a man be trained to know, but how a man be trained to act" (p. 49). From its first invention at Harvard and for many years thereafter, the case method was extensively used in its exclusively graduate program across all fields of business education.

What Is a Case and How Is It Taught?

In the 1930s the intended role of case studies is captured in the classic statement of Gragg (1954):

> A case typically is a record of a business issue which actually has been faced by business executives, together with surrounding facts, opinions, and prejudices upon which executive decisions have to depend. These real and particularized cases are presented to students for considered analyses, open discussion and final discussion as to the type of action which should be taken. (p. 6)

Lawrence (1953) more operationally remarked that

> a good case is the vehicle by which a chunk of reality is brought into the classroom to be worked over by the class and instructor. A good case keeps

the class discussion grounded upon some of the stubborn facts that must be faced in real life situations. It is the anchor on academic flights of speculation. It is the record of complex situations that must be literally pulled apart and put together again for the expression of attitudes or ways of thinking brought into the classroom. (p. 215)

More recently, cases have been described simply by Erskine, Leenders, and Mauffett-Leenders (1981) as

a description of an actual administrative situation, commonly involving a decision or problem. It is normally written from the viewpoint of the decision makers involved and allows the student to step figuratively into the shoes of the decision maker or problem solver. (p. 10)

Also fairly recently, Christensen (1989) somewhat more eloquently defined a case as

a partial, historical, clinical study of a situation which has confronted a practicing administrator or managerial group. Presented in narrative form to encourage student involvement, it provides data—substantive and process— essential to an analysis of a specific situation, for the framing of alternative action programs, and for their implementation recognizing the complexity and ambiguity of the practical world. (p. 27)

It is important to say here what a case is *not.* Teaching cases are not (1) fictional accounts of situations (so-called armchair cases and cases written for generalized experience), (2) sets of actual organizational data (e.g., balance sheets and other records), or (3) articles from business journals or newspapers about a particular company or industry. Although each of these "near cases" may create a great class discussion, they are not true cases. Neither are research cases, that is, real situations carefully documented to explore or elucidate some phenomenon of theoretic or pragmatic significance.

As those of use in the field have begun to appreciate, teaching cases may be short or long, broad or specific, and have an almost limitless topic range. Some have called cases a snapshot of reality, a slice of life, and other colorful but misleading labels. Several crucial features distinguish cases from other teaching approaches: (1) the source of every true case rests with the individual actually involved, (2) this source implies a process of data collection that forces the case researcher to go into the field, (3) completed cases must be approved by the key source person before use, and (4) there should be sufficient information in the case to allow the student to identify with the people, situation, and organization involved.

The case method clearly involves the clinical approach of learning by doing, blending both cognitive and affective learning modes. It has an extraordinary power to involve students in a highly personal learning experience; this involvement is the consequence of (1) having repeatedly to confront the intractability of reality (the absence of needed information, ever-present conflict of objectives, and the imbalance between needs and resources), (2) the imperative of relating analysis and action (the application of knowledge, always partial, to the complexities of reality, which requires double, concrete action) rather than waiting for complete solutions, (3) discussion in which students practice managerial skills (observation, listening, diagnosing, deciding, persuading, and intervening in group processes), and (4) the acquisition of a general administrative point of view (for which a person accepts responsibility for action with a sensitivity to the connectiveness of all organizational functions and resources, a sense of appropriate boundaries in specific contexts informed by a multidimensional perspective, and a sense of the critical and possible).

Effective case teaching, of course, depends on other factors beyond the repeated exposure to good cases. Having a classroom in which everyone can see and hear everyone else is necessary as is a class period of sufficient length for full discussion. Perhaps the crucial factor, however, is the role of the instructor. The case discussion leader guides a process of discovery. He or she forgoes the role and status of a center-stage, intellectually superior authority figure to facilitate a process of joint inquiry, providing information and monitoring the quality of student analysis and presentation. It is an art, of course, with aspects of asking questions that reveal the relevance of the discussion and invite advances in thinking, weaving together individual contributions into patterns that all can perceive, and intervening to speed up or slow down the pace of discussion. Artistry in case discussions lies in the mastery of details, the details of a case's facts, and the skill and technique details of leading the discussion process. The case instructor who tries to develop students' skills of observation, listening, communication, and decision making must also always model these skills.

What Are the Variations on the Classic Case Method?

Although cases and case instruction as described above are classic and common, the case method has evolved numerous variations and extensions over the years. Although originally used with mature students, graduate students, and executives in university programs, today the case method is used with undergraduates as well and, occasionally, in organization training and development settings. The early dependence on the individual discussion artistry of instructors has been supplemented by detailed written case teaching notes, modules (a sequenced set of cases and readings), and whole course curricula. In addition, there are often available today written conceptual and industry notes to supplement regular teaching cases.

Cases today also appear in several forms. There are *iceberg cases,* which offer a sample of a situation, thereby inviting students to determine what else would be useful to know about. There are *predictive series of cases*— for which the diagnosis and action recommendations of the first case may be compared with the reality of the chronologically next case and so on. There are now *multimedia cases* too, for which photographs or film or audio tapes augment a written case. *Living cases* occasionally are used, for which one or more executives are questioned by the class to discover the facts of the situation before analysis and action planning.

The case discussion format also may take several forms beyond the conventional instructor-led type. Individuals and student groups may be asked to lead the discussion. There are some case courses that use a standardized, step-by-step approach to case analysis. Role-playing may be used to have students experience what case characters experience or to test the feasibility of action recommendations. Cases used early in a course may be reassigned later to show a class its developmental progress. Sometimes experiential analogues to cases are developed, i.e., structuring the classroom organization and activities so that the student's experience parallels the major issues or dynamics of the case under discussion. Mini-lectures, mini-simulations, experiential exercises, films, field trips, and other instructional techniques are also sometimes used in case courses to supplement, enliven, or extend case discussions.

What Are Some of the Issues of the Case Method?

As has been implied throughout this introduction, the case method of instruction is a complicated interaction of case situation, individual student, the total class, the discussion leader, and the class's context. Not surprisingly, as has been noted, this configuration also raises the possibility of numerous tradeoffs and issues.

Some issues are the same as those with any pedagogical method, for example, class size (large enough to provide a rich variety of viewpoints but small enough to provide interaction opportunity), course length (enough cases to provide the acquisition of a personal way of thinking and acting), student feedback (through discussion involvement, written case analyses, and interim grading), institutional support (instructional resources and compatible pedagogies), and course materials (enough appropriate cases and ancillary materials). Some issues, however, are unique to case discussions. Faculty and student preparation requirements for the case method are high, and instilling and maintaining the discipline of thorough preparation is a perennial challenge. Case leaders must constantly monitor and choose among following or more actively guiding the discussion; relying on volunteer participation or calling on students; emphasizing situational analysis, problem diagnosis, or action planning; maintaining one facilitative style or alternating styles; working as individuals or groups; and so on. Other issues are associated with case sequencing: the degree of reliance on conceptual models and associated reading for knowledge acquisition, the amount and type of written work required, and how explicit to be about classroom dynamics. The interesting and personal involvement of case work requires an extraordinary vigilance so that students do not cross over the fine line between the learning from being upended and the emotional defensiveness of being upset by discussions. Another set of issues relate to keeping unintended learning to a minimum, for example, how to psych out the instructor or lesson plan, how to get called on or not in class, how to subtly put down others, and/or how to feed the instructor's ego to make oneself look good. In essence, most issues in case work reflect the tradeoffs and compromises among the validity of each student's developing a personal point of view, the validity inherent in the class's and each case's situational reality, and the validity of the generalizable knowledge of business and organizations.

About the Selected Articles

The case method has, from its inception, been a distinctive pedagogy. It is widely adopted. Many if not most of the best graduate and executive management programs use it extensively, as do those undergraduate courses and programs that emphasize the development of an action-taking, general managerial competency. The case method, for all of its distinctiveness and wide application, continues to be refined and elaborated in practice as the following articles illustrate.

Herman Gadon, in the first article, describes and carefully illustrates how he designs how cases are discussed to parallel the major case issues, thus increasing student involvement and experiential learning. Gadon's students essentially have a simultaneous, compound-learning opportunity for which the structure and dynamics described in the case and structure and dynamics experienced in the class are the same—for which "the medium and the message tell the same story."

Eileen Hogan then carefully describes an analytic model that she developed to overcome the confusion, frustration, and time consumption that can occur when students have to develop their own approach to work on cases. Unique to her approach is its emphasis on identifying casual chains in the situation—these chains both reveal primary problems and enable effective action planning. The systematic and logical ordering of steps to effective case analysis, such as described by Hogan, is seen more and more in the modern case method.

James Clawson and Sherwood Frey, in the final article in this section, provide an example of a technique for instructors to use in preparing for and leading a case discussion. They show how to map, or design, a productive sequence of questions that lead students through a consideration of problems, causes of problems, and selection among change strategies and alternative action plans. Teaching a case, they argue, is analogous to leading a tour—and the flexible use of a map reduces the chances of getting lost.

Recommended Resources on the Case Method

The Selected Readings provides a number of books that chronicle the origins, education, philosophy, and development of the case method as well as contain sensitive commentary on the instructor's role, classroom dynamics, and the case discussion process. The case method has not been without controversy and debate, as some of the articles in the Selected Readings show. Finally, I have included some sources that illustrate the continuing innovation in teaching cases.

References

Christensen, C. R. (1989). *Teaching and the case method.* Cambridge, MA: Harvard Business School.

Dewing, A. S. (1931). An introduction to the use of cases. In C. E. Fraser (Ed.), *A case method of instruction* (p. 49). New York: McGraw-Hill.

Erskine, J. A., Leenders, M. R., & Mauffette-Leenders, L. R. (1981). *Teaching with cases.* London, Canada: University of Western Ontario, School of Business Administration.

Gragg, C. I. (1954). Because wisdom can't be told. In M. P. McNair (Ed.), *The case method at the Harvard Business School* (p. 6). New York: McGraw-Hill.

Lawrence, P. (1953). The preparation of case material. In K. R. Andrews (Ed.), *The case method of teaching human relations and administration* (p. 215). Cambridge, MA: Harvard University Press.

Soltes, J. (1971). J. Dewey. In *Encyclopedia of Education* (p. 81). New York: Macmillan.

Whitehead, A. N. (1947). *Essays in science and philosophy.* New York: Philosophical Library.

Suggested Readings

Andrews, K. R. (1953). *The case method of teaching human relations and administration.*
    Cambridge, MA: Harvard University Press.
Argyris, C. (1980). Some limitations of the case method: Experience in a management
    development program. *Academy of Management Review, 5,* 291-298.
Berger, M. (1983). In defense of the case method: A reply to Argyris. *Academy of Manage-
    ment Review 8,* 327-333.
Gallos, J. V. (1992). Revisiting the same case: An exercise in reframing. *Journal of Manage-
    ment Education, 16*(2), 257-261.
Hunt, P. (1951, Summer). The case method of instruction. *Harvard Educational Review,*
    175-192.
Lombard, G. F. (Ed.). (1977). *The elusive phenomena.* Boston: Harvard University Graduate
    School of Business Administration.
Lundberg, C. C. (1989-1990). Case follow-up role plays: One way of creating realistic action
    experiences. *Organizational Behavior Teaching Review, 14*(1) 157-158.
McNair, M. P. (Ed.). (1954). *The case method at the Harvard Business School.* New York:
    McGraw-Hill.
Miner, F. C. (1978). An approach for increasing participation in case discussions. *Exchange:
    The Organizational Behavior Teaching Journal, 12*(2), 28-32.
Molstad, C., & Levy, S. (1987-1988). Developing experiential analogues to cases. *Organiza-
    tional Behavior Teaching Review, 12*(2), 28-32.
Reynolds, J. I. (1978). There is method in cases. *The Academy of Management Review, 3,*
    129-133.
Towl, A. R. (1969). *To study administration by cases.* Cambridge, MA: Harvard Business
    School.
Turner, A. N. (1981). The case discussion revisited (B). *Exchange: The Organizational
    Behavior Teaching Journal, 7*(4), 33-38.
Turner, N. (1981). The case method revisited (A). *Exchange: The Organizational Behavior
    Teaching Journal, 6*(3), 6-8.

Five
_____

Teaching Cases Experientially

HERMAN GADON
University of California, San Diego

The courses that I have taught through the years have evolved through several different stages. Initially, I relied primarily on lecture, then moved to a mixture of lecture and cases, and finally, relied heavily on experience-based methods. In the process of this development, cases often fell on hard times, as they seemed to be at odds with the new experiential pedagogy. This led to conflicts over the relative merits of case versus experiential methods and attempts to work out the right mix of cases and exercises.

After much experimentation, I discovered a way to move beyond an either-or solution and toward a method of integrating cases with an experiential approach. This combines the personal involvement of experiential methods with the wide variety of situations and institutional settings available through cases. The method is deceptively simple! I structure the class period so that the *manner* in which the students discuss the case will parallel the major *issue* in the case. Because the class reflects characteristics that are representative of any organization, a structure can generally be created that parallels the case.

By having the medium and the message tell the same story, the learning becomes very powerful. This approach has a further advantage in that it increases the willingness of students to examine their own experience. When they see that the issues contained in the case analyses are not dissimilar to the ones that they have just personally confronted, the threat in examining one's own behavior is reduced. This further permits the students to apply to themselves the concepts they are learning.

This chapter originally appeared in *Exchange: The Organizational Behavior Teaching Journal*, Volume 2, Issue 1.

One example that illustrates this process of integrating cases with experiential learning involves the "Case of the Changing Cage" (ICCH 8-460-001).[1] This is a sequential five-part case. After each part, the student is asked to make predictions, read the next part to compare these with what actually happened, and explain the reasons for any discrepancies. In this manner the student works his or her way through a dynamic situation of diagnosing, predicting, assessing, and correcting.

The case concerns a small work group of nine clerks under the supervision of a first-line supervisor, Ms. Dunn. The group is insulated from external influences by a wire enclosure reinforced by files to form a barrier to the prying eyes of the department head, Mr. Burke. The work group develops a stable culture in its isolation. In exchange for their autonomy, members of the cage group provide management with a reasonably high level of performance.

As part of a larger change in work layout, the cage is relocated so that it is no longer isolated and insulated but instead is subjected to the close scrutiny of Mr. Burke who frowns on many customs of the cage culture. The work group copes poorly with the change. Strain increases, performance falls, and satisfaction decreases. The scenario is a familiar one, and the case is a classic.

The method that was developed for an 80-minute class provides an experience in the classroom that roughly parallels the experience of the workers in the cage. An even number of groups of 6 to 10 members are formed in the class period before the session scheduled for the exercise (if work groups had been previously formed, these groups are used). Once the groups are formed, each selects a leader to facilitate the discussion of the case. The peer selection of a leader encourages closer association of the leader to the group members than to the instructor, thus paralleling the situation of Ms. Dunn. To continue the parallel further, the instructor should keep a low profile during the first part of the exercise, and at times even be absent from the room.

At the beginning of the class session, students assemble in their groups, read part one of the case, and have 15 minutes to make their predictions. These predictions are written and given to the instructor by the group leader. Students are then given part two and have an additional 15 minutes to explore the reason for any discrepancy between their initial predictions and part two. Again, they write their answers and give them to the instructor through their leader.

Before reading part three, half the groups are identified as A and half as B and then are paired. Each A group moves its chairs to B group's territory, encircled by B group members. B group members are told to observe the process of the other group's case analysis for the purpose of giving them feedback. The A groups then read part three and make predictions.

During this phase of the class period, the instructor changes his or her behavior and moves conspicuously about the room, stopping to listen and observe the discussions in each group. If the instructor notices inattention to the task, he or she admonishes the group leader with comments such as "Why is so and so laughing?" "Can't you keep these people working?"

The structure of this class provides rather clear parallels to the situation described in the case. Left to themselves, each group has developed a subculture as a function of its insulation from external influences. These established patterns of behavior are disrupted by changes that prevent established customs from continuing. In the class, as in the case, work groups leave familiar surroundings to occupy an alien space. The groups have been led to expect autonomy and have developed unique ways of using it and resent the loss of control as well as the disruption of prevailing practices.

In conclusion, the class can read parts four and five and discuss the options then available to Mr. Burke. The instructor can compare the feelings generated by the exercise in the classroom with the behavior of persons in the case. The instructor can also focus on emotional reactions because his or her behavior in part three of the exercise will invariably arouse resentment, which will persist unless it is confronted successfully. The parallels between Burke's and the instructor's alternatives can then be considered.

Integration of case analysis with classroom experience does not necessarily require elaborate structuring and shifting of groups. In the "Foster Creek Post Office" case, important learning is produced by a simple shift of one student (Elbing, 1970). In this case, Harry, a clerk for 24 years in a competitive, high-pressure, big-city post office, transfers by choice to the post office of a small town of 11,000. Harry's experiences in the city led him to internalize the required aspects of the job—he has learned to live by the book—the *U.S. Post Office Manual*—which prescribes the way work is to be done.

In Foster Creek, Harry encounters a different culture. Six mail carriers, with the knowledge of their supervisor, regulate their routes during the summer so that they can relax at home for 2 hours between 1:30 and 3:30 P.M. In the winter they work harder and longer hours than required. The post office personnel protect their summer practices by keeping patrons and inspectors happy. When an inspector on one of his irregular tours appears, all employees snap to and follow the book.

Unaccustomed to taking personal time during the day, Harry is unwilling to retire at home for 2 hours as do his peers. Instead, he returns to the post office early and "helps" others by doing their work for them. His help is apparently an attempt to ingratiate himself, behavior carried over from his experience in the city where such help was seen as an act of friendship. Harry's fellow carriers, however, perceive this assistance as an infringement, leaving them with idle time on their hands when they return to the office, which makes them look like slackers. This impression is reinforced when an inspector observes what is happening during one of his unexpected visits, posing a direct threat to the summer practices of the work group. In response, Harry is isolated, confined to a corner, where he is hidden from the public. Thus Harry's efforts to gain acceptance by his fellow workers lead to his being totally rejected.

The class structure again uses small groups of six to eight members, which begin the class period by discussing the questions assigned for the case. After 10 minutes, the instructor interrupts and asks each group to select a person to go to another group, preferably as a volunteer. After the shift is made, groups continue their discussion for 20 minutes. At the end of 20 minutes, groups are given 10 minutes for all members to write their answers individually to the following questions:

A. Strangers in the groups
   1. How did they feel as new members?
   2. How did they behave and why?
   3. What were their objectives?
   4. How did they perceive the way they were greeted in the new groups?
B. Old members in the groups
   1. How did they feel about the new member?
   2. How did they behave toward the new member and why?
   3. What were their objectives?
   4. How did they perceive the new member's behavior?

For the following 15 minutes, the old and new members in each group share their perceptions with each other. For the final 20 minutes, all information is shared in a general discussion in the class and parallels are drawn between experiences described in the case and the students' experiences in the exercise.

How well does this approach work with a sophisticated audience? Does it happen that, although successful the first or second time an instructor structures the class to parallel the case, it then stops being effective? Once participants know that's likely to occur, don't they see it coming, which deprives the experience of its impact? These problems have not occurred in my considerable experience.

This method not only offers high involvement but avoids another problem that often occurs in a straight case analysis. When there is only a cognitive discussion, the student may reject the importance of the message by seeing the phenomenon as either obvious or as unique to that setting. This sometimes occurs in a discussion of "Banana Time," a description by Roy (1960) of the social system of a group of four punch-press operators who work on a simple repetitive task. Norms and ritualized patterns of interaction have developed that exert strong control on the workers (including Roy, who has joined as a participant-observer). Roy observes behavior that at first seems meaningless to him but then becomes clear as rituals and norms with distinct social functions. Roy's (1960) growing insight is revealed by his sense of discovery:

> What I heard at first, *before I started to listen,* was a stream of disconnected bits of conversation which did not make sense. . . . What I saw at first, *before I began to observe,* was occasional flurries of horseplay that was so simple and unvarying in pattern and so childlike in quality that they made no strong bid for attention. (emphasis added)

Too frequently the students either see Roy's observation as obvious or conclude that such patterns occur only among workers who don't want to work. Students are unable as untrained observers in the early days of the course to see the patterns in behavior that develop as rituals and norms in their own work group and in the class.

Again, in this case the design for building a parallel classroom experience is a simple one. Six- to eight-member work groups are given Homan's Social System Conceptual Scheme to explain the behavior of the people in the case. After 20 minutes of discussion in their groups, I interrupt with a 10-minute lecture on the significance of rituals and distinguish them from norms. For the following 20 minutes, groups identify the rituals and norms that are emerging in their own groups and in the class, the significance of them, and the parallels to the case.

In this way the students become aware of the patterns of their own behavior. They experience in practice, as Roy does in the case, the significance of careful observation and clear analysis. I find that the combination of exercise and class discussion drives this lesson home more forcefully and with more lasting impact than case discussion alone.

It is sometimes possible to take advantage of demographic characteristics of the class to illustrate the main points of a case. "Anderson Manufacturing" (ICCH 13H25) is a case concerned with career choice: Ham Wilson, the protagonist, must choose between a managerial and technical career. By separating engineering, business, and liberal arts students into different groups, one can illustrate how differences in background lead to different definitions of the situation and different solutions.

In "RFK High School" (ICCH 9-747-183), a case about a new principal who must contend with warring factions in his school, one can design the class around the whites, minorities, and women in the course to provide parallels to the intergroup experience of your own students. The demographic features of our classes also provide other opportunities to explore the kinds of communication difficulties persons in cases sometimes have when they have learned different ways of thinking about the world.

This approach builds on the separate strengths of the case approach and experiential methods. Many cases lend themselves to arrangements of the kind illustrated in this article. The range of potential settings is wide, limited mainly by the imagination of the instructor. Furthermore, it allows case teachers to move toward experiential learning by building on their expertise rather than discarding it.

Note

1. Copies of all the cases mentioned in the article can also be found in Cohen, Fink, Gadon, and Willits (1992). The accompanying teacher's manual also contains a large number of other cases adapted to experiential use.

References

Cohen, A., Fink, S., Gadon, H., & Willits, R. (1992). *Effective behavior in organizations* (5th ed.). Homewood, IL: Irwin.
Elbing, A. O. (1970). *Behavioral decisions in organizations.* Glenview, IL: Scott, Foresman.
Roy, D. F. (1960). Banana time, job satisfaction and informal interaction. *Human Organization, 18*(4).

Six
_____

Using a Model for Case Analysis in Case Method Instruction

EILEEN HOGAN
Valdosta State University

One of the most difficult issues instructors face in teaching a subject by the case method is students' lack of a consensual approach for analyzing and resolving situations. That is, students vary widely in the nature, explicitness, and logicalness of their approaches to problem solving, decision making, and planning. Disparate definitions of analytical terms such as *problem, cause, decision,* and *solution* can also render case discussions ineffective.

One way teachers vary in how they deal with this issue is in how much structure they provide students for these analytical processes. Instructors vary from providing no structure at all, presumably in the hope that students will develop their own methods of analysis, to providing detailed procedures of analysis through which students are required to work. An instructor's choice of strategy should reflect his or her philosophy, beliefs about learning, and learning objectives, as the degree of structure provided has substantial consequences for the students' learning experiences. The *analytic process* approach, providing little or no structure, can be contrasted with the *subject matter* approach to clarify these differences.

The Analytic Process Approach

Some teachers argue that dealing with ambiguity in group problem-solving and decision-making processes is beneficial for students and that providing

This chapter originally appeared in *The Organizational Behavior Teaching Review,* Volume 9, Issue 2.

structure detracts from students' potential learning. The assumption is made that in deriving their own processes, students learn the nature of logic and argumentation more effectively.

In this pedagogy, the process of analysis, as opposed to the subject matter of the course, assumes the first priority among learning objectives. Learning how to learn is the focus, as opposed to learning about human psychology, accounting, or marketing. Within this framework, students' lack of consensus about how to work through problems becomes an opportunity for them to increase their capabilities of logical thought: They become more aware of their own mental processes through self-discovery.

The Subject Matter Approach

Within the subject matter approach, students' lack of consensus about problem solving and decision making becomes a problem to be overcome because of time limitations. Students' attaining their own order to analytical processes consumes valuable classroom time, and if instructors feel that the priority in learning should be placed on content areas more specific to the course title, they may begrudge this time. Although the process approach certainly does not preclude content learning, time constraints may make its use impractical. Furthermore, those methods for analyzing problems and decisions derived by groups are not guaranteed to be efficient or effective in the instructor's judgment.

An Alternative

Instructors explicitly or implicitly provide a guideline for case analysis or the process approach is chosen by default. Unfortunately, the process approach suffers if not well planned, prepared, and consciously managed by the instructor. Therefore, it makes sense for teachers to consider the implications of whatever level of structure they provide before moving ahead.

One alternative available is to provide students with a general model of the logic in problem-solving and decision-making systems and some definitions of commonly used terms. Models such as these have been quite popular in management development (e.g., Hale & Plunkett, 1982; Kepner & Tregoe, 1965) and extending these ideas to students' simulations of managerial situations can be useful.

Providing a general model is a compromise between the process and content priorities. Students can achieve awareness of their mental functioning through comparison with a given model and, if the model is not overly specific or constraining, be left freedom to establish idiosyncrasies within the framework. On the other hand, by providing a general ordering of analytical topics that need to be covered in a case discussion, a model can provide more efficient handling of cases, especially in early sessions.

Coupled with these advantages are disadvantages. Some students may find a given model difficult to understand or use; for example, a very logical method may not come across well to more intuitive individuals. Also, learning how to analyze does take some time away from content, although to some degree case discussions of management education content and analytical process can be held simultaneously.

For several years I have presented such a model to first-year MBA students during the first week of classes. Generally I have given a written description of the model to students at the end of their first case discussion (to allow some self-discovery), and then discuss the analytic process explicitly during the next several cases. The model then provides an expectation for discussions through the rest of the term. The results have been good: more orderly discussions at an earlier stage of the course, greater and earlier class participation, and positive response from students. Because of these factors, I believe that students are freed to learn more about course content during the term.

In doing so I have stated implicitly that I find the process of developing analytical methods too time-consuming given other constraints. However, because the model presented is general enough that students do need to deal with some remaining ambiguity and also because the approximately 55 cases put forth in the course in the first year give them ample opportunity to apply the model, I find their abilities to analyze quite satisfactory.

The objective of this article is to present this model. The model can be used by case readers in understanding and responding to case situations and, sometimes, by managers facing actual problems. The structure represents a logical flow that can aid in visualizing the present, understanding the past, and projecting into the future.

One Model for Case Analysis

Case studies typically describe an organizational situation. Case readers are expected to "understand" this situation, and "resolve" it. Understanding involves comprehending the causes and effects of various events or circumstances. Resolutions are courses of action (or nonaction) appropriate for case characters to take to relieve problems, adapt to adversity, take advantage of opportunity, or otherwise prepare for the future. These parts together can be called a case analysis. Effective performance in a case discussion or written format is that which covers these two elements to an appropriate depth.

DETERMINING THE PROBLEM

Most cases contain one or more problem situations, defined as a gap existing between what ought to be occurring and what is actually occurring. The first task of case analysis is to determine what, if any, problem or potential problem exists and whether or not it is important enough to be concerned about.

Although it may seem that determining whether a problem exists should be straightforward, defining a problem can be quite difficult. Several possible reasons for this exist. First, the *should* may be unclear—that is, one may not be sure of exactly what ought to be occurring. Second, the *actual* may not be clear—information about what is actually occurring may be ambiguous, biased, or even nonexistent. Either of these reasons make it difficult to define the gap between goals and reality.

Third, in organizations we often find that the definition of a problem differs, depending on who is doing the defining. In many case studies, it is possible to distinguish between problems as defined by various persons in the case, the case writer, and ourselves, the case readers. Therefore, part of determining whether a problem exists is deciding *whose* problem it is, that is, to whom is it important enough to require concern, analysis, and action? We should always be aware of these differences in perspectives and their impact on our understanding of cases.

BUSINESS VERSUS SOURCE PROBLEMS

After determining a problem exists and is worth further attention, a case analysis needs to describe the problem or potential problem in more detail. There are different types of problems that are encountered. The most obvious problems involve something that has gone wrong as measured against a business goal of the organization. Examples of this are insufficient quantity or quality of output, failure to deliver items on schedule, excessive costs of output, or decreased profits. These are called *business problems;* they are the primary concern of managers, of clear relevance to an organization's effectiveness. Other problems can be described as *source problems,* in that they often cause primary business problems but may not actually constitute problems per se. Examples are dissatisfied employees, failure to communicate, and high rates of turnover. Source problems are important because they frequently cause primary business problems. Almost all business problems can be traced at least in part to some problem of a deeper nature, and we often find that to solve a business problem it is

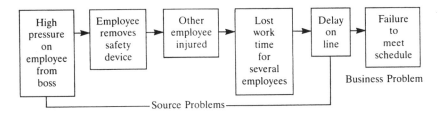

Figure 6.1. Example of a causal chain.

necessary to solve the source problems first. We normally are concerned with how an individual solves source problems, but we must always be aware that these source problems are important in that they may or may not actually lead to primary business problems. The business problems we are concerned about may be actual (already in existence) or potential; either may justify managerial concern, analysis, and action.

CAUSAL CHAINS

In some situations, there may be a whole chain of source problems that lead to a business problem. Thus an employee under high pressure to perform may remove a safety device without the boss's knowledge, which then causes another employee to be injured, which causes lost working time for several employees, which causes a delay in producing a product, which causes failure to meet a schedule. This idea of causal chains is important in understanding how many factors may act sequentially to produce a problem. Figure 6.1 depicts this causal chain.

We must recognize the semantic difficulty in the notion that the cause of one problem (source or business) may also be a source problem with causes of its own.

COMPLEX CAUSAL NETWORKS

Furthermore, source problems can cause more than one other problem, and several different factors may work simultaneously to cause another event (Fig. 6.2). The result is a complex causal network that the manager needs to make explicit and understand before trying to eliminate or adapt to a business problem.

LEVELS OF PROBLEMS

In addition to describing the type of problem as business or source, it is possible to categorize in other ways. One such way is to describe the level

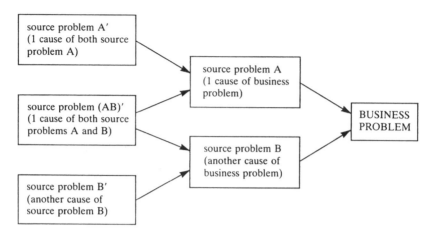

Figure 6.2. Example of complex networks.

of the problem. Levels define the extent to which the problem affects the whole organization, as opposed to only one individual in the organization. Some levels are (1) organization/environment, for which we might see that an organization's objectives and activities are not aligned with changing needs in its markets; (2) structural, for which, for example, responsibility and authority are not clearly communicated; (3) intergroup, such as disruptive competition between two departments of an organization; (4) group problems, such as the situations in which members of a work group suffer from low morale; (5) interpersonal, for example, conflict between two individuals; and (6) intrapersonal, that is, a problem an individual is facing within himself or herself. Causal networks can include problems from several of these levels, often intertwined with each other.

Recognizing the different levels involved in problems allows the analyzer to use appropriate knowledge of cause and effect. For example, interpersonal problems can be best understood by use of psychological concepts, whereas structural problems require a different set of ideas. The levels thus provide a checklist to ensure problems have been thought through in all appropriate ways.

THE NEED TO UNDERSTAND CAUSE

An individual might need to take some immediate action that deals with the effects of the problem (e.g., pouring water on the fire in the wastebasket). In the long run, learning the cause—the source problem(s) of the business problem (how the fire started and why)—gives a wider range of possible solutions, more robust predictions of the potential future problems associated with various courses of action, and an appreciation for the likelihood of the problem's recurrence. For example, causal chains are important in understanding the correction of problems, because by tracing cause-and-effect chains an individual can choose to intervene at various places to break the chain and correct the problem. The question of how far back to trace such chains must be answered by considering the costs (money, time, and energy) of further analysis versus the possible benefits to be gained.

THE PROCESS OF UNDERSTANDING CAUSE

This leaves the tasks of finding and understanding the causes of problems. Basically, this process involves looking to the past, collecting relevant data about the problem (when, where, and how big is it), and making reasonable assumptions and inferences to understand causal networks. Some guidelines may assist in this process.

1. When problems occur suddenly—that is, the gap between the *should* and the *actual* has developed in a short period of time—we should look for changes that occurred around the time the problem started to occur. This is because changes often cause problems, and identifying the timing of changes in this way can often help us understand problems.

2. On the other hand, problems that occur only in one area (e.g., low production on only one assembly line or low sales in Cleveland) provide an opportunity to understand cause by investigating differences between the area(s) where the problem is occurring and the area(s) where the problem is not occurring. This is especially valuable when problems occur in only one work group of several that are performing similar tasks. We ask what's different about the people, products, the physical location or facilities, systems, policies or procedures, or other items in problem area(s) versus area(s) that are still operating up to standard. Through these differences the manager can often get clues about why the problem occurs in certain places and not in others, yielding more understanding of the cause of the problem.

MOST PROBABLE CAUSE

We conclude what is the most probable cause (or causes) of a problem by deciding which of many possible sources is most consistent with available data about what the problem is, where and when it occurs, and how big it is. There are several guidelines for maintaining objectivity in this process. First, avoid jumping to conclusions about cause before seeking out and analyzing relevant information. Second, recognize assumptions and inferences and distinguish these from facts. Third, verify the accuracy of data. Fourth, after reaching a tentative conclusion about the most probable cause(s), test this conclusion before moving into action, recognizing that what is done may have significant positive or negative effects. Only when one is confident that he or she understands the source of problems behind the business problem should a move be made to a decision about solving the problem.

RESOLVING SITUATIONS

Once he or she understands the causes of a problem, an individual is better equipped to make an intelligent decision about the best course of future action. Even when no specific problem exists, those who understand the causes of good and poor job performance are best equipped to make effective decisions. We define a decision as a choice between alternatives—in this case, alternative courses of action. The best alternative will be that which best meets the goals for the decision (what the decision should achieve) and the constraints within which it must operate. By objectively evaluating each alternative against these goals and constraints, the best choice of action is often obvious.

SELECTING CRITERIA

The process of selecting the criteria against which the alternatives will be measured should include these steps. First, the goals of the organization, the unit, and various case figures should be considered. Second, limits on time, money, resources, and policy should be noted. Third, potential problems (i.e., gaps between *should* and *actual* that may occur in the future) caused by implementation should be anticipated, and the risk of their occurrence and the size of such potential problems should be considered (i.e., some solutions have been known to cause bigger problems than they were originally meant to solve).

Examples of factors a manager might use as criteria for making this decision are the following:

- Eliminating a specific problem
- Least time elapsed before getting back to an acceptable condition
- Fewest negative side effects
- Cheapest in money, in time invested in implementing, or in energy
- Human values, such as subordinate development
- Receptivity of organizational members to a possible solution

By comparing how well several alternatives meet criteria simultaneously, a decision maker can choose the best solution.

IMPLEMENTATION AND EVALUATION

After making a decision about what to do with the problem, the decision must be implemented. Implementing begins with setting out an action plan. This action plan builds on work already done in analyzing potential problems and risks in making the decision but is more specific. Action plans should specify who does what, when, where, and how. Also, contingency plans—"What I will do if event X occurs"—are important features of action plans. Action plans do vary in detail—more important problems, more complex problems, and situations in which many and/or large potential problems are anticipated or that involve changes in individuals' long-term habitual behavior patterns should involve more detail. As this is true between action plans, it is also true within action plans—some parts of plans may be much more complex and detailed than others.

THE ANALYSIS PROCESS AS A CYCLE

A dilemma often occurs as action plans are implemented. On one hand, people need to be committed to the course of action they have chosen. Without this commitment, other people they expect to implement the solution may withhold their full effort. On the other hand, individuals need to be aware when things are not going as expected and be willing to change the plan at that time. Therefore, although they must be committed to what they are doing, they need to seek out data actively that indicate whether things are or are not going as they should, and they should continue to evaluate. As they evaluate, they may also become aware of better information about source problems, potential problems they had not foreseen, new factors entering the situation, or changes in goals and constraints. Any of these may lead to a "recycling" of the analysis process: A return to defining the problem (if goals have changed, perhaps it is no longer a problem), a more involved search for cause; remaking a decision, or defining a different action plan. The problem-solving process often is not straightforward but instead is a course of trial, error, learning, and retrial.

The process of analyzing a situation can be conceived of as a four-stage, potentially recursive process (Fig. 6.3). First, an individual identifies a problem as something wrong, its type and level(s), and the various cause-and-effect chains as far as known. Perhaps interim action is initiated. Second, an individual seeks to understand further the causes of the problem. He or she does this by looking at the changes that have occurred, differences that may be present, verifying information and testing ideas with others, and eventually selecting the most probable cause(s) from a list of possible causes. Third, an individual makes a decision about the best solution to the problem. He or she selects the alternative that best meets the criteria for solving the problem. The alternative may be to remove or minimize a cause of the problem, thus removing the problem itself, or may be to live with or minimize the problem's negative effects. In the fourth stage an individual plans action in detail, implements the choice, and observes the situation. Based on observations, he or she evaluates and decides future analysis and action. He or she needs to be both committed to the decision and flexible in its implementation as well as be aware of the possible need to recycle and be willing to do so.

Summary

This article has presented one model of a logical ordering of the steps needed in effective case analysis. Students can benefit from being presented with such a model by being made aware of their own intuitive analytical processes and forced to confront inadequacies when they exist. In addition, the model provides benefits for groups in its definitions of terminology and systematic methodology for working through the problem definition, data collection, deduction, criteria setting, and alternative evaluation phases of analysis. For case methods instructors, such a model can cut down on time spent working through these issues during class sessions, providing more time to cover management and organization topics.

References

Hale, G., & Plunkett, L. *The proactive manager.* New York: Wiley, 1982.
Kepner, C., & Tregoe, B. *The rational manager.* Princeton, NJ: Kepner-Tregoe, 1965.

	I. Defining the Problem	II. Understanding Cause(s)	III. Making a Decision	IV. Implement & Evaluate
Content	"SHOULD" ↕ Gap = Problem "ACTUAL"	PC —?→ Problem PC —?→ PC —?→	A1 A2 A3 **?** Best Choice	Action Plan ⌂ Solution
	Something's wrong—	*Why has this gone wrong?*	*What's the best way to resolve this problem?*	*Is this going as I expected?*
Procedure	Define: What is/are the gaps? Important Type and level of problem. Cause and effect chains, as far as known. Interim action, if needed.	Understand: Changes, differences Gather information. Organize, schedule. Verify information. Test. Select most probable cause(s) from possible causes.	Specify criteria for choosing best alternative (results, limits, risks of potential problems). Compare alternatives to each other based on how well they meet the criteria. Choose alternative that meets criteria the best.	Develop action plan (who, what, where, when, how). Communicate with others. Watch for disconfirming data. Evaluate. Decide to continue or recycle.

Figure 6.3. The case analysis process.

69

Seven

Mapping Case Pedagogy

JAMES G. CLAWSON
SHERWOOD C. FREY, JR.
University of Virginia

Have you ever had an experience like the one our colleague described?

I walked out of class one day feeling very agitated and very frustrated. The discussion had been extremely lively, hands up all over the room, and a lot of excited and eager student participation. But I was concerned because in the middle of the discussion, I felt like an infantry commander caught in the middle of a raging battlefield, surrounded by tumultuous energy but unable to see clearly, much less control, the ebb and flow of the contest and having little confidence about where or how it would end up. I remember wishing several times in the class that I had an observation balloon so that I might rise quietly and unobtrusively above the dispute, survey the territory, and figure out what to do and where to go before coming back down into the midst of it. I thought I was well prepared for the case and its content, and I knew the students fairly well, but I needed something more, a better way of visualizing the interaction of me, them, and the material. What I needed was a way of surveying the territory of the discussion from a higher vantage point, to look at its topography, so that I could chart a course through it that would get us where I thought we as a class needed to go. This concern may reflect my own intolerance of ambiguity, but there have been many times when I have felt just swamped by the speed and erratic nature of the discussion.

In our experience, this is a common phenomenon among case method teachers who have moved from a concern about mastering their content

This chapter originally appeared in *The Organizational Behavior Teaching Review*, Volume 11, Issue 1.

area to a concern about how to teach the content or, better, how to help the students learn the content or, best, how to balance the three.[1] In the desire to be student centered and, therefore, to be as concerned about teaching the people as the material, case teachers sometimes follow student leads without having a means of anticipating where the discussion will go or of managing that discussion or of making sense of it afterward.

We have found that mapping our case pedagogy is an effective process in dealing with these concerns. *Mapping* is an appropriate word here, because we have found that one can lay out a chart of the discussion with various sites and a variety of routes for moving among them. We have found that the process of constructing these maps is an excellent way to prepare for a case class, to develop a teaching note, and to record after a class new wrinkles that may have emerged. We have also found that one can develop a variety of maps for any case, depending on the particular audience or the particular objectives for the day. An analogy may best introduce what we mean.

Teaching a Case Is Like Leading a Tour

Let's compare teaching a case with leading a guided tour, where the tour guide is the instructor, the tourists are the students, and the scenic region is the topic of the day's class. At first, the tour guide has some discretion over where the tour will begin. If the scenic region is Tokyo, for instance, the tour guide may suggest that the tourists meet at any of a variety of places: Mitaka in the north, Hakone in the west, Yokohama in the south, Chiba in the east, or perhaps at the Imperial Palace right in the middle. The tour guide will send out these instructions in advance along with some reading material about the sites they plan to visit so the tourists will know where to gather and be better prepared to enjoy the day.

If the tour guide tells people to start at Mitaka and then waits for them at Yokohama, the tourists are likely to be upset for all of the wasted effort they made getting to Mitaka and for the resulting confusion, which usually lasts throughout the tour. Alternatively, the tour guide might not give any instructions, expecting the tourists to show up at the travel agency office and there to make the decision of where to begin together. This is more time-consuming, but for more experienced tourists, it has distinct benefits.[2]

Having chosen a starting point, the tour guide then consciously or subconsciously makes decisions about how much influence to have over the group. Should the tour guide lay out a specific itinerary with detailed times and foci at each stop along the way? Or should he or she allow the tourists to decide at each stop what they want to see and which site they want to see next? Of course, the interests and experience of the tourists will make a big difference. If they are new to the Tokyo area, the tour guide may wish to conduct one or two highly structured trips. If the group is generally familiar with the city, the guide may wish to give them several options along the way.

In either event, the tour guide will have his or her own idea of which stops are the most interesting. The tour guide, for instance, may conclude in advance that the day's tour of Tokyo should include the Tokyo Tower, the Imperial Palace, Ginza, the Tsukiji fish market, the Kabuki Theater, and a public bath in Akasaka for general interest.

Furthermore, the tour guide may have his or her own opinions about what aspects of each stop are important to note. He or she may determine that when the group stops at the tower, any tour guide worth his or her salt will make sure the tourists note the function, height, earthquake precautions, and history of the place. Other guides may wish to consider only the aspects of the tower that the tourists find interesting and bring up themselves. The sites and their important features when taken together begin to form the elements of a map, but as yet they have no relationship to each other.

Now, suppose the tour guide has contacted the tourists and asked them to meet at Mitaka. The tour guide arrives, meets the tourists, and is faced with a decision: Should he or she choose where the group goes from here or should he or she let the tourists choose? In fact, the tour guide will be faced with this decision at each stop. If the tour guide decides to choose, he or she might say, "We'll begin at Tokyo Tower today," and then load everyone on the bus. Upon arriving at the tower, the guide may ask the tourists what they think is significant about the structure. In the course of that discussion, all or part of the elements on the tour guide's list of important features may arise, but if he or she is convinced that all of the aspects are truly important, he or she is not likely to leave the tower before the group has considered them all. Of course, not all of the tourists may be interested in the history of the tower or even aware of it, so the tour guide may have to explain a few things when faced with such apathy or ignorance.

Finished with the tower visit, the tour guide again must decide where to go next. On his or her map of Tokyo, he or she can see that there are many ways to go, each with its own interests and intricacies. If the group went to the Imperial Palace next, the jump in historical perspective might be overwhelming for some and an interesting contrast to others. They might visit in succession the Ginza, the fish market, the palace, and then the theater to give a reverse chronological flow to the tour. Or they might bounce back and forth between the modern and the historical. In any event, visiting the public bath, interesting as it is, at the outset would tend to dampen the interest in and excitement for the rest of the stops; one seldom likes to leave a hot bath and proceed traipsing around the countryside. In all probability, the tour guide may choose to end the tour at the public bath where all can relax and reflect on the day's events.

If the tour guide is a good listener, he or she might hear something in the discussion at the tower that would indicate the route the tourists would prefer to take. Asking them straight out where they want to go at each stop might undermine the confidence the tourists would have in the tour guide, so that tour guide may determine to be more subtle about it. Instead, he or she notes on his or her tour plan or maybe even in the margins of the city map along each different route, transition phrases and/or questions that might naturally lead from the tower to each of the other stops. That way, no matter what alternative the tourists may suggest or not suggest, the tour guide is prepared to move from one stop to the next.

Of course, not all of the alternatives make much sense, especially to the experienced tour guide. If someone suggests going to the bath immediately the tour guide has ready an explanation as to why that would hinder rather than facilitate their collective learning experience on the tour.

As time passes, the tour proceeds in this fashion, visiting preselected sites, noting significant aspects about each site, and then deciding explicitly or implicitly where to go next. Occasionally, a tourist may request a side trip, say, to see a quaint Japanese inn that the bus passes. The tour guide notes the level of interest, assesses quickly whether or not this would be of interest to the group as a whole, notes how much time is left and how much this little trip would take and decides whether to respond or not. Too many of these little side trips will leave the tourists confused about what they have done and angry that they did not get what was promised them, so the tour guide is careful to keep the number and length of these diversions under control.

In fact, in observing other tour guides at work, our tour guide notices that new ones tend to stick much more closely to their preselected routes by forcing the tourists to follow them. Sometimes this leads to apathy or rebellion among the tourists. The more experienced tour guides focus less on the sites and more on the tourists. They are willing to make adjustments along the way, all the while trying to build the right balance among the tourists, the sites, and the tour guide's own interests and experience.

Our tour guide has realized that it takes confidence in one's own familiarity with the sites and confidence in the tourists' judgments and interests to be able to deviate from one's personal itinerary and follow tourist suggestions. A wise tour guide also knows that although following only the tourists' suggestions can eventually lead to deep appreciation for

Tokyo, that can be a very lengthy process. So our tour guide decides to try to balance the decisions between his or her own educated judgment and the interests of the tourists. After all, even if the guide's own itinerary has been covered completely, if the tourists haven't appreciated it, little more than dragging a bunch of unwilling foreigners around a crowded city has been accomplished.

Finally, at the end of the day, the tour guide suggests that they stop on their way home and take a bath. Soaking in the hot tubs (*o-furo* for you Japanophiles), the tourists reflect on the sights and insights of the day, each drawing his or her own points of interest and memory. On some trips, the tourists are more confused than others, and the tour guide will sum up the day, maybe with an invitation to come back for another similar tour. On other days, the trip may have been so clear in its themes and learnings that no wrapup is necessary from either tour guide or tourists.

DEBRIEFING THE TOUR

Although we expect that the parallel elements of this analogy and case teaching are clear, let us be explicit. The tour guide is the instructor, and the tourists are the students. The advance instructions are the study questions, and the background readings are any technical notes or expository pieces that accompany the case. The mismatched starting points are what happens when an instructor opens with a question that is not congruent with the advanced assignment. The travel agency office is the classroom. The sites are the key topics of discussion in that day's class, and the significant features of each site are the important facts or principles associated with each topic of discussion. The route comments are the transition questions that lead from one topical area to another. Explanations offered at the sites are lecturettes. Finally, the bath talk is the summary at the end of the class.

Of particular interest to us is the city map that the tour guide used. What is the analogous element in case teaching? We think it is a *case map,* and we have begun using them in our own teaching to great advantage.

Constructing a Case Map

The first step in preparing a case map is to list the topical areas to which the case provides entry. We have found writing these topics on small cards to be helpful in later steps. Next, one lists with each area (card) the significant facts or principles that can or should be addressed when visiting that topic in that case. Of course, some of the topical areas may be appropriate for some audiences and not for others. Not all sites will be visited by each audience so that an instructor might have several maps for each case depending on his or her audience and the class objectives.

Once the instructor has completed these cards, in effect completing a personal analysis of the case, he or she must begin to map the pedagogy or androgogy of the class. The instructor considers the audience, what they have done in previous classes, where the course will be going in subsequent classes, and chooses the most relevant set of cards.

Spreading the cards out on a paper desk pad, the instructor can then begin to play with different sequences and structures, different maps, if you will, of the territory represented in the case by the cards.[3] Once a reasonable structure is ready, laid out on the desk pad or computer monitor, one can begin drawing reasonable arrows from one card to the next. Some transitions won't make sense and get no arrows. With the arrows drawn in, one can then begin to write out on the desk pad itself, or on the monitor, transition questions and phrases that could be used to move the class from one topic (site) to another.

We believe that this question phrasing is an *extremely* important part of case teaching. If a good picture is worth a thousand words, then a good question is worth a dozen answers. Questions that yield yes-or-no answers don't often lead to full discussions. Questions that press students to think about underlying reasons and causes or to think about consequences and results tend to generate enlightening discussions.

The benefit of this mapping technique is that almost regardless of which way the discussion goes, the instructor has a mental view of the topography of the discussion, a map of the territory, that he or she can use to move from one part of the map to another. Student discussion will usually fall into reasonably predictable chunks, outlined by the sites or topical areas. Within these, the instructor can be alert for the key facts and principles. If they all come up and the class begins to dawdle without moving itself on to the next topic, the instructor can suggest the next tour site through a directive transition question. If the key points don't all emerge from the discussion, he or she can ask some questions that will highlight those aspects left unmentioned.

We have found this an excellent way to be able to rise mentally above the discussion, look down on it and maintain some perspective. The benefits of being able to see what's going on yields additional confidence and subsequently skill in managing a case discussion.

An Example

We have outlined the classic Dashman Company case (Harvard Business School case #9-642-001) using the mapping approach introduced above.

As you can see from the sample map in Figure 7.1, we often start this case
at the "travel agency offices" by asking, "What are the problems here?"
You might wish to take a more focused approach to a particular topic
(emphasizing one of the sites/cards), therefore beginning with a different
question and thus producing a different map. Once we have opened the
topic of problems in the case (the first tour site), we want to make sure that
the class sees the situation from the perspectives of the several parties of
the case, so we list them on our map in the box titled "Problem Identification." You can also see that we often use this site as a springboard into a
little side discussion on the generic nature of a problem. During this
diversion, we want to make sure that four elements of problems—wants,
gots, want-got gaps, and problem owners—are all clear before returning
to the specifics of the case. These are listed in the "Generic Problems" box.
This diversion can be used as a means to broaden the problem discussion
if it shows signs of being too narrow. When we use the case early in a
course or module when we will be returning to the problem model later
on, the diversion becomes part of the main route.

When the class has explored the perspectives of the key stakeholders,
we usually either lead or follow the class to a consideration of the causes
of those problems. Several sources seem important to us in this discussion,
and these are noted in the box on causes. We are not limited to those listed
here, but because we have a map, we are aware when students add things,
fail to mention things, or take a different tack.

From the causes box, one could branch out in several directions, depending
again on the tour strategy, the audience, the focus of the course/seminar, and
other conditions. Again, the importance of the map for us is that we are much
more aware when these detours occur and whence and thence they take us. If
the students have a lot of energy for a discussion of the ways in which one
might design and implement systems to control the heretofore independent
plant purchasing managers, we might follow that energy confident that given
our map, we can put perspective on the discussion by being able to explain
where we were and how we got there or even be able to direct the discussion
both subtly and constructively back to the main route.

If necessary, we will follow the causes discussion with the action
question, "What should Mr. Post do?" or more generally, "What should be
done by whom to address these problems?" We usually try to press the
specifics of action planning and so chose to include the journalistic six
imperatives (who, what, why, when, where, and how) in our box in addition
to the various alternatives that are often suggested in class and that are
shown in Figure 7.1, but you might have other approaches you would like
to emphasize here. For instance, you might have preceded this discussion
with a site/topic called "alternatives" or "action options," which we have

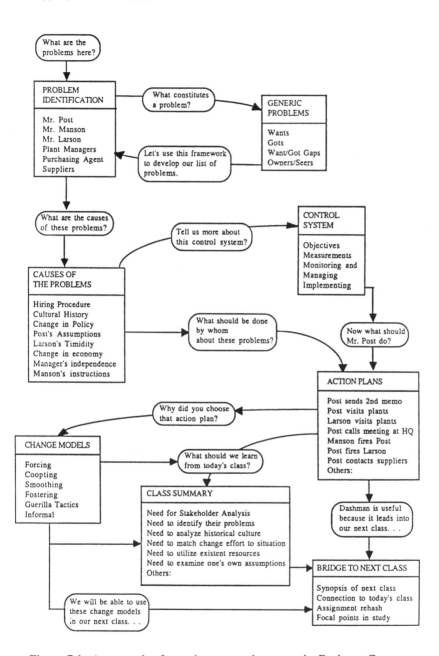

Figure 7.1. An example of mapping case pedagogy— the Dashman Company.

done on occasion. Sometimes seeing alternative courses of action is the single most constraining factor in managerial decision making, so this can be a very useful discussion.

Because we often use this case as an introduction to managing change, we usually end with a discussion of models of change by asking students to consider why they chose the action plans they did to make explicit their change theories. This sets up successive cases in the change module in that it gets students thinking about their personal change models and makes it easier for them to compare and contrast them with the ones we will introduce in the module.

You may have other topical areas (represented by the boxes on the diagram) or additional principles (the lists within the boxes) that you would use in mapping this case. But this example does illustrate the general framework and approach we are suggesting.

This mapping approach does not constitute our entire preparation for teaching cases. We usually do extensive additional analyses of various parts/sites in a case and add other things like a board plan and supplemental information and quotes. But mapping gives us excellent perspective on the teaching topography of a case. We encourage you to try this technique several times to see if it works for you by providing additional perspective on your case teaching both before you enter class and while you are in the thick of things in front of a forest of hands. If you do, we expect that you will be much less likely to become a casualty or to experience the confusion of the battlefield that our colleague expressed at the outset.

Notes

1. The editor's introduction to Athos (1979) outlines briefly four stages of teacher development: material focus, pedagogical focus, student focus, and skilled integration, which we find to be a powerful and useful model.

2. It also changes the theme of the article from mapping case *pedagogy* to mapping case *androgogy*, because it follows the androgogical concept developed by Knowles (1990) for which the learning desires of the students are solicited and included in the class design. Pedagogy refers etiologically to the teaching of children, whereas androgogy refers to the teaching of adults.

3. We have experimented with doing this on microcomputers with good success. Drawing packages like *Draw Perfect, GEM-Draw, Dr. Halo,* and *MAC-Draw*—which have boxes, ellipses and circles, arc drawing capacity, lines ending with arrowheads, and small text fonts—work well.

References

Athos, A. G. (1979). Contingencies beyond reasoning. *Exchange: The Organizational Behavior Teaching Journal, 4*(2) 7-12.

Knowles, M. S. (1990). *The adult learner: A neglected species* (4th ed.). Houston: Gulf.

Simulation, Video, and High-Tech Applications

JOAN WEINER
Drexel University

GIL BOYER
St. Josephs University

Humans, in the heritage of their various cultures, possess awesome power. In a technologically shrinking world, the social use of that power for the optimum benefit of any one person or any one culture increasingly requires the active, mutually benefiting cooperation of other people and their cultures. It is in the actualization of human cooperative interdependence that the constructive future of human beings lies. Affluence, in self-actualized terms, is a cooperative venture. Our classrooms need to reflect this.

That is what this volume is all about. The Organizational Behavior Teaching Society has been dedicated to improving the interface between the student and the professor, and that interface has been changing quite rapidly, ushering in a new era in pedagogy. An effective learning environment must address two issues: (1) teaching students the concepts, skills and techniques necessary to understand and solve problems while interacting effectively with others in group and organizational settings; and (2) structuring classroom teaching in such a way that makes the first issue possible.

Our lecture halls are probably the poorest learning environment we could devise to prepare our students to be effective in today's interdependent, interactive world. All too often, as the statement goes, the notes of the professor are transmitted to the notebooks of the students without passing through the brains of either. Better would be discussions in which the students are actively involved *and* the professor gets some feedback about the effectiveness of his or her comments. Better still would be involving the students in actually using the new information as a way to learn. If the real thing is not feasible in the classroom (too expensive, too dangerous, not readily available), then try a simulation. The whole idea is to shift the emphasis from the teaching of the instructor to the learning of the student. To do this the delivery system changes—lectures alone won't do. Power relationships change—student centered not instructor dominated. Even the definition of classroom changes, and boundaries of space and time take on new possibilities. The world outside the classroom has changed so much that classroom can become a very exciting, interactive, and even fun place to be.

Now with video and computer technology far less expensive, much more powerful, and in most universities readily available, Tomorrow is already here, and it looks vastly different from our obsolete lecture halls. No need to imagine new and futuristic inventions. We certainly will have some, but we have enough now to construct this new era without imagining anything else. We already have powerful, high-speed chips, data banks, networks, video phones, satellites, fiber optics, laser disks, teleconferencing, and so on. The list is long, and each new connection envisions new possibilities. We are redefining our world—classrooms and the art of teaching included. The task is to do it (make it happen).

Let's offer a couple examples. In the early 1960s some students at New England Educational Data Systems (NEEDS) at Harvard were playing around with the computer of the day—a huge IBM 7094 mainframe that cost $10 a minute to operate. Their goal was to put all of Shakespeare's writing in one large (for then) file, develop lexicons of the words Shakespeare used as his characters' moods and attitudes changed, apply them to the text file to select the passages that used similar words, and thus rewrite the bard's work in such a way as to reveal new meanings. The students called this having "Dialogs with the Dead." The theory was there, but affordable hardware to implement it was not available for another two decades. This development took place, mind you, while most computer programs were little more than page turners. Not surprisingly, we tend to first use new technology to replace an old one and we tend to use it in the same way—computers as a substitute for textbooks or as a substitute for typewriters, for example. Many of our current uses are of this substitution type and do not take advantage of the technology's capabilities. New *uses* have to be discovered or invented.

For instance, more recently, in a St. Josephs University honors class designed to teach the essentials of the business curriculum to liberal arts students, we assigned a competitive, computer-driven business simulation game, put the game on our mainframe, gave students their own disks, and told them to try to win the game. No lectures or textbooks were given. Then we gave them a very comprehensive test covering both the vocabulary and concepts typically covered in introductory business texts. They all passed with flying colors! And they reported that it was fun! (Should we have given the test? Possibly not, but we were stuck with the need to introduce the new while satisfying the requirements of the old.)

Our library card catalogs are now binary files, searchable in Boolean notation. If you want to see what high-tech plagiarism can look like, turn a bright student loose to use a Dialogs with the Dead technique on one of your library's data bases, and then ask yourself, "Is this plagiarism or some new form of research?" Programs like Hyper-text pick up where the card catalog leaves off and allow the development of concept dictionaries as a new form of manipulable text that puts the sequencing of the content of the text in the control of the reader.

Although commonplace now, only a few years ago computer rental stores began to allow customers to rent a computer by the hour—complete with programs and a printer. Several years ago, we asked a young college student (an English literature major) who was running a computer rental store in Westwood near UCLA's campus what he wanted to be when he graduated. His prompt reply: a computer programmer. That surprised us, and we asked, "Why a programmer?" His thoughtful but ambitious answer, "I want to be the Shakespeare of the 21st century." Think about it. We did.

Up until the spread of railroads, standard time did not exist—local time was quite good enough. Now standard time is universal, and never mind hours or even minutes, most everyone takes even the second hand on their watch for granted. Distance is measured more often in lapsed time than in miles or kilometers. And where depends on what you need. High-tech communications has made manufacturing of most items an international shuffle-board game, where components are made wherever it is cheapest, assembled wherever it is most convenient, and sold wherever the markets are. So diversity, a buzzword of the 1990s, is an economic fact waiting for the politicians to catch up with reality.

If you want to see and experience today's most advanced classroom, get friendly with the pilot-training director of a major airline and get a ride in a Link Trainer. It is a box (the interior of which is a replica of an airplane cockpit—controls, instruments, and windows that are video displays) sitting on three hydraulic legs, all of which is controlled by a computer that responds to the student's actions in the cockpit. With such simulated reality, it makes actual experience in a real airplane virtually unnecessary, and the student pilot learns by doing without paying the expensive and potentially fatal cost of learning in a real airplane. You can't find a training director? Okay, try Disneyland or Walt Disney World or the Epcot Center. They all have rides that embody most of the technology of a Link Trainer. They all include frighteningly realistic experience that unfortunately lacks one key ingredient—there is no part that allows the participant to participate. There are no controls—only the ride. And for the participant, the ride is passive, rather like our lecture halls. It is not education, but rather just entertainment. However, the feel of virtual reality is there, and it is worth the ride just to experience it even though you cannot control it.

Another good example of high-tech feedback systems is your local electronic amusement center. Time was, not so long ago, when they contained only pinball machines. Then, in the 1970s, along came Pong, and the game changed, literally. Now these establishments have interactive computers driving videodisks whose various tracks the player selects as responses to the movement of the controls. To the player it seems very real and under his or her control. At a quarter a pop they are almost addictive. Similar but less extensive games are available using a home computer. The best known is probably Nintendo. Less dramatic games now teach typing without an instructor. The teaching of typing has been taken over by a computer program that makes a learner-paced fun game out of learning to type, and is faster, more effective, and much cheaper than a typing instructor. No classroom or schedule is needed. (Actually, today's kids won't need typing instruction at all. They will have mastered it as part of growing up much as they learn to tie—oops! use Velcro fasteners on—their shoes until, of course, verbal input command computers become common).

Beyond electronic books and gadgets that combine words, sound, pictures and animation are the programs to preserve unwritten languages by inventing a written form, such as those sponsored by the J. B. Du Pont Foundation. And then there are translators. Small, pocket-size electronic dictionaries that translate words in one language to another language—or several languages—have become common. Some even pronounce the word, and some handle not just words but whole phrases. Although useful to the tourist, these are but toys compared with the serious translating programs that now make it possible to translate whole texts by machine. Not perfectly to be sure, but well enough to put a very big dent in our Tower of Babel. To that end, in 1990, the University of Pennsylvania hosted the first International Symposium on East Asian Information Processing. Besides the expected presentations on the challenges of translating Chinese, Korean, and Japanese, there were vendors selling software packages that purported to do just that—translate to and from English.

While the potential of advances in technology is to change dramatically how, when, where, and what we teach, the reality is that many stumbling blocks remain. Economics is one of them. For many colleges and universities, the next decade will be a fight for survival, and enhancing management education classrooms through technology may be perceived to be more a luxury than a necessity. In the business sector, similar difficult economic pressures also are present, but in general, corporations have moved further faster than the collegiate environment in introducing new technology into management education. This gap between business and education may even increase.

A second resistance point comes from responding to change itself. It seems to take an inordinate amount of time for people to become used to a new idea, and they do it by casting new technology in an old mold before taking off and using the new technology for what it truly can do. As an example, the reality is that the touch tone phone, with its calculator-type key pad, merely increased the speed of dialing for over a decade before its potential as an input device for a variety of other functions began to be utilized—and not yet anywhere near its full potential.

In our management education programs, many think of the VHS camera and tape as merely an easier-to-use version of the old 16-mm camera and film. Many of our best texts are now in video format (often the poorest of them are copies of our better lectures, but we are learning). They are just video substitutes for our old 16-mm film collection. In the same way, word processing programs enable students to submit typed, formatted, spell-checked reports that are easier to read than before. Technology again has moved us ahead, but in old terms. We are just beginning to learn how to really use the power of video effectively. The 8-mm cameras are opening up new venues for students to record and share their own experiences. Our students already make presentations in video format rather than paper or lectures. It will take some getting used to (and some of us won't make it) to accept the potential of the Minicam or power pack or e-mail to change what we do, with whom we do it, and how.

Perhaps, most difficult, changes in traditional relationships in management education are perceived by some as threatening or inappropriate. Advancements in realistic learning experiences in the form of simulations (whether computer driven or not) and high technology bring tools that facilitate the shift in relationships, and for the most part they shift the Power in the classroom from the instructor to the student.

In the meantime, in our universities where resources are not yet up to Link Trainer types of expenditures, there are things we can do. Cohen's beginning piece in this section attempts to extend beyond simulation to reality. He tells us how to reorganize the classroom into a business (be one rather than talk about it—a big step forward in shifting the classroom control to the students without any high technology at all).

The use of video in management education can have a powerful effect by increasing interest, adding dramatic realism, and providing effective models for learning. There are many video programs and cases that can enrich the learning experience, especially when used purposively and not just for entertainment or to fill time. We strongly recommend Marx, Jick, and Frost's (1991) *Management Live: The Video Book,* a recently developed collection of video clips used with readings and exercises to provide a powerful presentation and encourage discussion of a variety of management topics. In their article, Gioia and Sims recommend the use of homegrown video and provide some useful guidelines. Although novel and challenging over a decade ago when they first reported on their work, these helpful guidelines would now make only modest demands on the technology available at most institutions. Now, with the availability of video formats and laser discs controlled by a readily programmable desktop computer, it is possible with video to approach the interactiveness of the Link Trainer. In the last article in this section, Bigelow surveys available computer software related to management education and chronicles a field that is moving so rapidly that much of it will be obsolete before you read about it (but then you'll be able to catch up all the faster).

How can we keep up on what is happening in this rapidly changing world of simulations and technology? The first answer is simple—go to your local elementary school, talk to the kids, watch what they are doing, and think about how it is changing their expectations and world of learning. Next, keep up to date with the media and, in particular, how the corporate world is responding to the technology challenge. The fact that 25 Yale professors can be recruited by Arthur Andersen & Co. to work on artificial intelligence models that will be used to develop training programs for the corporate world should give some picture of where the action is.

But more to the point, bibliographies are too static to form a realistic picture of what is happening in the world. Check out Kinko's latest catalog—a prime source for faculty-developed software that can be used in the classroom. Other vendors are following suit.

Groups like the International Simulation and Gaming Association (IS-AGA) hold conferences and, perhaps more important, are developing programs that link students throughout the world in collective decision making. The Association for Business Simulation and Experiential Learning (ABSEL) holds yearly conferences focusing on the use of simulations and experiential learning. There also is the Sage journal, *Simulation and Games.*

As John Bigelow points out, there are different classes or approaches to using computers in management education. Expert systems focus on decision-tree-types of programs that attempt to rationalize and formalize how the expert solves a problem. Simulations attempt to emulate reality in the hopes of teaching management how to recognize and deal with problems they can anticipate facing in their jobs. For example, the Strategic Management Group (SMG), formed in 1981 by three Wharton School professors, now is doing business worldwide with computer simulation workshops for managers, featuring tailor-made adaptations to various industries. A third approach in some ways merges parts of both expert systems and simulations into games to be won or solved by the participant. Yet another class deals straightforwardly with issues like translation from one language to another, what-if-type spreadsheets that can be used to explore the impact of decisions. Also, there are search programs that facilitate finding and/or recombining data from large files. There are more and other ways of looking at the set of ever-growing computer programs. When the fight for the next generation of video systems is finally resolved, it is most likely to be in digital rather than the analogue formats now in use around the world. In our shrinking world, there is room for only one such system, and the stakes to supply it are very high indeed. Digital video coupled with computer controlling programs, fiber optic networks, and satellites has mind-boggling potential. Our education systems will have to achieve this potential or become obsolete. This electronic revolution is still in its infancy, and it is difficult indeed to predict where it will be even a few years from now.

The major theme of the December 1992 Second International Organizational Behavior Teaching Conference in Perth, Australia, was the impact of technology on our classrooms, and a new partnership became obvious—the art of management and the science of technology have merged.

It is difficult to see when you are a part of a revolution and, in fact, in the middle of it. Your running to your library is helpful but not enough. However, the place to look is where the action is. And, as usual, the first application of a new revolution starts as play. So look to the kids and their toys.

Reference

Marx, R., Jick, T., & Frost, P. (1991). *Management live: The video book.* Englewood Cliffs, NJ: Prentice-Hall.

Suggested Readings

Barton, R. (1972). *A primer on simulation and gaming.* Englewood Cliff, NJ: Prentice-Hall.
Delbecq, A. L., & Scates, D. C. (1991). Teaching with television: Assessing the potential of distance education. *Journal of Management Education, 15*(3), 340-351.

Gery, G. (1988). *Making computer-based training happen.* Boston: Weingarten.

Gordon, J. (1985). Games managers play. *Training Magazine, 22,* 30-47.

Horn, R. & Zuckerman, D. (1976). *The guide to simulation/games for education and training.* Lexington, MA: Information Resources.

Schleger, P. (1984, October). What, me produce video? *Training and Development Journal,* 40-48.

Eight

Beyond Simulation
Treating the Classroom as
an Organization

ALLAN R. COHEN
Babson College

No matter what style of teaching is used, the classroom is an organization. As in other organizations, goals must be set; decisions made; work allocated; and members recruited, motivated, controlled, and rewarded.

Whether or not the instructor chooses to make explicit the parallels between other organizations and the classroom, issues such as leadership, structure, and control still must be handled, and how they are handled will have great impact on student learning. Students probably learn as much from our classroom managerial behavior as they do from the content of our teaching. Because of the correspondence between what we teach and how we teach, we have a marvelous opportunity to exploit the organizational parallels and illustrate our subject matter with our behavior.

The idea of using what is going on in the classroom is familiar to many instructors of management and organizational behavior, and many experiential exercises are designed to do just that. But my colleagues and I have gone beyond that by structuring the entire course to highlight the organizational parallel. This has led to far-reaching consequences for our role in the classroom, the sequencing of subject matter, and the activities of students. This article will describe the methods we have developed for making use of the opportunities inherent in a classroom and will explore

This chapter originally appeared in *Exchange: The Organizational Behavior Teaching Journal,* Volume 2, Issue 1.

some of the wider implications. The course I will describe is introductory human behavior in organizations, meeting two to three times a week for 14 weeks with a section size of about 50. This same approach, with minor modifications, can also be used in other management education courses such as human resource management and management principles. We use essentially the same format with undergraduates and day and evening MBA students.

The Classroom as an Organization

At the beginning of the course we make explicit to students our concept of the class as an organization. We maintain that although not all organizations have the learning goals of the classroom, it is possible to make analogies with other organizations on the basis of what will transpire in the course. We explain that we will manage the class in the best way we know to maximize learning about behavior in organizations, and that to do so we will create a particular kind of organization that is subject to analysis using the conceptual tools available in the course. Throughout the semester we continually point out parallels between what is happening in the classroom, what is happening in the case studies of other organizations, and what is happening in outside organizations to which the students belong.

Our objective is not to *simulate* an organization but rather to create genuine organizational *issues* for students, to put them in the position of an organizational member who must deal with such problems as how work gets allocated; how one works with others who bring different expertise to tasks; how one influences and motivates subordinates, peers, and superiors; how one copes with ambiguity in solving difficult tasks that do not have any obviously correct single answer; how disagreements among coworkers can be resolved; and how decisions will be made. We accomplish this by the way we handle the class structure, reward system, chain of command, span of control, and leadership style. Like other organizations, we use job descriptions, performance appraisal, differential authority, task groups, and other such organizational devices to manage the class and make parallels clear.

STRUCTURING THE CLASSROOM

Because we have 50 or more students in a class, one of our first concerns is to structure the class into more manageable units. Heterogeneous work teams of six to eight persons are formed by having students sort themselves along such dimensions as work experience, class standing, and knowledge of social science.[1] Most class time is spent in these teams, usually analyzing cases, occasionally doing exercises, simulations, or negotiations. Whatever the task, there is some kind of output that in many cases is measured and evaluated.

We also create a layer of middle management. Once groups have been formed and have solved three or four tasks together, we ask each group to select a group leader. This leader reports to the teacher and is held responsible for his or her group's performance. As much as possible we try to relate to the groups through the group leaders.

We meet with the leaders outside the class for about 1 hour a week to help them in their role, gather data on what is going on within the groups, make decisions about assignments and pacing, and so on. We try to build the group leaders into a team whose members can support one another in the very difficult role of managing a group of peers whose external status is comparable with theirs. Occasionally, the instructor meets with the group leaders during class while each of the groups is working on a task, thus creating dilemmas for the leaders in that they have to manage their groups while spending time with fellow managers and the boss.

A time-honored way for organizations to try to clarify members' expectations about required work is the distribution of formal job descriptions. Because we have a fairly clear idea of what we want from the students, we have written the equivalent of job descriptions for students, group leaders, and the teacher. These are distributed early in the course.[2] Just as for other organizations the existence of formal job descriptions does not guarantee the desired behavior, their distribution for a class does not necessarily result in the full commitment and dedication to learning that we would like. But we think it is important for students to see both the possibilities and limitations of such a document.

REWARD SYSTEM

The reward system in the course is also designed to raise issues parallel to those facing any organization trying to decide how to allocate rewards. Class members are judged partly by their performance on group tasks and partly on their individual performances on other tasks such as papers and exams. Roughly one-third of the final grade is based on group projects; one-third on individual papers, quizzes, and exams during the course; and-one third on an individual final paper in which all concepts in the course can be used to analyze what happened in the student's task group.

Because we hold the group leaders responsible for their group's performance, we ask them to take some responsibility for evaluating the members' individual performance. For those tasks in which the entire group has to come up with one product, the teacher assigns a grade to the total product, but that grade is then distributed among members by the group leader. The leader can use any basis he or she desires for determining the allocation, including asking group members to participate in the process.

The group leader receives for group products whatever grade is given to the group by the teacher, because it is assumed that the group's overall performance is partly a reflection of how well the leader did his or her job. The group in turn evaluates the leader's overall performance. This plus the leader's self-evaluation and the teacher's evaluation are considered in determining a final grade for each group leader. Again, this is organizationally real in that evaluations of managers at least in part reflect the opinions of their subordinates as well as their superior.

One of the hardest tasks for any manager is to do performance appraisals of subordinates in a way that genuinely helps them grow. One form of feedback is the allocation of individual grades on group tasks, but we attempt to go beyond that. During the leadership section of the course I use a case in which a subordinate's poor performance is an issue (Dominion Acceptance Corporation). In discussing the case, students often recommend that the manager be more direct and open. Building on that I then ask each of the group leaders to give a performance appraisal to their group members. Their appraisals are then critiqued for constructiveness by the group members who have been appraised. In this critique, students frequently refer back to the case and the concepts covered. This allows us to draw parallels between managers in outside organizations and managers we have created in the classroom.

Some Variations of Classroom Structure

Because all students in the course presumably intend to be managers, we have been trying to work out a way to give everyone in the course the valuable experience of being in a leadership or managerial position. At first we rotated group leaders every week, but this was a difficult system to administer and was not organizationally convincing. Lately, however, we asked group leaders to delegate to individual members leadership on particular tasks, and to give feedback on performance to each person who has been in that temporary leadership role. This not only gives everyone a chance to experience at least some leadership dilemmas but parallels normal informal leadership assignments.

Another variation we have tried is having students switch groups two-thirds of the way through the course when we get to the intergroup unit.

Although this gives students a chance to try out new behaviors and get out of roles they have fallen into in their first group, it has seldom produced in the new groups the same kind of loyalty, commitment, and peer pressure for group performance that makes the task group structure so valuable. We have begun to experiment with a more matrix-like organization in which the old groups continue but new, temporary groups are formed to do certain tasks. Such a structure is very complicated to administer but appears to be a promising way both to allow for experimentation in a new group and raise fascinating intergroup questions about primary group loyalty, multiple membership, and so on.

One further device we have developed is to use undergraduates as course assistants. When we have been able to find interested and competent undergraduates, we ask them to work with us, either as assistant managers or as assistants to the manager. They have often helped resolve difficulties that individual groups were having, meeting with the group leaders, grading papers, or conducting exercises. This not only adds more managerial levels to the organization, but gives valuable teaching-managerial experience to the better students.

Wider Implications of This Method

The method described—treating the instructor as the manager of the student organization created for the course—has a large impact on the role and teaching methods of the instructor.

Using task groups that meet during class time places the burden for work activity on the student rather than on the teacher. They carry out the work; my job as teacher is to manage the learning process of the members of the class. Only occasionally do I lecture; as a manager I would seldom make speeches to 50 people at once and I only do it in the classroom when that is the most efficient way to convey information quickly. More often I will direct students to concepts in the text, discuss a problem they are experiencing, consult on group processes, respond to questions, and so on.

This is a major shift in the locus of responsibility, one which means that for considerable amounts of class time I am neither talking nor focal. A considerable amount of my influence comes from the way I organize the class, the questions about cases that I want answered, the sequence of assignments—factors that are separate from my interpersonal style and not always immediately apparent to students.

Even the role of the teacher as top manager is subject to analysis. During the leadership section of the course, the instructor usually explores student feelings about his or her behavior and role in the class and its effects on the class as a learning organization. Often we can pick up on comments that students make when discussing cases involving leadership and compare those to our own behavior to date in the class. Some of us temporarily initiate a crackdown on the class on the day when groups are discussing a case with an authoritarian but successful manager (Multi-Products, Inc.). A few students have even been willing to admit they prefer such authoritarian behavior and claim that, despite their fear, it would facilitate learning.

Even though there are differences in how each of us manage our class, most of the faculty who have used the class-as-organization model have moved to a somewhat more controlling managerial style than initially preferred. We teach contingency thinking about leadership, in which the motivation of subordinates and the nature of the tasks influence choice of leadership style, and we have had to learn to practice what we preach. For example, although all of us believe that intrinsic motivation is more desirable than extrinsic, we have found that there are too many other pressures on students to rely solely on intrinsic motivation. We are, therefore, no longer apologetic about using exams, quizzes, or papers to guarantee that work is done and material mastered; we trust that the material is valuable enough to be worth the effort we coerce from them. Likewise we have felt freer to pressure the group leaders to monitor and enforce performance (which again is different from the much greater autonomy we initially gave them). We talk about all this with the students and give them a chance to help us modify our leadership styles in accordance with our collective diagnosis of what is needed to introduce maximum learning. Whatever the choices we make, we try to help the students become comfortable talking about the issues and in seeing if they can learn from having been on the receiving end of the particular managerial style of their teacher.

Other Devices to Implement the Model

Another approach we have used is to structure case discussions in such a way that the *issues* in the case also occur *within* each discussion group.[3] If, for example, a case centers around the attempts of a new member to gain entry into an ongoing, well-developed group, then I might ask a member of each group to carry out some task with another group during the discussion and then use the accompanying feelings as a vehicle for further group discussion. Thus within each group as well as for the class as a whole, we are constantly trying to make the medium the message.

We have found it important to sequence course topics so that the material matches the students' in-class experience. For example, we do not begin with a unit on the individual, although that seems logical, because it does not fit the classroom dynamics. Until students have resolved their membership needs and developed trust, they will not readily identify with individuals in cases or be open about their own self-concepts and values. Only after groups have formed and gelled can such sensitive areas be explored. Thus we match content sequence with group development so that the group's tasks dovetail with what they are going through collectively and individually as organization members.

The criterion for introducing concepts, cases, and exercises becomes "What do the task groups in my organization need to maximize their learning?" Conceptual material does not just build on itself but helps explain both phenomena in the case and the classroom. This gives greater meaning to the course content because their ongoing struggles to complete tasks in the face of problems of differentiation, coordination, and commitment make any tools welcome.

Advantage and Disadvantages

As suggested above, using the class as an organization has positive effects on student motivation. Even MBA students, usually most skeptical about experiential teaching innovations, appreciate the tough organizational situations in which they find themselves. And they respect the thought and organization required to structure and sequence the course.

Some undergraduates squirm and resist a method that requires active participation and interdependence with others for grades, and every semester there are a few who plead to be allowed to write all papers themselves. As I have become increasingly convinced of the appropriateness and legitimacy of creating a realistic organization, I have gotten better at facing such students with the implications of their desires. While the most passive students would probably prefer to remain anonymous, they respond no more negatively than such students always have, and a number of them find themselves reluctantly getting interested.

A major benefit is the freeing up of the faculty member to use a more contingent leadership style. Whether lecturing about participation or allowing great freedom to unmotivated students, teachers have been hardpressed to match leadership style to student needs in the classroom situation and to the concepts being taught. By taking a managerial role, using student middle managers, and using a group structure, it becomes possible for the instructors to use their greater knowledge and expertise without constantly telling students exactly what to do or abandoning all influence and control.

The most difficult problem is deciding when to intervene in a group that is having difficulties. Do I let them struggle with an unmotivated member, an impossible division of labor, or a misunderstood concept? Deciding when to bite my tongue, when to ask a loaded question, when to offer help, or when to insist on their facing a problem is continually difficult. But I believe it is the right kind of difficulty, the exact tension between performance and development that every good manager faces.

This method places on the instructor different time demands from other methods. During much of class time the instructor observes groups, saying little. A great deal of time is required before the semester begins to decide on sequence of classes and activities. About 1 hour extra per week is needed for meeting with group leaders, but many class hours require less preparation once the instructor knows the case. The self and group analytical term papers are long, but they are an integral part of the course and more interesting to grade than most final exams.

The quality of the time is very demanding. One must be a good manager, not just a clear lecturer or direction giver. If one's leadership style is to be examined, one has to be able to listen to student criticism or confrontation and respond nondefensively and constructively. Student feelings about one's style are always there, but other methods can more easily insulate one from hearing them! And it is not easy to know how to "develop" one's "subordinates." In any management course, students are only willing to learn a new behavior or skill when they see the instructor demonstrating its efficacy in real time.

Nevertheless, I am convinced that no other way so clearly and forcefully puts students in a live organization, allows them to experience issues while studying them, and creates the willingness to learn and use concepts. Students do not complain that what they are learning is unreal or irrelevant when they need to learn it to understand and cope with the organizational forces created in the classroom.

Notes

1. See "Task-group Forming" in Cohen, Fink, Gadon, and Willits (1992). Several articles discussing nuances and benefits of using the classroom as an organization are also included in this text's teaching manual.

2. See "Role Descriptions for Instructors, Students and Student Group Representatives," in Cohen et al. (1992).

3. For further details on this method, see Chapter 7.

Reference

Cohen, A., Fink, S., Gadon, H., & Willits, R. (1992). *Teacher's manual for use with* Effective Behavior Organizations. Homewood, IL: Irwin.

Suggested Readings

Balke, W. M. (1981). The policy learning co-op: Treating the classroom as an organization. *Exchange: The Organizational Behavior Teaching Journal, 6*(2), 27-32.

Barry, D. (1988-1989). Twincorp: Extensions of the classroom-as-organization model. *Organizational Behavior Teaching Review, 14*(1), 1-15.

Betton, J. H. (1991). Simulating organizations: A student-documentary history of emergent behavior. *Journal of Management Education, 15*(2), 193-205.

Greenhalgh, L. (1979). Simulating an on-going organization. *Exchange: The Organizational Behavior Teaching Journal, 4*(3), 23-27.

Miller, J. A. (1991). Experiencing management: A comprehensive "hands-on" model for the introductory undergraduate management course. *Journal of Management Education, 15*(2), 151-169.

Nine

Videotapes in the Management Classroom
Creating the Tools to Teach

DENNIS A. GIOIA
The Pennsylvania State University

HENRY P. SIMS, JR.
University of Maryland

One of the aims of any instructor of management and organizational behavior is to grasp the attention of the students so that they will be actively involved in the learning process. In this article, we describe our experience in using videotape technology as one approach to student involvement.

Generally, our motivation for using this technology stems from our own fondness for the medium as well as our belief that it is a powerful technique to teach through modeling. We find it interesting and fun, and it helps us in our attempts to find common ground with our students. The general principles of learning through videotape technology are based on theories of modeling and vicarious learning (Manz & Sims, 1981; Sims & Manz,

This chapter originally appeared in *Exchange: The Organizational Behavior Teaching Journal,* Volume 7, Issue 3.

AUTHORS' NOTE: This article is based on a presentation that was given at the Eighth Annual Organizational Behavior Teaching Conference, held at Harvard University on June 16-19, 1981. We are indebted to several colleagues who have worked with us in the development and use of videotapes, especially Daniel Brass, Robert Griffin, and Charles Manz. This work has been supported through various grants from The Pennsylvania State University.

1982). For the most part, the theory is based on principles of social learning theory (Bandura, 1977). The efficacy of modeling as a basis for teaching has been widely demonstrated (Bandura, 1977; Latham & Saari, 1979; Manz & Sims, 1981).

In this article, we will focus on two aspects of videotape use that are drawn from our own experience. We will discuss the problem of developing video materials, with a special focus on local production of tapes. We will also share some of our experiences in the ways tapes can be presented and used.

Although modeling videotapes can be constructed to demonstrate almost any management concept, we have chosen to focus on several major topics that we teach as examples of "content" that can be covered with modeling tapes, for example, the effective use of contingent positive and punitive behavior (Sims, 1977, 1980) and the effective use of goal setting by managers and subordinates (Locke, Shaw, Saari, & Latham, 1981).

When teaching these concepts, we usually start with a learn from doing approach. We ask several student dyads to role-play a management by objectives performance appraisal interview between a manager and a subordinate. In this role-play, we typically see many examples of both effective and ineffective verbal behaviors. A critique is then provided by observers of the role-play. We next provide theoretical lecturettes on these topics. Then after the students in the classes have been exposed to the experience and the lecturettes, we show a series of four short (7 to 10 minutes each) videotapes that demonstrate alternative ways for managers to render positive, punitive, and goal setting statements. Respectively, these four tapes focus on (1) noncontingent positive reward behavior, (2) noncontingent punitive behavior, (3) goal-setting behavior (without positive or punitive feedback), and (4) a combination of contingent positive, contingent punitive, and goal-setting behavior.

We usually have a discussion with the class after each tape. It is important, of course, to tie in the tapes with the theoretical and conceptual material that we present in the lecturettes and the supplemental reading. Depending on the time available, each tape can be debriefed in a short time, say 30 minutes, or, as we sometimes do, can be covered over several class days with virtually a whole class devoted to one or two tapes.

Perhaps we can best expand on our approach by answering specific questions that are typically raised when we describe how we produce and use tapes.

How long have you been using videotapes in the classroom?

In one form or another, we have been using videotapes since 1976. We produced our first set of home-grown tapes in 1979. By now, these tapes have been used with thousands of students. For example, the tapes are a central part of presentations to introductory large lecture classes of several hundred students. We also use the tapes in both undergraduate and MBA classes of 20 to 40 students. In addition, the tapes have also been used extensively in executive development forums. Last but not least, we have also used the tapes with executives in one-on-one feedback and coaching.

You seem pretty confident that tapes can be used for virtually any management topic. Are there any areas where you think they might not be useful?

We think that modeling tapes can be constructed to demonstrate almost any management concept, but it seems to us that they can be best used when specific behavior concepts are the focus of attention. We would guess, however, that tapes might be less useful to teach about topics such as organizational design or topics that are more abstract. But as soon as we say it can't be done, someone is sure to do it.

Production of Tapes

Why did you choose to produce your own tapes? What about commercially available films and tapes?

We do use commercial films and tapes in other parts of our courses, so we have no inherent bias against them. But films generally run 20 to 30 minutes. That is a long time to spend making one point. We also feel that too many commercial films talk down to our students—even our undergraduates, by being overly simplistic and repetitive. Visual images can speak volumes in very short order, and we felt we could make points just as effectively in much less time. Besides, we were not able to find films or tapes that dealt with behaviors to the degree of specificity that we considered desirable. Therefore, we decided to create our own. Looking back, we're sure we were also motivated by our fascination with the technology itself.

How can tapes like this be produced?

There are at least two ways to produce modeling tapes: an economy method and a professional method. The economy method depends on ultracheap labor (colleagues and students) and uses home video equipment, which that can be purchased for less than $1000 to $1500, or possibly university-owned portable equipment. Perhaps a step-by-step procedure would be most clear.

THE ECONOMY METHOD

Step 1. After some experience with a class, it is possible to identify who the best role-play actors are. Ask these students to engage in a role-play outside the class setting to play the manager and the subordinate in front of the videotape camera. (They can receive either course credit or student wages for their participation.)

Step 2. The filming can be done in any seminar room with chairs arranged to represent an office. The manager is coached to behave in four distinctly different ways for each of the tapes to be produced. For example, in the noncontingent punitive videotape, the supervisor is coached to review each of the objectives shown on the role-play sheet with the subordinate, and to find something wrong or express disappointment with some facet of the subordinate's performance on each objective. For the noncontingent positive videotape, the actor is coached to reinforce positively the subordinate or express satisfaction with the performance on each objective and especially to avoid being negative even when performance is poor. For the goal-setting videotape, the actor is coached to concentrate only on the future-oriented setting of goals, avoiding any past-oriented evaluative verbal behavior and especially the rendering of either positive of punitive statements to the subordinate. (Our experience shows that this tape is by far the hardest to produce, simply because students have difficulty acting as a pure goal-setter, without evaluation overtones.) Finally, for the combined videotape, the actor is carefully coached to reward good performance (objectives met) positively, to reprimand poor performance (objectives not met), and to shift into a future-oriented, goal-setting mode with the subordinate.

In all cases, the subordinate is coached to react normally, but consistently, across all four tapes. The object of the construction of the videotapes is to have a consistent scenario, consistent actors, and consistent levels of performance, and to demonstrate both the ineffective and effective ways to conduct a performance appraisal interview (especially as related to the theoretical frameworks of contingent verbal behavior and goal-setting).

Step 3. These procedures are rehearsed individually until a good role-play is obtained. Each interaction should be as similar as possible, *except* for the variance in managerial verbal behavior. The role-play should be targeted for no more than 5 to 7 minutes with only approximately 1 minute spent on each objective, to emphasize the critical verbal behaviors.

Step 4. The role is videotaped after rehearsal. Usually, the final taping can be done in one or two takes.

Step 5. The best of the takes is transferred to a single videotape to create a master teaching tape for use in all future classes.

THE PROFESSIONAL METHOD

In actuality, the professional method is quite similar to the economy model, except for a few changes. It still should be labeled home grown, but in our case, this approach used professional resources that were available in the university community.

First, we used professional actors instead of students. We recruited by posting a call for actors in the theater department. Using professional actors has several advantages. First, we can usually get people somewhat older than students, which adds to the credibility of the product. Also, professional actors are very adept at learning lines rapidly and providing more realistic interpretations with fewer rehearsals and takes. Overall, we were amazed at how quickly our actors were able to adapt to our conditions.

It also turns out that this approach is not that expensive. We've found that actors want to act and will do so given any opportunity. We did pay a small honorarium, but it was indeed very small. Our actors were more interested in seeing themselves in the end product.

In this situation, we also used a professional studio. This studio is an internal instructional production facility at The Pennsylvania State University. Their business is producing instructional tapes, so we were able to take advantage of this internal resource. (Many schools have such a resource; before making tapes on one's own, the availability of such a facility should be checked out.)

We did the taping in this studio set, with three high-quality color cameras. The most important resource was an experienced and extraordinarily competent technical director. We were frankly amazed at the richness that this director was able to add to the tapes.

How long did the taping last?

Believe it or not, we were able to complete four tapes, averaging about 8 minutes each, in one evening. The actual time was about 3 hours. It was a very exciting process. The professional experience of the actors and the director were invaluable.

You mentioned a script. Where did that come from?

We keep our eyes and ears open for ideas that might suggest possibilities for videotape scripts. For instance, many current television shows portray organizational settings that provide a rich source of ideas. We are not above borrowing the germ of a good concept and adapting it in our own fashion. We also draw on our own organizational experience for script ideas. We both have a repertoire of war stories that can serve as the basis for videotape scripts. Finally, our teaching itself leads to script ideas.

For the tapes described here, we had the advantage that we had previously done more than a hundred role-play exercises with experienced executives and students in our classrooms. We also knew fairly well the behaviors that we wanted to portray. To create the script, we started with role-play scenarios and built on them. For example, we did about a dozen role-play episodes, using the scenarios as a basis and working with just about anybody that would be willing to sit down and work with us. We found that experienced actors were especially creative and experienced managers were also extremely useful. We recorded each of these episodes on audiotape.

We used the audiotapes as input to write the scripts. Basically, we just listened to the tapes to get good ideas about the lines and wrote the script for the first videotape on a word processor. This tape was the noncontingent positive reward tape. We then used this script as a framework for creating each of the other scripts. The main thing we changed was the verbal response behavior of the manager in the scenario. Instead of replying positively to a subordinate's statement, he or she would reply negatively for the punitive tape.

We ended up with four scripts in which the characters were the same, the circumstances were the same, the initial behavior of the subordinate was the same. The main difference was in the verbal behavior of the manager, which, of course, enables us to focus on the teaching points we wanted to make.

How about nonverbal behavior?

Actually, we didn't initially set out to create differences in the nonverbal behavior, but the nonverbal interpretations of the actors was a surprising and pleasing bonus. Now, we find the tapes are also very useful as a stimulus for discussing nonverbal behavior.

Is it really worth your time to produce a tape yourself? How much time did you spend on producing these four tapes?

Probably 100 to 200 hours were spent by the faculty alone. Of course, you can double this when the technical and acting people are included. The net results of this effort were less than a half hour of videotape. Is it worth it? We think it is, especially when you experience how marvelously effective the tapes can be in class. However, one would certainly not want to put in all that effort for only a one-time use. In the end, we believe that if the professor has fun doing the project, then this enthusiasm will come through in the final product. In our case, we did indeed have fun with it, and we have certainly gotten our mileage out of the tapes. Besides, you end up with much more of what you want, not some adapted compromise.

It is important to point out, however, the amount of input and resources for a relatively short output. In our case, we put hundreds of hours in planning and organizing, tens of hours in taping, and the actual output was less than 30 minutes of tape. With this kind of input/output ratio, you must really *want* to do it.

Is it possible to make a kind of training tape that shows a situation, then asks the viewers to decide how a manager should respond to it, and then show some alternative responses?

Yes. In fact we have created such a tape by selective editing of the modeling tapes we previously described. This tape shows a basic scenario of a manager interacting with a subordinate who performs either excellently or poorly. An edited pause in the tape allows viewer decision time about appropriate managerial responses. Then, short reward, reprimand, and goal-setting clips follow, allowing the class and the instructor to comment on their relative effectiveness as managerial behaviors.

How is the editing done?

Videotape editing is an electronic process. The tape isn't hacked up like a piece of film and then spliced together. Actually, the electronic editing is considerably easier than film editing.

I think most people would feel overwhelmed by the process of making their own videotapes. Convince the technical idiots among us that it can be done.

It's less of a technical problem and more of a management problem. The main effort is in specifying the content and finding, coordinating, and scheduling the resources to get the job done. We think good technical help is typically available.

Use of Tapes

How do you use tapes in large classrooms?

Our general approach is to use the tapes in short segments to illustrate a particular pattern of behavior. For example, we might talk about goal setting in the abstract and present the theoretical aspects of goal setting, but the tapes become invaluable when we want to answer the question of how managers actually go about the process of setting goals with subordinates. So after introducing the topic and presenting the concepts, we say, "Let me show you an example of what I'm talking about. Let's look at this short tape to get an idea of how this might actually be carried out." The next step, of course, is to turn around and press the button that starts the tape. Usually, we follow up the tape with a short discussion. Even in classes of hundreds, we have found that we can briefly carry on a limited dialogue with the class about what the tape portrayed.

Of course, technical facilities for showing the tapes are necessary, and we are fortunate at Penn State to have large lecture halls that are designed to use this technology. We think most people would be surprised, however, at how far even a single television monitor can project in the classroom.

Any problems with using videotapes?

We suppose it might be possible to get carried away with the technology itself and forget the original learning objectives. Also, we would guess that most people would typically underestimate the time and effort required to organize and carry out a tape production effort. Last but not least, when you are using tapes in the classroom, it is important to have a backup procedure ready to go. Technical material has a nasty propensity to fail at the most inopportune moment, and we have found that it is usually wise to be ready to go to Plan B.

Can you describe a useful strategy for the utilization of videotapes and other audiovisual material?

From our viewpoint, we do see a strategy that we generally find useful. We think the strategy mainly consists of providing excellent technical equipment and excellent technical consulting services but leaving the conceptual creativity mainly in the hands of faculty. Also, nothing is forced. This policy tends to produce a form of entrepreneurship among the faculty. Furthermore, several teaching-development grants are available yearly, a number of which are now being used to create new videotapes for classroom instruction.

For example, our college has implemented an outstanding MBA communications course in which each MBA student participates in a series of presentations that are taped and individual feedback (i.e., looking at oneself on tape) is provided. We have colleagues using videotape to construct strategy cases, and to create ongoing behavioral cases. Furthermore, our behavioral lab is used for more traditional videotaping and feedback of group interaction exercises. Use of tapes tends to be catching; seeing one faculty member do it frequently leads others to try something on their own.

Would you summarize your impressions of the main advantages of creating and using your own classroom videotapes?

Sure. They grab the viewers' attention. They allow teaching and learning specific concepts by modeled example. In many cases, they represent a lively and different teaching pedagogy that enhances their effectiveness as a teaching tool. They also are a very flexible medium: the tape can speak for itself, the instructor and/or the class can interact with the tape, or it can simply be a supplement to a good lecture. Finally, we've found creating our own tapes to be interesting for it's own sake.

References

Bandura, A. (1977). *Social Learning Theory*. Englewood Cliffs, NJ: Prentice-Hall.

Latham, G. P., & Saari, L. M. (1979). Application of social learning theory to training supervisors through behavior modeling. *Journal of Applied Psychology, 64*, 239-246.

Locke, E. A., Shaw, K. A., Saari, L. M., & Latham, G. P. (1981). Goal setting and task performance: 1969-1980. *Psychological Bulletin, 90*, 125-152.

Manz, C. C., & Sims, H. P., Jr. (1981). Vicarious learning: The influence of modeling on organizational behavior. *Academy of Management Review, 6*, 105-112.

Sims, H. P. (1977). The leader as a manager of reinforcement contingencies: An empirical example and a model. In J. G. Hunt & L. L. Larson (Eds.), *Leadership: The cutting edge* (pp. 121-137). Carbondale: Southern Illinois Press.

Sims, H. P., Jr. (1980). Further thoughts on punishment in organizations. *Academy of Management Review, 5*(1), 133-138.

Sims, H. P., Jr., & Manz, C. C. (1982, January). Modeling influences on employee behavior. *Personnel Journal*, 58-65.

Ten

Using Microcomputers in Management Education

JOHN BIGELOW
Boise State University

We live in interesting times, and one of the interesting things that is happening is a technological revolution in information processing. The increasing power and decreasing costs of computing have spurred the widespread use of computers in business as well as in business education. The diffusion of microcomputers into these areas, however, has been uneven. Although one sees a great deal of computer use in the quantitative business disciplines, such as accounting, finance, and operations research, much less has been done in the qualitative areas, such as management, organizational behavior, organizational theory, and human resource management. It has been only very recently that this situation has begun to change, and we have begun to see computer applications pertinent to the qualitative areas of management.

In this article, I review some computer programs that have been or are being developed that are relevant for management learning. My focus is twofold: first, I focus on qualitatively oriented programs, which are not based on quantitative processing or modeling. Consequently, I do not consider spreadsheets, data bases, class-grade management packages, accounting programs, and the like. I do not get into decision support systems, which tend to be predominantly quantitative, although the qualitative/ quantitative bifurcation is becoming less clear here. Second, I focus on programs implemented on microcomputers, because this is the predominant

This chapter originally appeared in *The Organizational Behavior Teaching Review,* Volume 10, Issue 4.

way by which such programs are available to learners. Later in the article, I discuss some of the larger issues of using these programs in the service of learning. I conclude with an epilogue, in which I review what we have accomplished in the 8 years following the first publishing of this article.

Some Qualitative Microcomputer Programs With Relevance for Management Learning

In the first part of this article, I look at a variety of programs that don't fall into any neat overall category. In the second part, I review a number of expert, or knowledge-based, systems. These are programs that draw on expertise or some other body of knowledge to provide advice about some problem area.

ELIZA

Eliza (by Steve Grumette) is a program that attempts to mimic—not simulate—a therapist. The program starts up by printing on the screen, HOW DO YOU DO. PLEASE TELL ME YOUR PROBLEM. The person keys in whatever response comes to mind, in natural English, and the program responds. A sample dialogue included with the program gives an idea of what an *Eliza* session may be like. The person's statements are in regular type; *Eliza*'s are in small capital letters:

All men are alike.

IN WHAT WAY?

They're always bugging us about something or other.

CAN YOU THINK OF A SPECIFIC EXAMPLE?

Well, my boyfriend made me come here.

YOUR BOYFRIEND MADE YOU COME HERE—THAT'S INTERESTING.

He says I'm depressed much of the time.

I AM SORRY TO HEAR YOU ARE DEPRESSED.

It's true. I am unhappy.

DO YOU THINK COMING HERE WILL HELP YOU NOT TO BE UNHAPPY?

I need some help, that much seems certain.

WHAT WOULD IT MEAN TO YOU IF YOU GOT SOME HELP?

Perhaps I could learn to get along with my mother.

TELL ME MORE ABOUT YOUR FAMILY.

My mother takes care of me.

WHO ELSE IN YOUR FAMILY TAKES CARE OF YOU?

My father.

LET'S TALK ABOUT YOUR FATHER.

You are like my father in some ways.

WHAT RESEMBLANCE DO YOU SEE?

You are not very aggressive.

WHAT MAKES YOU THINK I AM NOT VERY AGGRESSIVE?

You don't argue with me.

WHY DO YOU THINK I DON'T ARGUE WITH YOU?

You are afraid of me.

DOES IT PLEASE YOU TO BELIEVE I AM AFRAID OF YOU?

My father is afraid of everybody.

REALLY, EVERYBODY?

My father is very fearful.

WHAT ELSE COMES TO MIND WHEN YOU THINK OF YOUR FATHER?

Bullies.

DOES THAT HAVE ANYTHING TO DO WITH THE FACT THAT YOUR BOYFRIEND MADE YOU COME HERE?

This dialogue may sound sexist, but the program is only picking up key phrases from the person and feeding them back. In my own interactions with the program, the dialogues are not always as coherent, although the program not infrequently comes up with a gem. For the past three semesters in my organizational behavior course, I have made this program one of the optional programs a group could select for a group project. In the project, members of the group would use the program, and then as a group, write a paper relating the program to one of the chapters covered in the course. So far, no group has chosen *Eliza*. It seems that the groups have generally preferred programs more directly related to management. I think that *Eliza* could be used in relation to a chapter on communication. An analysis of the program could lead to some basic principles of nondirective, supportive listening. *Eliza* is an unprotected basic program, and it is possible not only to run the program but also to list it out and see how it is constructed. The program could be perfect for teaching a computer hacker about principles of listening.

EXECUTIVE SUITE

The goal of *Executive Suite* (by Armonk Corp.) is to start out at the bottom of an organization and work one's way into the executive suite. At the start of the game, the player is interviewed and offered a choice of beginning jobs. The player is then presented with a series of job situations and is asked to choose from a menu of responses. The situations may include deciding whether or not to join a political subgroup, choosing the kind of company car one wants to use, deciding whether or not to tell on one's boss upon discovering an indiscretion, whether or not to confess to a serious problem with one's own project, etc. The player's choices are assessed according to unstated criteria and are used in periodic job evaluations. If the person has chosen well, higher-level jobs with more salary and perks are offered. If one chooses poorly, this decision can haunt the person through the rest of the game, leading to lower-level jobs or even to being fired. Ultimately, if one plays the game well, the executive suite is attained.

For me, this a game about organizational power and politics. I have used it in my classes and linked it to chapters on power, politics, and influence. The game is not explicit about the criteria it uses. However, if one plays the game for a while, criteria such as loyalty, honesty, and age become apparent. I have found that students are attracted by the gamelike quality of *Executive Suite*—even students who are not assigned this program will play it. I've generated some very useful discussions by asking student groups to induce the criteria in the game, to decide whether or not the criteria are realistic, and to speculate on the likelihood of encountering similar dynamics in their careers. However, I suspect that the credibility of the game suffers simply because it is gamelike. I've found that students tend to rate this program lower than other programs I've assigned, such as some of the Human Edge programs. I'm pretty sure that part of the reason for this lower rating is because of the political, adversarial nature of the game, which some students find distasteful. Thus the lower average rating may be taken as a plus or a minus for the program.

MANAGEMENT TRAINING SERIES

Thoughtware provides a series of software packages for managerial diagnostics and training. These packages include assessing personal management skills; evaluating organization effectiveness; understanding personal interaction styles, leadership, and motivation; defining goals and objectives; improving employee performance, performance appraisal, and time management; conducting meetings; managing by exception; and dealing with stress management and life and career planning. These packages were developed specifically with managerial training in mind and are designed for use by individual managers.

I've run through the management assessment package and the leadership package, and have mixed feelings. The packages are organized in a hierarchical (tree) format, which is easy to grasp and get around in. The IBM-PC version that I had requires 128 kilobytes of memory and a color graphics card. The program uses different colors for different parts of the text and to emphasize points. I found I enjoyed having a color presentation. In addition, the program made use of graphics, such as talking heads, graphs, and illustrative pictures. In the diagnostics part, the program tests the user and then provides feedback on the score. For example, the program may display the user's score on the screen and graphically compare the score with that of a larger population.

On the other hand, much of the program involves simply reading what appears on the screen. The later programs include assignments relating the material to the user's job. Finally, obtaining these programs is an expensive proposition because the programs are priced more according to the managerial training market than the educational market. Even with the discounts available to higher education institutions, getting these programs up and running involves a sizable investment.

The financial issue notwithstanding, the programs provide what appears to be an effective individual study format for teaching students about management topics and provide some recognition of the individual user. I wonder if a class that taught management in a traditional format could be discriminated by tests from a population of students who had studied management via these programs.

INTERACTIVE CASES

At the June 1985 Organizational Behavior Teaching Conference, Dennis Moberg and David Caldwell (University of Santa Clara) demonstrated two of their interactive cases. These cases are designed to facilitate the teaching of diagnostic and application skills by providing students with information and requiring them to make decisions, observe the effects of their decisions, make further decisions, and so on as the case unfolds over time.

The authors developed these cases because they had problems with commonly used cases, which (1) provide no direct feedback to students and (2) deal with single, big decisions, instead of the series of incremental decisions more typical of managerial decision making. In response, the authors developed a number of cases for management and organizational behavior topics that contain a series of decision points. Each decision may change the rest of the alternatives or create a different set of problems. In going through a case, students typically make anywhere from 10 to 30 decisions. The program provides feedback to students based on their paths through the case and compares what they've done with associated theories.

The authors have developed interactive cases on organizational change, motivation, socialization, developing an effective group, performance appraisal, politics, organizational design, and a problem employee. They have tested the cases extensively with people in management training, MBA students, and undergraduates. They report that although these cases will not accomplish the same kinds of educational goals as will the more commonly used cases, they are effective in illustrating theory, drilling in theory application, and generating discussion.

COMPUTERIZED PERSONAL ASSESSMENT INSTRUMENTS

When teaching a management course, it's sometimes useful to have students fill out some kind of personal assessment instrument, for example, the *Jenkins Activity Survey* on stress, the *Kolb Learning Styles Inventory,* and the *Fundamental Interpersonal Relations Orientation Instrument.* There is some experimentation occurring with putting assessment instruments on a computer. Instead of filling out a pencil-and-paper form, the assessee reads the questions on the computer screen and records choices using the keyboard. The advantage to computerizing an instrument (besides saving paper) is that the computer can then score the person's answers and present the results in a number of ways. For example, the computer might present the score results, explain what they mean, compare them with a sample population, present a graph (with the person's score as a blinking or different colored dot), and assign a follow-up project tailored to the person's particular score.

The Thoughtware series has woven in it this kind of assessment. For example, in the *Management* package, one fills out a management styles survey and learns about how one tends to manage. Jack Webber (University of Virginia) has computerized the *Jenkins Activity Survey.* In his class, he assigns a case to his students (the John Wilford case), which has to do with stress and its consequences. He then assigns (but does not require) that students go to the computer lab and fill out the survey. Once students key in their answers, the computer prints out their scores and what the scores mean.

I think that computerization of personal assessment instruments is an area in which microcomputers can provide a positive contribution to management learning. Computerized instruments can save the learner the time, effort, and possible mistakes of scoring the instrument by hand. In addition, the computer can do a lot to make the results more intelligible to the student. Ultimately, once one starts collecting a series of scores on the computer, one can start thinking of how to use them collectively. However, before this can be done, we need to have some broader theory that can be used to integrate a variety of personal assessment scores.

A potential issue in developing computerized personal assessment instruments is that of copyrights. If an instrument is copyrighted, unauthorized use of the computerized version could constitute a copyright infringement. The Fair Use Doctrine raises the possibility that such a use may be legally permissible without first obtaining permission of the copyrighter. However, the particular kind of use discussed here gets a mixed score according to five criteria commonly used to assess fair use (Bixby, 1984). These criteria are (1) purpose of copied materials (educational use is a plus), (2) economic effect on the market (the computerized instrument doesn't compete with the original—a plus), (3) extent of copying (the entire instrument is copied—a minus), (4) length of time used (the instrument is intended for repeated use—a minus), and (5) the nature of the copyrighted work (the work is not intended to be copied—a minus). With this pattern of pluses and minuses, the developer of a computerized instrument is probably better advised to seek permission of the copyrighter.

COMPUTERIZED ACTION EXAM

An action exam is one for which individual students are put into a series of realistic situations and scored according to how competently they apply course learning to handling them. Waters, Adler, Poupart, and Hartwick (1983) pioneered this exam approach for the classroom. I have modified their approach to fit Whetten and Cameron's (1991) text *Developing Management Skills*. More recently, I have developed a *HyperCard* program for the Macintosh that generates exams, allows me to score people directly on the computer screen, and automatically puts the scores into the students' records. In addition, the program can provide instant exam and course feedback to students immediately after exams. This was quite a chore to program, but is now starting to pay off as a labor and paper saver.

In giving the exam, I scheduled each person for a 15-minute period in my office. I have at one side the computer, which is displays the criteria that I'm using to assess the examinee's responses. The student comes in and is seated. I give the person a sheet of paper (generated by the program) with a number of paragraphs, each describing a situation. I ask the person to read a situation, to respond as though he or she were in the situation, and to do something like resolving conflict, communicating a certain way, or making a motivational statement. The early chapters of the Whetten and Cameron (1991) text are not interpersonal, and in testing on these chapters, I ask the person to do such things as identify stressors and how he or she would respond to them, develop a creative program definition to a given situation, and so on. I score by the extent to which the person demonstrates the appropriate competency and also by the extent to which he or she can explain what he or she is doing in terms of the text. This latter criterion screens out the occasional bullshitter who just does what he or she always does and accidentally tweaks one or more of the criteria. I score by using the Macintosh mouse to click the appropriately numbered button on the computer screen.

Once the exam is finished, the program automatically updates the person's semester record and summarizes the updated record on the screen. I then briefly feed back this information to the person. I generally weigh the exams so that they constitute something over half the total semester score. The remaining score is based on group work—I have been giving no written exams in this course.

I like the face-to-face interactions with students in the action exam. Whereas students can slide by a question on a written exam, I can probe further in the face-to-face situation. I wind up feeling like I really know the extent to which they've accomplished course goals. In addition, I feel that I'm personally developing in my coaching ability as I gain experience in giving these exams. However, the exam is repetitive and time-consuming. I have learned the pattern by heart as well as many of the typical student responses. Examining a class can pretty well fill up a couple of days, but I estimate that the exams are not much more time-consuming than essay exams, because action exam scoring is done in situ and requires no further work beyond the interview.

Student response is decidedly positive overall, but not unambivalent. On the plus side, students generally like the exam as a credible and sensible way of testing course accomplishment. Some are even elated to have a course that does away with the bullshit of written exams. On the minus side, some are concerned about so much scoring in so few minutes, and most experience distinct stress concerning the exam—especially just before, while waiting for their turn.

The program itself is usable, although the user should have a knowledge of *HyperCard*.[1]

Expert Systems

There are a number of programs that I would put into the category of expert, or knowledge-based, systems (depending on whether they draw on expertise or some other forms of knowledge), which provide advice in some problem area. In general, these systems use one or both of two ways of reasoning. The first is *crisp* reasoning, which assumes that knowledge can be expressed as a series of if-then statements and that when asked a question the user can point to a single answer. The second is *fuzzy* reasoning, in which knowledge is expressed as probabilities, which are combined using Bayesian statistics. In crisp reasoning, an answer is found when the conditions on which that answer is contingent are established. In fuzzy reasoning, an answer is found when the probability of that answer rises above a given critical level of probability, usually .7 or so.

I'm pretty well convinced that of the two, the crisp-reasoning expert systems are more appropriate for most business applications. Although the fuzzy reasoning systems sound attractive in that they can handle ambiguous, uncertain situations and can sometimes derive conclusions from incomplete knowledge, they are useful only in situations in which probabilities are known, for example, in geological or medical situations. It is usually very difficult to get a fuzzy reasoning system to work sensibly in an area where probabilities are not normally used. For example, in a review of *Expert Edge,* Pountain (1985) attempted to use the fuzzy reasoning capabilities of the expert system to identify whether a fungus was edible and if it should be eaten. He comments:

> I discovered just how difficult it was to make sensible estimates of probability that would lead to any answer at all: a lot of my systems refused to commit themselves until the acceptance level was set absurdly low. My favorite system was one that produced the advice that there was an 80 percent chance that I should eat the fungus and a 30 percent chance that it was poisonous. (p. 376)

Fuzzy reasoning systems may be useful in business areas where research has produced a body of statistical data. For example, it might be possible to generate a fuzzy system drawing on the vast number of correlational studies done on performance and job satisfaction. However, in most areas of business theory and expertise, it's my belief that the crisp reasoning systems match much better the nature of the knowledge represented.

For this reason, I limit my review to systems that use crisp reasoning. I'll start by discussing a number of systems that provide advice on specific topics. I'll then discuss two expert system "shells" that can be used for creating expert systems.

THE EDGE SERIES

The Human Edge group has produced a number of applications that provide expertise on specific management topics. These include the *Management Edge, Communication Edge, Negotiation Edge,* and *Sales Edge.* All work in essentially the same way: The user is asked to answer a number of questions about himself or herself. These are forced choice pairs having to do with whether the person perceives himself or herself as a leader or follower, group or individually oriented, and so forth. The user is then asked a somewhat shorter list of questions about some person the user wants to manage, communicate with, negotiate with, or sell to, respectively. Once these lists are completed, the program provides a printout of extensive and specific advice as to how to proceed, given who the user is and the kind of person with whom he or she is dealing with.

For the last year I have used these programs in my undergraduate organizational behavior course. I ask work group members to think of situations they are in for which these programs are relevant, to run the program based on the people involved, and then get together in their groups and collectively write a paper about how the programs do and don't correspond to similar topics in their texts and whether or not they learned anything new from using the programs. A number of themes have emerged in the papers. The groups do not think that the advice is always accurate and occasionally the advice seems quite inaccurate. On the whole, however, the advice seems on track and appropriate for the individuals involved. Occasionally, the program makes a real hit, which the user sees as an important insight or idea. Students appreciate the programs because they take the people involved into account and provide specific, doable advice, whereas the text tends to be less specific and personalized. Students sometimes complain that they don't know the other person well enough to fill out the form or that they are uncomfortable with the absolute, dichotomous nature of the questions—there's no room to waffle. Sometimes students complain that they are not in any kind of management situation and have no expertise on which to use the program. I then ask them to use a situation about which they know. Alberto Zanzi (Suffolk University) has students use Human Edge programs to analyze written cases. He reports that although his approach guarantees that all students will be considering a common, management-relevant problem students may complain that the case doesn't provide enough information.

In comparing the programs, my students tend to rate the *Management Edge* and the *Communication Edge* highly, and the *Negotiation Edge* rather lowly. Student feedback indicates that the main reason for this is that the students are less comfortable thinking about the zero sum game approach that this program takes: They are more comfortable with the win-win situations represented by the communications and management programs.

Overall, I am positive about the Human Edge programs and plan to continue using them. They flesh out some of the concepts I use in my course by making them more personal and provide individuals with specific tips about how to proceed in certain situations.

GROUP DIAGNOSTICS

At the June 1985 Organizational Behavior Teaching Conference, Roger Volkema demonstrated his program (*Group-DX*) that diagnoses problems experienced by groups. The program starts by asking a few questions about the nature of the group, then asks educated questions and offers suggestions on how to deal with 11 common group problems. I had a chance to sit down with the program for a while, and I found it very easy to use and filled with what I though were pertinent suggestions.

It seems to me that this program would be an excellent resource to make available to any class organized around groups. In my experience, class groups frequently do experience problems of the types that Volkema describes. Making this program available might be an effective way of inducing group members to think about how their group is doing and what options are available to them.

MANAGEMENT ADVANTAGE

Management Advantage's (from Thoughtware) cover states "I'll give you a big advantage. Not just an edge." This gives the impression that the program is intended to compete with the Human Edge series. The program is aimed at a single user and, after initial startup, assumes a certain individual, managing a certain unit, in a certain organization. The program offers support to that person by providing managerial expertise in 12 areas: motivation, delegation, improving productivity, interviewing, monitoring and directing performance, developing subordinates, coaching, constructive competition, rewards and recognition, job satisfaction, new employees, and cooperation and collaboration. In each of these areas the program contains a set of managerial principles relevant to the area, which can be used in three ways: (1) the user can simply request to see what these principles are, (2) the program will use the principles to lead the user in thinking through a plan in detail, and (3) the program will use the principles in helping the user troubleshoot a specific situation. While going through these uses, the user may indicate which screens should be saved for printout and may type in his or her notes. At the end, a summary, including indicated screens and notes, is printed. The program's knowledge base appears to be a combination of management rules of thumb and some recognized management theory. For example, the motivation base appears to draw on Hertzberg's two-factor theory.

In its troubleshooting mode, the program is quite reminiscent of the group diagnostics program described earlier: The program raises a series of hypotheses about what may be causing the trouble and asks which the user thinks is the case. If the user indicates a yes, the program may ask further more focused questions and eventually comes up with suggestions as to what to do about it.

Overall, I'm favorably impressed by this program. It is easy to use (after installation), draws on an extensive knowledge base, and has given useful, often theory-based advice—at least in the situations I chose. I could see this as a useful adjunct to a managerial skills class.

MICROEXPERT

MicroExpert (by Beverly Thompson and William Thompson) is being marketed by McGraw-Hill. It is an expert system shell that enables any interested individual to create his or her own expert system. The person must decide on an area of expertise and organize it into a series of if-then statements. In addition, the person must provide prompt questions, which the program uses to ask questions of any user. The person writes a file using any word processing program that can save a text file (e.g., *Word-Star*), and saves it to disk, with a ".KO" suffix. When run, *MicroExpert* allows a choice of what system to run. It loads the system of choice and asks a series of questions, based on the prompts. When it has enough information, it provides an answer to whatever question the system is based around.

Having received a copy, I thought a nice initial project would be to program Vroom's (1982, p. 598) decision process flowchart into it. It took about 2 hours to translate this flowchart into 23 if-then statements. A sample statement appears as follows:

    If group problem is yes
    and quality requirement is yes
    and enough information is yes
    and member acceptance is yes
    and my decision accepted is no
    and members share goals is no

and conflict likely is no
then leader behavior is consult-individual
and leader behavior is consult-group

In addition, I wrote out seven prompts, one for each of the seven yes-or-no questions asked in going through the chart. Finally, I included a number of "translations" for the key concepts involved. These served the function of replacing the brief concept phrases I used in the system with longer, more descriptive phrases. The program uses these translations when communicating with the user, and this helps a great deal in making the computer's communications understandable. However, the translations apparently do not work with the conclusions, so the recommendations of the program are briefer than I'd like them to be.

After correcting a couple of minor errors in formatting, the program loaded (this took about 45 seconds) and ran just fine. At each point in working through it, the program offers the opportunity not only to answer the question asked but to review possible answers and to ask some questions about what the program is doing. When an answer is found, the program provides not only the answer but a review of what it learned that enabled it to provide that answer.

The program has some advanced features as well. A program called *Crossref* is provided that helps in debugging an expert system under development. It is possible to develop systems that use quantitative data in addition to more qualitative information. It is possible to create a number of smaller expert systems and to link them together into a larger system. All of these are features that a serious developer would find valuable.

The thing that most intrigues me about *MicroExpert* is its low cost and openness. The program and manual cost under $100 and need no further investment (aside from expertise and a computer) to run. The program was written in *Turbo Pascal,* and the source code is included on the disk. Thus those with an interest in developing the program itself can do so—given a knowledge of *Turbo Pascal.* One enhancement I can think of would be a "Say more" command, which would provide a paragraph or two about how to operationalize variables used in the system.

Dave Whetten (University of Illinois at Urbana-Champaign) has been using *MicroExpert* as a basis for developing an expert system that teaches people how to manage conflict. The program starts with a sketch of a situation that involves conflict. The system then tells what strategy is appropriate and presents guidelines for implementing the approach. The student is then asked to type out a 20-line action plan, and the program provides a printed copy of the transaction. Whetten reports that *MicroExpert* doesn't provide some things he'd like to do, such as provide fuller descriptions and display additional text and graphics.

I'm currently using *MicroExpert* as a basis for a group project in my junior-level management class. Student groups are assigned the task of identifying an area of expertise, researching it, making a flowchart, and programming the system into *MicroExpert*. Areas of expertise chosen by groups include assessing employee performance problems, evaluating and selecting a supplier for a company, deciding whether or not a company needs a computer, choosing a company to work for, predicting the attendance of an entertainment production, and choosing an organizational structure to fit a particular environment. I've found that many students have an "exam" mentality, by which they want to make a system that asks a large number of questions, then tallies up the score to get an answer. Of course, an expert system works on a rather different approach. Currently, the groups have produced flowcharts of their systems and are translating these into statements for *MicroExpert*. It seems that all the groups are progressing successfully and are learning a lot about how an expert system works. After their projects are completed, each group will present its system to the class. Following that, I'll discuss how they may be using expert systems in their business careers.

EXPERT EDGE

Expert Edge is an expert system shell, released by the Human Edge group. It differs from *MicroExpert* (and from Human Edge's other expert system shell, *Expert-Ease*) in that it has the option of using fuzzy reasoning in addition to crisp reasoning. In effect what this means is that the user has the option of entering probabilities in addition to selecting among fixed choices. For example, if asked, "Do you arise early in the morning?" the user can answer that there's, say, a 60% chance that he or she will do so. In *MicroExpert* this same question might be dealt with by offering discrete choices, for example, always, sometimes, and never.

Expert Edge is a full-featured program that offers quite a few alternatives in generating, editing, organizing, and using expert systems. By the same token, this is not program one masters in one or two sittings. I would have no question about having students use expert systems generated on this program: It's not difficult to start up the system, access a particular advisory system, and run it through. However, I'd guess that it would take a substantial effort by a student group to get up to speed in developing an expert system on this program. For this reason I would not use it simply as a way of introducing management students to what expert systems are.

It would be more appropriate in a class with more emphasis on qualitative applications of microcomputers in business. Eventually, this kind of alternative access to expertise is bound to have some effect on the human experts who make their living practicing their expertise.

Issues in Using Microcomputers in Education

It is clear to me that programs of the types described above have a place in education and that we are going to see much more of them in the future. However, I also see some issues with which we are going to have to deal in developing and implementing educational programs—I discuss three of these below.

WHAT KIND OF LEARNING IS ACCOMPLISHED?

The application of computer programs toward educational ends can be considered as one kind of educational methodology. In general, most educational methodologies are more effective in accomplishing some educational ends and less effective in accomplishing others. For example, a textbook is helpful in assimilating information but not directly helpful in applying the information to live situations. Cases can be helpful in learning to analyze and apply concepts but are not as helpful in assimilating information or using information in live situations. Skill practice exercises may help a person to use a skill in a certain type of situation but are not as helpful in preparing a person to think through complex situations.

What kinds of learning goals can be accomplished by the use of computer methodologies? I think that computer programs can be effectively used to help accomplish many of the *cognitive* goals of education (e.g., assimilation of material, diagnosis, decision making, and application of concepts). Computer methodologies are *less* effective in helping the learner to interact effectively with situations, for example, in taking in information about and making sense of complex situations, in implementing a plan, and in interacting competently with others.

This suggests that the educational use of computers will impact existing courses differentially, depending on what kinds of goals they are intended to accomplish. We can expect computers to have a great deal of relevance for courses that are designed around largely cognitive ends (e.g., introductory and theory courses). On the other hand, we can expect computers to have less relevance for courses that deal with situational interaction (e.g., courses involving field projects, experiential exercises, or skill practice). In these courses computers may help with cognitive learning before interaction and may serve as productivity enhancers (e.g., word processing), but they cannot entirely replace actual interaction between learner and situation.

HOW CAN THE KNOWLEDGE UNDERLYING A COMPUTER LEARNING SYSTEM BE VALIDATED?

Most of the programs described above contain some kind of knowledge, derived either from a study of experts and/or from the public body of social science knowledge. It seems a reasonable expectation that the user be provided with information that would be helpful in assessing the validity of the advice offered. There are at least three ways that this can be done. First, with expert knowledge, a panel of experts (different from those who generated the system) can evaluate the system's advice. Second, with social science knowledge, the specific theories and studies used can be cited. Third, when advice for a particular situation is offered, the line of reasoning used to reach the conclusion can be explained.

The programs above are mixed in their provisions of this kind of information. *Eliza, Executive Suite,* and the Human Edge series provide no information about the bases or how they were validated. When queried about this, a Human Edge representative responded that they had a quality group of social scientists who did a lot of research before constructing the Human Edge programs. However, this kind of reassurance does not take the place of the kind of information discussed here. The Thoughtware management training series, the interactive cases, the computerized personal assessment instruments, the group diagnostics program, and *Management Advantage* do provide some information about the knowledge base being used. However, none of these programs adequately explains how the knowledge base is used to reach particular conclusions.

In sum, most of the computer programs reviewed are not entirely satisfactory in their validation of their underlying knowledge. This makes it difficult to assess the reliability of the advice given. Acceptable methods of validating knowledge bases have been established. To be credible learning tools, future programs need to include more careful validation of their underlying knowledge bases.

ARE THESE COMPUTER SYSTEMS LEARNING TOOLS OR LEARNING REPLACEMENTS?

In my experience with the programs described above, I found the particulars of the advice or gain very easy to comprehend. However, it was seldom apparent to me what broader principles were at work. I found that if I used one of the programs a lot, I'd start to induce some principles: For example, in *Executive Suite,* be open about problems and don't try to hide them and in the *Communication Edge,* try to assess the needs of the other person. However, this kind of inductive learning is a slow process, and I'm never sure that I have all of the principles the program is using. If one regards these programs as productivity tools that are to be kept on hand and referred to during one's career, then this is not a problem; the programs provide an easy way to use a fairly complex body of knowledge. However, if one regards these programs as educational tools, intended to transfer the knowledge to the learner and eventually to wean the learner from the program, then it is definitely a problem.

One might argue that it would be enough simply to make explicit the underlying knowledge base. However, this may not be enough to ensure knowledge transfer, because sometimes the knowledge base is arranged for the computer and not the human. For example, the Vroom flow chart described above is based on a very explicit body of information. However, although the procedure for using it is easily grasped, I don't understand why it recommends what it does. I've taught the decision process flowchart a few times but have never learned it in the sense of internalizing what it means.

This has to do with a quality of knowledge that Michaelsen, Michie, and Boulanger (1985) call *surface representations* versus *deep representations.* Surface knowledge is cookbook-like in that it tells one what to do without understanding why. Deeper knowledge contains a greater understanding of the underlying relationships involved. A prerequisite for a computer program to be useful in learning is that its knowledge base not only be available to the user but also have depth. This means that expert systems usable for learning will have to be more complex than those that simply give direction. In addition, it means that this knowledge will have to be organized in ways that are useful to people.

In a broader sense, this issue is analogous to the use of calculators in the classroom—students learning how to do arithmetic calculations often argue that because they know how to accomplish the results using a calculator, why should they learn the more time-consuming and tedious methods using paper and pencil? Similarly, once an area of expertise is fairly convincingly encoded as an expert system, students may ask the same question: Why memorize, when an expert system is easier, faster, and more thorough? This could become a very important question in the near future.

Conclusion

We are just beginning to learn about how to apply microcomputers in the qualitative areas of management and management education. I have described some computer programs that are now available or in development. I believe that we are now seeing the tip of the iceberg of what is to come. Currently, a great deal of research is being done in a number of artificial intelligence areas, such as natural language, voice, and visual interfaces, and in the ability for computers to learn and impart knowledge. In addition, the power of microcomputers can be expected to steadily increase for the next several years, while at the same time prices can be expected to steadily decrease. Within three years, useful microcomputers will probably be within the economic grasp of most college students.

However, capability does not equal effectiveness. Raw computer power means nothing unless it is effectively directed toward useful education ends. I think that the coming decade will see significant changes in how management is taught—indeed, in the very concept of education and educational institutions. There are now great opportunities to innovate for management teachers who are willing to leap into the current gap between management education and computer use. As with any methodology, computer learning-programs have their strengths and weaknesses. It is our task to develop and capitalize on the strengths of this methodology without giving up other effective methodologies or compromising our educational goals.

Epilogue: 1985-1993

I ended my 1985 article on an upbeat note, predicting that the programs reviewed were the "tip of the iceberg of what was to come." What developments have since occurred in using microcomputers for management teaching? Certainly, computers themselves are much more available to students, and are much more powerful than the typical computers of 1985.

A lot of change has occurred. On the down side: Armonk and Human Edge are out of business, Thoughtware is no longer courting the academic market, McGraw-Hill is no longer offering *MicroExpert,* and I don't see as many faculty developing programs as before. The Organizational Behavior Teaching Society's Microcomputer Interest Group has discontinued, mainly because there's nothing much to report. Use of qualitative programs in management classes continues to be low.

If nothing else, we have learned that anyone wishing to develop software for university use has some difficult obstacles to overcome. Whereas the quantitative disciplines draw on the programs that businesses use (e.g., *Lotus 1, 2, 3,* and *dBase*), there are as yet no equivalent programs for managers. Thus would-be program writers must develop for the much smaller and poorer university market. Faculty may endeavor to develop their own programs, but it has become apparent that universities offer faculty little incentive for program development (Bigelow, Gacia, Rude, & Warfield, 1987-1988).

Still, there has been progress. Book publishers have managed to provide an outlet for management software by bundling it with texts. Computerized test banks have been a common text companion for some time, but we are now seeing increasing numbers of computer simulations; for example, *Io,* included with Lewis, Garcia, and Jobs's (1990) text. Computerized self-assessment instruments are becoming available in the same way, for example, the instrument included with Quinn, Faerman, Thompson, and McGrath's (1990) text. Whetton and Cameron (1991) include not only computerized skill preassessment instruments but also computerized skill application exercises for their chapters on power, motivation, and conflict. Interactive cases also seem to be receiving broader attention (Moberg & Caldwell, 1988; see also Bigelow, 1990, chap. 6; Rude, 1988-1989; Sherman, 1988-1989). Use of expert systems seems to be in a lull, but we also see some experimentation here (Szewcsak & Sekaran, 1987-1988). In addition, some new types of qualitative programs have been introduced that are possibly relevant to management education. Those interested in reviewing the kinds of programs available might obtain Mindware's catalog.[2]

I think two newer directions are worth noting. The first is programs aimed at stimulating a person's creative processes. I did some work with *The Idea Generator* (Bigelow, 1988-1989), but a number of like programs are now available, for example, *Merlin's Version* and *Idea Fisher.* These are representative of a line of programs that attempt to develop a person's capabilities, rather than provide direct solutions. Given the increased attention given to creativity and innovation in colleges of business, such programs could prove to be quite relevant.

The second direction is microsimulations, or programs that simulate key aspects of another person in interaction. The early work here seems to be going on in special education. For example, Strang (1986, 1987) reports success in teacher training using computer-generated pupils that made "off-task" comments. Similarly, Murphy (1987) reports increases in appropriate classroom management responses using computer-generated student talkouts. I think there is a lot of potential for using computer-simulated dialogues as preparation for actual management dialogue.

In sum, we've learned a lot over the last 8 years about producing viable programs for management courses. As with any new area, we've seen a considerable shaking out as less viable ideas and approaches fall away. However, we've also seen some signs of development, as viable marketing and software approaches are established. Consequently, in the long term, my predictions of development and increased use of qualitative programs for management courses continue to be positive. I believe that computers can provide powerful benefits to management education. Although these benefits will probably not be realized soon, I believe that they will come in time.

Note

1. I will be happy to send copies to anyone who sends me a Mac disk. The only stipulations are that the header stay the same, that the program not be sold for profit, and that I receive copies of any developments. For more information on action exams, see Bigelow (1991, chaps. 10-11) and Whetten and Cameron (1991, pp. 20-46).

2. Mindware's toll-free number is (800) 447-0477.

References

Bigelow, J. (1988-1989). Review of *The Idea Generator. Organizational Behavior Teaching Review, 13*(3), 149-153.

Bigelow, J., Garcia, J., Rude, D., & Warfield, A. (1987-1988). A software developer's job is never done. *Organizational Behavior Teaching Review, 12*(4), 34-51.

Bixby, M. (1984). *Photocopying in education: What is "fair use"?* Unpublished manuscript, Boise State University, College of Business, Boise.

Lewis, C., Garcia, J., & Jobs, S. (1990). *Managerial skills in organizations.* Boston: Allyn & Bacon.

Michaelsen, R., Michie, D., & Boulanger, A. (1985, April). The technology of expert systems. *Byte,* pp. 303-312.

Moberg, D., & Caldwell, D. (1988). *Interactive cases in organizational behavior.* Glennview, IL: Scott, Foresman.

Murphy, D. M. (1987). Using microcomputer simulation to teach classroom management skills to preservice teachers. *Behavioral Disorders, 13*(1), 20-34.

Pountain, D. (1985, October). Computers as consultants. *Byte,* pp. 367-376.

Quinn, R. E., Faerman, S., Thompson, M., & McGrath, M. (1990). *Becoming a master manager: A competency framework.* New York: Wiley.

Rude, D. (1988-1989). Review of interactive cases in organizations. *The Organizational Behavior Teaching Review, 13*(3), 146-147.

Sherman, D. (1988-1989). Interactive cases for introductory courses in organizational behavior: An emerging computer aided instructional technique. *The Organizational Behavior Teaching Review, 13*(4), 112-120.

Strang, H. R. (1987). Acquisition of fundamental behavior management skills with microcomputer-simulated pupils. *Journal of Special Education Technology, 8*(3), 14-28.

Strang, H. R. (1986). Training classroom management skills via a microcomputer-based simulation. *Teacher Education and Special Education, 9*(2), 55-62.

Szewcsak, E., & Sekaran, U. (1987-1988). Introducing personal computer technology in the teaching of organizational behavior courses. *The Organizational Behavior Teaching Review, 12*(1), 74-83.

Vroom, V. H. (1982). Can leaders learn to lead? In D. Hampton, C. Summer & R. Webber (Eds.), *Organizational behavior and the practice of management* (pp. 597-607). Dallas: Scott, Foresman.

Waters, J. A., Adler, N. J., Poupart, R., & Hartwick, J. (1983). Assessing managerial skills through a behavioral exam. *Exchange: The Organizational Behavior Teaching Journal, 8*(2), 27-44.

Whetten, D., & Cameron, K. (1991). *Developing management skills* (2nd ed.). New York: HarperCollins.

Suggested Reading

Bigelow, J. (Ed.) (1991). *Management skills.* Newbury Park, CA: Sage.

Experiential Method

DOROTHY MARCIC
Czechoslovak Management Center
and
Metropolitan State University

Rationale for Experiential Learning

Many teachers and trainers went through 16 or more years of schooling during which the teachers talked while the students presumably listened and took notes. This is commonly called learning. Such approaches were more refined in college, where instructors, particularly in business, showed a near addiction to overhead transparencies—as if this new twist on an old technique would greatly enhance the learning involved. Assumptions under this model include the teacher as expert and fount of knowledge, with the student as empty vessel eager to be filled with pure gems of wisdom. Unfortunately for so many who have toiled under this system, such learning has great limitations, for it only goes so far.

Learning, as a field of study, has fascinated psychologists and educators for many years. Numerous theories abound on the actual process of learning, whether it be conditioned learning of the Skinner (1968) variety or a more holistic approach from someone like Bruner (1966). Many management professors are familiar with Kolb, Rubin, and McIntyre's (1974) learning model. That process describes learning as starting from concrete experience in which the learner sees something unusual or new, followed by reflective observation, conceptualization, and finally experimentation.

Some writers have argued for the existence of a hierarchy of learning, most notably the earlier work of Bloom (1956) with his taxonomy of educational objectives, which are

Knowledge (Primary Level)
Comprehension
Application
Analysis
Synthesis
Evaluation (Highest Level)

Clearly, the lecture and multiple-choice exam approach generally deals with the primary level and perhaps the second level of comprehension. Reasons why methods at these lowest levels of learning are used include the speed and relative ease of teaching and the assumption that what is presented to the learner is assimilated. In addition, it is by far easier to evaluate the effectiveness of teaching knowledge and comprehension than determining how well the learner can synthesize or evaluate.

Experiential education, when done well, can involve all of the six levels of Bloom's model. However, what is sometimes called experiential education is little more than a highly controlled and even coercive classroom situation that may, in fact, hinder learning. More on that later.

Knowles (1978), one of the leading writers in the field of adult education (and we are, after all, not talking about teaching 10- to 12-year-olds), describes a number of assumptions about learning for adults based on the work of Lindeman (1926). Some of these are

1. Adults have a life-centered orientation to learning. Therefore, life situations are more appropriate for adults than abstract subjects.
2. The richest source of learning for adults is experience. Hence the base methodology should be analysis of experience.
3. A deep need to be self-directing is a characteristic of adults. Therefore, teachers are more effective as engagers of mutual inquiry rather than transmitters of knowledge and evaluators of their conformity to that style of learning.

Types of Experiential Learning and Advantages of Use

Hoberman (1992) identified two types of experiential learning: synthetic and natural. Synthetic learning involves any devised activity, whether case study, game, simulation or role-play, whereas natural learning is a more sophisticated form of on-the-job training. Both types of learning involve analyzing a situation, coming to a decision, taking action, and handling the consequences. These activities require implementation, which makes experiential learning different from passive learning. In natural learning, the learner uses day-to-day work problems and experiences as means for applying theories, testing models, exploring new approaches, and helping to educate those on other levels about the nature of problems.

Classroom learning can actually incorporate both types of experiential learning, provided the students are employees somewhere, particularly if they have some level of responsibility. By assigning students the task of analyzing real-work problems (rather than only those from a book) or doing organizational assessments, for example, the students are applying classroom theories to their work venue.

Training programs often use experiential learning as well. And here the facilitator has an excellent opportunity to make use of natural methods. In addition, the trainer can use such techniques as simulations, which can compress 1 or 2 years of a problem situation into 1 hour and can bring a worldwide system of plants and offices into one room, with a great deal of learning involved. Actions can be analyzed, with immediate feedback and comparison with other groups. Games, too, which have the capacity to engage students quickly, can create a positive classroom environment, one in which risks are more easily taken. Games have been shown to have a great short-term impact but low long-term learning. However, if used in conjunction with other learning techniques, the results are likely to be more positive (Hoberman, 1992).

Issues in Experiential Education

CONTROL

Experiential learning began as "laboratory learning," with the natural open-endedness of a laboratory setting. In such a venue, student learning is high, for what ever results is used as a topic of analysis. However, in these situations, the teacher must be extremely flexible and willing to take risks, perhaps even looking foolish. Many instructors are not comfortable with this, instead preferring to control more tightly the outcome. What results is a well-devised and organized classroom activity, which may be timed to the minute, turning the teacher into a "manic clerk," and a manager of learning experiences. However, manic clerks are not educators (Vaill, 1979). In these settings, students who react differently from the teacher's expectations are given some type of negative feedback. Here learners quickly deduce how to please the teacher. Learning, though, is often then confined to only that ingratiation, and the students feel duped and manipulated.

RISK TAKING

Closely related to control is the ability of the instructor to veer off the plan when the opportunity arises and to take advantage of a natural-learning situation in the classroom. Is there a severe conflict between two members of a team? How about dealing with that issue right in class if the content of the class relates in any way to conflict management? Or have some members psychologically withdrawn from class or from the activity? Again, if related to class content, the instructor has the chance then to use that withdrawal behavior as a point of analysis and learning. However, this diversion requires wading into unchartered waters. Those who have done it, though, report that some of the most important learning from the entire course takes place then.

EMOTIONS IN THE CLASSROOM

Even though the subject here is management and organizational behavior, many textbooks and instructors act as if emotions did not exist or at least were not important. Yet there are many arguments that support emotion as a basis for many of our behaviors. And if they are not discussed as class material, most likely they will not be used in the classroom for laboratory learning. Again, here is potential for intense learning. Someone gets angry at the teacher. Is that here-and-now issue addressed? Or another student shows a great deal of enthusiasm over a certain point of view. Why not explore where that emotional rise comes from? As with risk taking, though, the instructor here has few role models to emulate when reacting in these situations (see Chapter 4, this volume).

GRADING CLASSROOM PARTICIPATION

Grading classroom participation, argues Gilson (1992), only rewards those students who possess the wherewithal to verbalize their learning. Therefore, extroverts and majority students do better, for it has been shown that women and minorities are less likely to contribute to class discussions (Hall & Sandler, 1984). And when they do, the results are often not as positive as for majority students. The glass ceiling starts, then, in the classroom (Gilson, 1992).

PSYCHOLOGICAL TYPES AND LEARNING STYLES

Related to classroom participation, it has been demonstrated that certain types of people do well in different learning situation. Kolb et al.'s (1974) work indicates that some learners prefer more abstract problems with little interaction of other students. Others, though, want action-oriented learning and to be involved in groups. A classic study by Killmann and Taylor (1974) used the Myers-Briggs Type Indicator to determine which students preferred and learned the most in a t-group setting. For example, extroverts, intuitives, and perceptives felt the most comfortable but did not necessarily learn the most, because the setting was so similar to their natural state. These results demonstrate once again that some learners do better in certain types of environments.

PRACTICING WHAT IS PREACHED

Instructors may teach the elegance of participative management but run an authoritarian classroom. An instructor may think he or she is not an authoritarian, but he or she then must answer these questions: How much input do students have in the development of the course? In the planning of their work assignments? In their final grade? In the grading of other students, papers, and so on? As Vaill (1985) states, "it is hard to be ethically powerful about the ethics of power, hard to be accepting of feedback about one's own lecture on feedback" (p. 549).

STATUS AND CAREER ISSUES

There is probably no experientially based management or organizational behavior professor around who has not been criticized by fellow faculty (particularly those in the hard quantitative disciplines) for not really teaching. After all, they say, doing simulations is so easy and allows the instructor to just take it easy. Therefore, those professors who would like to be respected by their colleagues (and perhaps get tenure and promotions on the way) face the challenge of educating each and every colleague on the theories of adult learning or, easier, giving up and doing the lecture method like most everyone else.

Introduction to Section Articles

In these days of tight budgets and cost cutting, it is not unusual to see even more large lecture classes in universities. How does one teach experientially in these settings? In Chapter 11, Lindbergh Sata has developed several techniques for breaking down the anonymity and formality of huge classes by using various verbal and nonverbal exercises to create a more informal relationship between students and teacher and among the students themselves.

In Chapter 12, Jeffery Weil discusses a course in which students are given the power to plan, organize, staff, lead, and control their class. What is required is a restructuring of student-teacher relationships as well as a new look at such issues as grading, attendance, service to the classroom, presentations, and so on. In the end, students have become empowered through planning and implementing the course. Weil reports that he has never himself given a grade in the many years of teaching this course. All he does is copy the grade that students have assigned.

Our conceptually dividing experiential learning from other teaching strategies is questionable, as Donald Bowen debates in Chapter 13. He explores such issues as locus of responsibility, process involved, teaching skills and values versus knowledge, and level of student involvement. Bowen describes the need for a refocusing of the argument, having the course developer look carefully at the needs of the students, goals of the class, and needs and skills of the instructors.

Kim Cameron and David Whetton's names have become almost synonymous with management skills development, an approach that is inherently experiential because it relies so heavily on observation, personal application, and reflection. Their approach described in Chapter 14 involves teaching students to manage rather than to teach about management. Key components of their skill learning model are skill preassessment, learning, analysis, practice, and application.

Recommended Resources

Anyone interested in learning more about experiential education and how to use it in management education can refer to the following sources:

Christensen (1991)
Cross (1981)
Hoberman (1992)
Rossman and Rossman (1990)
Vaill (1985)

Try any of the volumes in the Pfeiffer and Jones/University Associates Series of Structured Experiences for Experiential Education (San Diego; 619-578-5900).

There are many textbooks and supplements that include myriad experiential exercises. For example, see Marcic (1992), Whetton and Cameron (1991), and Gordon (1993).

References

Bloom, B. S. (1956). *Taxonomy of educational objectives.* New York: Longman.

Bruner, J. S. (1966). *Toward a theory of instruction.* Cambridge, MA: Harvard University Press.

Cross, P. (1981). *Adults as learners.* San Francisco: Jossey-Bass.

Christensen, C. R. (1991). *Education for judgement: The artistry of discussion leadership.* Cambridge, MA: Harvard Business School Press.

Gilson, C. (1992). *Of dinosaurs and sacred cows: The grading of classroom participation.* Unpublished manuscript.

Gordon, J. (1993). *A diagnostice approach to organizational behavior* (4th ed.). New York: Allyn & Bacon.

Hall, R., & Sandler, B. (1984). *Out of the classroom; A chilly climate for women?* Washington, DC: Association of American Colleges.

Hoberman, S. (1992). *Experiential management development.* New York: Quorum Books.

Killmann, R., & Taylor, V. A. (1974). Contingency approach to laboratory learning: Psychological type vs. learning norms. *Human Relations, 27,* 891-909.

Knowles, M. (1978). *The adult learner: A neglected species.* Houston: Gulf.

Kolb, D. A., Rubin, I. M., & McIntyre, J. M. (Eds.). (1974). *Organizational psychology: An experiential approach.* Englewood Cliffs, NJ: Prentice-Hall.

Lindeman, E. C. (1926). *The meaning of adult education.* New York: New Republic.

Marcic, D. (1992). *Organizational behavior: Experiences and cases* (3rd ed.). New York: West.

Rossman, M. H., & Rossman, M. E. (1990). Applying adult development stategies. San Francisco: Jossey-Bass.

Skinner, B. F. (1968). *The technology of teaching.* New York: Appleton-Century-Crofts.

Vaill, P. B. (1979). Cookbooks, auctions, and claptrap cocoons: A commentary on the field of organizational behavior. *Exchange: The Organizational Behavior Teaching Journal, 4*(1), 3-6.

Vaill, P. B. (1985). Integrating the diverse directions of the behavioral sciences. In R. Tannanbaum, N. Margulies, & F. Massarik (Eds.), *Human systems development* (pp. 547-577). San Francisco: Jossey-Bass.

Whetton, D. A., & Cameron, K. S. (1991). *Developing management skills* (2nd ed.). New York: HarperCollins.

Eleven

Experiential Methods in a Large Classroom Setting

LINDBERGH S. SATA
Saint Louis University

Tightening budgets, which increase pressure on faculty to be more "productive" with their time, lead many schools to have large introductory courses of several hundred students packed into one lecture hall. Faculty have reluctantly accepted such large class sizes at the introductory level to ensure smaller student-teacher ratios in the advanced classes.

Whatever the economics, students enrolled in such classes uniformly dislike the feelings of confusion and alienation that they experience. Motivated students attempt to arrive early to find a seat in the first 10 rows to gain some sense of personal contact with the professor. This is necessary because despite public address systems, large projection screens, blackboards, and video monitors, once eye contact with the instructor is lost it is difficult to maintain a sense of involvement and personalized interaction in the learning process. The size of the lecture hall, its acoustics, and the requirement of projecting one's voice in order to be heard, alter the communication style of the speaker, which may further increase the sense of alienation.

These problems are compounded in such settings by the difficulty students have in making contact with each other. Not infrequently, members of large classes report that it may be past mid-semester before they recognize the presence of friends among the sea of strange faces.

This impersonalization, when added to the distractions common in large classes, tends to discourage student involvement. Question-and-answer

This chapter originally appeared in *Exchange: The Organizational Behavior Teaching Journal,* Volume 3, Issue 1.

sessions at the conclusion of the lecture, if employed, are frequently taken as rituals and elicit responses primarily from the verbally aggressive students. Attendance problems and examination by proxy are some of the other undesirable consequences. Finally, the structural constraints that inhibit student-faculty interaction make it extremely difficult to identify with the professor or his or her discipline.

Faculty also report difficulties. Large classes tend to formalize the professor's role, confining it to the transmittal of knowledge and relegating feedback and clarification to study section discussion. The dilemma of transmitting information clearly and concisely to several hundred students, and the impossibility of responding to more than a token number of questions, further contributes to the formalization of the lecture, the solidification of hierarchical roles of teacher and student, and the creation of social distance. Professors who have prided themselves on recognizing and knowing each student individually find themselves frustrated and cynical as a consequence of large classroom teaching assignments.

Not only does classroom size produce this formalized and distant type of interaction but faculty report that their range of teaching approaches is seriously curtailed. The first to go are experiential techniques; teachers resign themselves to the goal of helping students acquire cognitive information, abandoning their hope that students will be able to experience and integrate the material on a personal level.

One commonly used solution to the problem is to break large classes into study sections of manageable size. This alternative has, however, been less than satisfactory. The smaller sections are typically delegated to teaching assistants who might have some competence in clarifying content but lack sophistication and experience in creatively working with students in ways to inspire enthusiasm for the subject content.

This problem could be lessened if the teacher would change his or her role. Maier (1971), for example, defined his role primarily as a consultant to students rather than as a lecturer. He used a small-group format within 100-student classes and was able to have participation and involvement comparable to that which is possible with much smaller classes. A variation of this theme is to have the instructor redefine his or her primary audience. Bradford (1969) and Bradford and LeDuc (1975) defined the core student group as the teaching assistants and devoted most of his attention to helping them better plan, develop, and implement their teaching goals; he views the lecture to the total student group as an ancillary supplement to the basic learning that occurs in the smaller sections.

This article describes some relatively simple approaches I have used to break down the anonymity and formality of large classes. My interventions include some simple experiential techniques integrated into the lecture period. I have had two goals: first, to break down the formality and increase the interaction between teacher and students and among students themselves in an effort to build a classroom climate that is more conducive to learning and, second, to provide the skills and personal learning that are more appropriately gained through experiential techniques rather than through formal lectures.

To illustrate some of the approaches adopted to achieve these two goals, I will describe the initial days of an introductory course in clinical medicine. This particular segment was to focus on the ethical and philosophical concerns of physicians in modern society. The goal was to encourage students to examine fundamental concepts of the physician's role—not so much the medical component of the role, but rather the personal and interpersonal issues the physician faces in dealing with colleagues, staff, the hospital, and patients.

The content had personal meaning and importance to the instructors; however, the concepts as they had been taught in previous years were sufficiently removed from the day-to-day experience of freshman medical students to cause them to be poorly received. Parenthetically, the students, for the most part, were heavily involved with mastering basic science requirements and had only minimal contact and exposure to patients and medical practice. My reaching these goals was particularly difficult in a 150-person class that met for 90 minutes in a large lecture hall—hardly the sort of setting that would encourage anyone to become personally involved or very empathetic to these medical dilemmas.

The first goal was to confront directly the potential distance and impersonality that was virtually inevitable in a large class. Because one could not rely on the increased contact that occurs between teacher and students and among students in small courses, my challenge was to create a new learning environment.

I began by sharing the dilemmas of lecturing to a large group and indicating that any social distance is created less by my personal intention than by the structural constraints of class size. I expressed what I want in the educational process and shared my feelings about this large class size. I find that the more I can express my personal feelings, the less I am seen as a distant and impersonal object. I also share my difficulties in recognizing students out of class and request their help through identifying themselves in out-of-class encounters with me.

I then turned to the issue of student contact with each other. They had been studying together for two semesters so there was time for relationships to develop. I asked them to look around and identify what percentage of their classmates they knew. Conducting an impromptu survey through raising hands, students can identify whether they know 100%, 75%, 50%, 25%, 10%, and less than 10% of their classmates. The vast majority of students respond to the 10% figure, and the rest distribute on the 25% and less than 10% dimensions.

Feeling statements were then randomly elicited regarding the large numbers of strangers constituting their peer group. Responses were examined in terms of feelings of alienation and exclusion and the discomfort experienced under such circumstances. Student responses were then compared with surveys conducted on medical care patients receiving treatment in public hospital settings and their common complaints of institutional indifference, dehumanization, and alienation that comes from the impersonal waiting room, long lines, uncomfortable periods of waiting before care is given, and unsympathetic personnel—all conditions the students could identify with on the basis of their academic experience.

Students were then asked to pair with someone who was unknown to them and to spend 5 minutes getting to know one another. The animated interaction period was reluctantly interrupted with the suggestion that ample opportunities to become acquainted were available over the following years of study. Statements were elicited about "humorous surprises" such as rediscovering a high school classmate, having been competitive suitors for the same person in an earlier college romance, or living in the same boarding house without being aware of one another's presence. The interaction demonstration was discussed in light of the relative ease of conversing with strangers when appropriate structure and sanctions were given for open and authentic engagement and, conversely, the difficulty that most individuals experience when structure is not provided and one must take a risk to initiate such an interactional opportunity. The physician-patient relationship was appropriately introduced in this context.

The following class period focused on different aspects of the physician-patient relationship. The previously formed interactional pairs were requested to participate nonverbally for a period of 10 minutes in a blind walk. One student of each pair was asked to close his or her eyes and be sightless. He or she was then accompanied by the sighted partner through the halls of the school. Following the 10-minute demonstration the students were to reverse roles while maintaining the nonverbal climate so that each member of the pair could experience sighted and sightless roles.

After their return to the classroom, randomly elicited comments were paraphrased on the blackboard and volunteers were encouraged to share feelings with their classmates. The leader-blind roles were then articulated in terms of the affective component of what was meant by responsibility and what was meant by helplessness. Issues of control and dependency inherent in the patient-physician role were also discussed.

The nonverbal experiment was subsequently repeated with specific instructions to consider the degrees of freedom possible even with such an infirmity and to test the limits of freedom under such conditions. Students quickly found themselves climbing over furniture, dancing, skipping, exploring both the physical and human environments. Following their return and the sharing of experiences, the lecture then focused on the helping relationship and the conditions under which physicians constrain or free patients in their dealings with them. Students became aware of the awesome meaning of the word *responsibility,* and of the difference between *helping* and *helping the hell out of someone.*

These are some examples of activities that can be used to modify the formality of a large classroom and also to provide the personal learning usually lacking with the lecture format. Obviously, not all subject areas have such experiential aspects, but the instructor who explores these alternatives will be surprised at the number of times a simple activity can be developed to illustrate a conceptual area. All of this is not to suggest that it is inappropriate to lecture or that entire periods might not best be spent lecturing. Rather, the point is that even with the constraints of a large classroom, there is often more flexibility in teaching styles than is first apparent.

A second point is that the instructor in a large class must be aware of the powerful impact that structure has on student involvement, motivation, and learning. In the small class, the teacher does not have to expend extra effort to increase involvement, interaction, and feedback to the instructor, for that develops out of the normal interactions. But in large lecture classes, the instructor has to set up conditions where two-way communication can occur.

Such communication is important, not only to facilitate student learning but for feedback to the instructor. When lecturing to a large sea of faces, it is difficult to know to what extent one is on-target or off—and if off, whether one is aiming too high, too low, with too many or too few examples, and so on. An advantage of including experiential techniques is that the teacher quickly learns the extent to which he or she is on target.

There are other methods the instructor can use. Student representatives can be selected from study sections to meet periodically with the teacher and assistants to discuss student concerns regarding content and teaching style. Or, as McCaskey illustrates, student surveys can be taken throughout the course to monitor progress and make whatever changes are necessary (see Chapter 19).

Using experiential techniques and increasing the amount of personal two-way communication between teacher and students requires a set of skills above and beyond being able to deliver an adequate lecture. Far too often lecturers find themselves unduly preoccupied with content at the exclusion of examining group-process issues that if ignored may undermine their effectiveness. The teacher's sensitivity to students' ability to attend to and absorb content information reflects the adequacy of the sequential flow of the material presented, being conscious of the dynamics of the group, and being aware and adjusting to the discovery of being too far ahead or too far behind the students' ability to absorb new information. In the final analysis, teaching is the art of sensitively integrating the learning objectives of teachers and students in a collaborative process whereby both are interested in mastering such objectives successfully.

References

Bradford, D. (1969). *The use of para-professionals in higher education: Seniors as college instructors.* Unpublished manuscript.

Bradford, D. & LeDuc, R. (1975). One approach to the care and teaching of introductory O.B. *The Teaching of Organization Behavior, 1*(1), 18-24.

Maier, N. R. F., (1971). Innovation in education. *American Psychologist, 26.*(8), 722-725.

Twelve

Management Experientially Taught

JEFFREY L. WEIL
Manhattan College

Cohen (1976) and Zanzi (1983) describe course methods that break the traditional professor-lecture/student-listen mode. Cohen (1976) used the classroom as a microcosm to study organizations. Zanzi (1983) advanced the *contract* method of meeting course requirements into a *cafeteria* method. This article reports my experience with a course strategy that not only builds on the above methods but also defines as the goal of the course to transfer to students power and responsibility for planning, organizing, staffing, leading, and controlling *their* class (operational details will emerge as the article progresses). Thus the course itself has become formatted as a business experiential exercise wherein students learn and practice academically acquired knowledge as will soon be required in everyday business life.

Concept

The concept and its execution are flexible and can be adapted to such variables as the individualisms of different professors and particular classes, that is, students. This article is not, therefore, intended as a session-by-session protocol for the course but only as a report on some of my own practices and observations. I hope that the recounting will inspire some readers to go forward with one or more of the key elements.

This chapter originally appeared in *The Organizational Behavior Teaching Review*, Volume 12, Issue 3.

Basically, the design is a departure from the normal business course, especially for the soon-to-graduate business senior at Manhattan. Many of our lower undergraduate courses are lecture style, and over the years, teachers and students develop modes of interaction that may be ideally suited for academic environs but are potentially devastating if projected to the business world. For example, by the time business students are in their senior year, they politely come in, sit down, open notebooks, and pen in hand, wait to be told course requirements, which they will conscientiously execute. This behavioral repertoire is entirely dysfunctional in business in which initiative is assessed early on. I use the strategy described below for a senior-level interpersonal behavior dynamics course. But it can be generalized to other courses and student clubs (Weil, 1983).

Student Accountability
and Restructuring of Classroom Roles

I abandon the conventional relationship of professorial superiority over student acolyte in favor of a boss-employee relationship in which, in a working relationship, students are expected to question my authority (diplomatically, of course), to challenge competitors, to voice opinions, and generally, to think independently. I share with students as much power as possible to decide the following aspects of the course, and then hold them accountable through grades based largely on their success in executing their decisions.

STUDENT ROLE DEFINITION

The role of students in their prior courses has most often been passive acceptance of professorial decree. In this course design, students are held accountable for the creation of their course. Therefore, they are forced into a role that must confront and resolve task uncertainty, time and goal orientation. Specifically, students are accountable for defining, planning, organizing, staffing, directing, and controlling all operational aspects of their course. There is, in addition, topical content (which is listed in the college catalog, is logically sequential to the topics covered in the prerequisite textbook course in organizational behavior, is an area of interest to senior business students, is an area that we judge to have potential utility for the students, and/or is an area that has burst upon the discipline). This must be identified and defined because the end take-away knowledge should be process and content. In this scenario, the ultimate goal is to have students not only run the course in a business mode but also take on all management functions. Students must decide course requirements within a specified set of overall objectives and number of class sessions. Perhaps, for the first time in their college careers they must consider teacher needs, student needs, school policy, accreditation requirements, academic requirements, course policy, and content. Each one of these variables must be taken into account when the students pursue their first goal, to design a product—the course.

PROFESSOR ROLE DEFINITION

As the professor, I initially preside as an owner-president who decides final policy, retains ultimate authority, and is responsible for efficient employment of student resources. Ideally, this role can be diminished over time as students assimilate management functions. My goal is to become limited to being a natural resource and supplier of information, role-plays, and minimal guidance and to interweave presentation of the substantive content required in the subject area; all this in lieu of my being a general manager.

This reality of creating their own course, with objectives and realistically redefined student-professor roles, becomes a first experiential exercise analogous to students' future business tasks. Students must apply their own knowledge and skills in the creation and execution of this course with accountability to each other for that performance.

The Process of Course Definition and Finalizing Requirements

Given the new expectations applied to both professor and students for responsibility and accountability, the goal of defining a creditable course can now be pursued. The process has been facilitated with a linear progression through three questions: (1) What do you want to do? (2) Why do you want to do it? and (3) How do you want to do it?

WHAT DO YOU WANT TO DO?

When students are asked this question in the opening moments of the first class they initially think the professor is kidding or trying to relieve tension. Then I center my conversation on their college history analyzing the roles adopted reflexively by students and professors. Each term I hear the same story, that students have learned to take on the role of "sit back and relax" while the professor performs. The skills involved in this role include listening, accurate note taking, memorization competition (i.e., against a grading curve or each other), reading, and paper writing. In addition, they have learned some devious methods of satisfying course requirements, such as fraternity test files, departmental garbage cans, and old term papers from friends. From campus to campus the specifics may vary, but by the time students become seniors they have developed a general strategy of "I'll wait to hear what the professor wants and then I'll do it."

As a result of this, I wanted to design a course that accomplishes two goals. First, to break the predisposition of students to take on a subordinate, passive, and reactive role. That of coworker is desired in its place. Second, to teach students experientially the dynamics of human intragroup interaction. In a senior-level behavioral dynamics course that is intended to be experiential, the most active role-plays and active participation work best. In contrast, if this method is used for other courses in which the primary emphasis is different (e.g., business policy, small business management, and nonbusiness courses), then naturally, the priorities of material would be different.

WHY DO YOU WANT TO DO IT?

Learning by doing is different from learning by lecture or by reading. This thesis and the pros and cons of experiential learning have long been amply covered (e.g., Kolb, Rubin, & McIntyre, 1974; Maier, Solem, & Maier, 1957).

HOW DO YOU WANT TO DO IT?

The question of *how* has two possible meanings. The first centers on the method that the class will use to define a course. In other words, how do I get this process started? The second centers on how the course will be executed once it is defined and on finalizing course requirements.

Over the years I have relied on open discussion to help define the course. Students tend to reality test to determine whether I am serious about having them define and conduct their course. Thus an early question has been, "Are we going to assign grades to ourselves?" An affirmative answer usually leads to, "Why don't you give us all A's?" with associated jokes and giggles. I then inform them that (1) students and professors must maintain professional self-respect and credibility; (2) therefore, because I am responsible for course requirements, an irrational assignment of A's is unacceptable; (3) their course has accreditation ramifications that extend well beyond a three-credit course; and (4) irrational grade assignments that are not based on clearly defined operational and behavioral definitions could result in my, the chairman's, or the dean's falling back to typical requirements such as three tests and a paper.

I make clear that I would be very pleased with a decision whereby my needs and the students' are mutually satisfied. Students want to earn A's. With this I have no argument. In fact, all will be ecstatic if we can hand in a valid, defendable, and rational grade sheet with straight A's. Thus the course orientation becomes vividly clear—they must compose course requirements that allow all students to learn by doing and to earn valid grades that are perfectly respectable without penalty for learning errors en route.

At this point the open discussion becomes a deadly silence. I inform the class that I will return in 1 hour to review their decision. Most often, students formulate a shopping list of topics that will become the content of the course. If they have not, then they request 1 day to conduct library research. Oftentimes, 3 or 4 hours are required to formulate course requirements. Next, I inform the students that once course content is agreed on, they must then be ready to organize, staff, lead, and control. They have now reached the second meaning of question three, that being exactly how they will conduct and finalize the course. At this point other questions arise—paraphrased conceptually: "Who is going to do which topics?" "What behaviors will be required?" and "What performance measures will be made of us for grading purposes?".

I usually leave the students alone at this stage in the planning process, during which many possibilities are stated. Discussions often go in circles, and some brave student may assume a leadership role in a valiant attempt to guide the class through the assigned task of answering the above questions. Students want to be fair and honor everyone's opinion, and they find it exasperating when no resolution is in sight. At this point, I come back and suggest the formation of special committees that will have defined functions, line, and staff authority. For example, a secretarial committee can be immediately created and will initially keep minutes of the class proceedings. Having started, students usually see the efficiency of specialized committees in contrast to having all class members participate in everything; they quickly suggest potential other committees. A contract committee will write up an agreement describing all aspects of course requirements, participation, grading, and committee functions for all to sign. An evaluation and compilation committee is created to study the literature on performance evaluation and to construct proper performance evaluation tools. A steering committee keeps track of and reports the progress of all groups and assignments. A grievance committee settles any differences of opinion, such as in assignments, grading, or deadlines. An end-term party committee makes all arrangements for that happy ending.

Staffing of committees usually occurs when students volunteer for specific ones. If there are no volunteers for a given committee, students are elected or assigned by the coordination committee. If human resources are thin then students serve on two or more committees as needed. Additional committees can be formed in response to class needs as they develop.

Committee organization is only one method that distributes students into different groups, because interests in course content topics varies. Assignment of students to topic groups is made in the same fashion as committee assignments. Job interviewing has been of particular interest to the senior group; otherwise, topics are various assortments seen in human behavior in the organization texts. There is, however, an emphasis on experiential exercises for those topics, because the standard literature review occurs in a prerequisite course.

"For Example" and "What If"

This course strategy has produced some interesting outcomes that can be roughly separated into two nonexclusive categories—"For Example" and "What If." "For Example" will include some typical results of the process. In the "What If" category I will discuss stalls and frustrations that have occurred in the process of course definition and of finalizing course requirements.

FOR EXAMPLE

Grading. Students define grading policy and assign each other grades. In most classes, each requirement has been assigned a percentage weight contribution to the final grade. In one class, the overall course performance was separated into four components—major project (35%), minor project (10%), committee service (25%), and role-play activities (30%). Each of these four behavior categories was further calibrated by the unique behaviors required within each of these four components.

Independent of the constituent requirements, students have decided to grade each other on all requirements, which so far have included role-plays individual papers/presentations, group papers/presentations, class participation, class committee assignments, exams, student's teaching competency, and case studies. I have had groups present a topic, conduct a role-play, write study notes, and then write, administer and grade an exam within their topic area. Each presentation group would subsequently be evaluated by the remaining class members on the quality of the presentation/study notes, the fairness of the exam, and its grading (exams were graded on a 100-point scale). Thus on this particular requirement of a group class presentation, in a class of five groups, each student would have four exam grades and one group grade.

Response evaluation of any of these group performances or other requirements was conducted in some quantitative form. For example, the popular five-point scale with the anchors "strongly agree" and "strongly disagree" was used for papers/presentations within statements such as: "I found the content interesting." "I feel I learned new information from the presenters." "I enjoyed the delivery style of the presenters." "The presenter was well organized." "The handouts were appropriate and helpful." "The presented information had practical impact, and I can see myself using the information in the future." and "There was a clear relationship among the ideas presented." One class conducted evaluations on the behavioral categories of role-plays, case studies (these were reports from on-site interviews), exams, participation in class activities, and term papers. These students also used a five-point scale with "excellent," "quite satisfactory," "satisfactory," "barely college level," and "not college level" for each of the five behaviors. However, different behaviors had to be assessed differently. For example, in role-plays a student could be scored from "excellent" through "not college level" on five different attributes: "desire to participate," "presence," "quality of input," "attitude," and "realism." For case studies the attributes were "general style: vivid, direct," "personality: enthusiastic, confident," "volume," "quality of case," "grammar/writing," "preparation," and "overall impression," again rated along the same five-point scale. The evaluation committee then collected all individual student evaluation forms and computed a final course grade. One evaluation committee loaded all assigned grades onto the computer so students could check their progress at any time. The file was protected so students were not able to manipulate grades.

Attendance. Attendance is critical in a class for which daily interaction occurs through scheduled role-plays, individual presentations, group presentations, or other class business. Attendance takes on an additional impact when students grade each other. If there is a protest both parties need to air their positions in front of the grievance committee. Obviously this interaction is impossible if either is absent.

Other Requirements. Other requirements beyond attendance, committee service, presentations, papers and role-play evaluations are often specified. One class decided on a living paper. They selected, contacted, and visited managers in different organizations. Preformulated human behavior questions were presented to these managers, and their resulting responses about disruptive workers, communications, leadership, conflict, and other areas of interest were reported in term paper form to each class member. Another interesting requirement was a thumbnail paper. Students selected 10 texts or research topics in the management literature, reviewed them, prepared abstracts and then graded the document on its practical orientation and utility. All thumbnails were placed on 3 × 5 index cards and duplicated for all classmates. As a finished product, all students had a basic expandable reference file as a functional management tool for their future careers. Another class decided to visit other business schools in the New York City-New Jersey area. Their goal was to size up their upcoming competition for jobs. Students attended the competition's classes to assess depth and breadth of course work, which was then compared with their own background. Most thought that they had better training and, as a result, felt more confident for the onset of job interviewing.

WHAT IF . . .

A Student Refuses to Sign the Course Agreement? Some years back one student refused to sign the course agreement. Oddly enough, this particular student was very active in formulating and guiding the entire class to that agreement; his refusal to sign surprised everyone. The contract committee, the objecting student, and I first met with the dean of the business school to verify the validity of the course requirements and to develop a policy responsive to the one student's dissent. The final result was a modified course agreement offering a selection of three alternative methods by which students might take the course. The first was the traditional model as in years past: an assigned text, readings, three tests (two essays and one cumulative multiple choice), and a term paper. The second was the current and new version. The third allowed any dissenting student to write his or her own alternative to the first two, which had to go through proper channels, that is, the class committee and then the dean.

There Is a Disagreement on a Grade That One Student Assigns Another on One of the Above-Mentioned Course Behaviors? There have been disagreements of assigned grades, that is, some students believed their fellow student had assigned a lower-than-deserved grade. The grievance committee then reviews oral and/or written evidence. After making a decision, they levy penalties, which have been creative. For assigning an unjustifiably low grade or needlessly protesting a fair (even though low) grade, grievance committees have levied deductions in grades and referred unacceptable student behavior to the dean of students; for minor but valid miscommunications and misunderstandings, "six-pack" penalties were collected at the class party.

The Students Assign Every Member of the Class an A? Well, first of all, this just has not happened. Once I have delegated to students the authority and power to assign grades, I have never had to rescind it. In senior courses my grade distribution is generally 20% A's, 30% B's, and 50% C's and D's. Even though it is a smaller sample size, the students' grade distribution in this experiential course is generally 10% A's, 35% B's, and 55% C's and D's.

As one can see, the output of this process is very different from that of conventional courses, contract courses, and courses for which the professor takes on the role of general manager. The most obvious differences are that students not only plan, organize, implement, and measure from day one until the end of the course but also have authority and power to assign grades. In fact, I have never assigned a grade in this course in all the years that I have taught it; I have rewritten on the grade sheet only *the grades assigned by the students.* I have many gratifying observations and recollections of students' talent, ingenuity, creativity, professional demeanor, and pride toward their responsibility and self-reliance, all of which will be essential for their ultimate success as business managers.

References

Cohen, A. R. (1976). Beyond simulation: Treating the classroom as an organization. *Exchange: The Organizational Behavior Teaching Journal, 11*(2), 13-19.

Kolb, D. A., Rubin, I. M., & McIntyre, J. M. (Eds.). (1974). *Organizational psychology: An experiential approach.* Englewood Cliffs, NJ: Prentice-Hall.

Maier, N. F. R., Solem, A. R., & Maier, A. A. (1957). *Supervisor and executive development.* New York: Wiley.

Weil, J. L. (1983). *Teaching managerial skills experientially with student clubs.* Paper presented at the 10th annual meeting of the Organizational Behavior Teaching Society, Norman, OK.

Zanzi, A. (1983). *The use of a psychological contract and "cafeteria style" assignments.* Paper presented at the 10th annual meeting of the Organizational Behavior Teaching Society, Norman, OK.

Suggested Readings

Herbert. T. T., & Lorenzi, P. (1981). *Experiential organizational behavior.* New York: Macmillan.

Napier, R. W., & Gershenfeld, M. K. (1973). *Groups: Theory and experience* (2nd ed.). Boston: Houghton Mifflin.

Verny, T. R. (1974). *Inside groups: A practical guide to encounter groups and group therapy.* New York: McGraw-Hill.

Whiteley, J. M., & Flowers, J. V. (1978). *Approaches to assertion training.* Belmont, CA: Wadsworth.

Thirteen

Experiential and Traditional Teaching of Management
A *Dubious Distinction*

DONALD D. BOWEN
The University of Tulsa

Over the past several years, I have developed a wide variety of experiential learning materials for undergraduate, graduate, and executive development courses and have been a frequent spokesman for experiential teaching at professional conferences. If I am such a confirmed proponent of experiential teaching, the reader might justifiably expect me to begin this discussion with an authoritative definition that distinguishes experiential from other teaching techniques and to develop a closely reasoned argument for the necessity or superiority of experiential strategies in management education.

However, for some time now, I have grown increasingly less confident that we can, or should, sharply distinguish experiential learning from other teaching strategies. Granted, the distinction between experiential and non-experiential (usually labeled *traditional*) teaching modes is a popular one in the literature (e.g., Green & Taber, 1978; House, 1979; Mezoff, Cohen, & Bradford, 1979) and in virtually every discussion of teaching among management and business faculty. On the other hand, I have heard colleagues apply the term *experiential* to computer simulations, all types of field experiences, internships, cases, debates, and plant tours as well as to t-groups, various types of structured exercises, and role-plays. Thus a lot

This chapter originally appeared in *Exchange: The Organizational Behavior Teaching Journal,* Volume 5, Issue 3.

of my own skepticism about the usefulness of the distinction was triggered by how broadly people actually use the term.

In the next few paragraphs, I will develop a number of arguments against both the validity and usefulness of the distinction. The reader should be forewarned that what follows makes no pretense of being a comprehensive literature review. At the end I will attempt to offer a few tentative suggestions for making progress on some of the problems identified, but it will be quite obvious that I do not have all the answers. I am still struggling with many of these questions in my own teaching, and it will be helpful to me if these remarks stir a vigorous response from others.

Typical Definitions of Experiential Learning

It may be useful to begin with a fairly standard definition of experiential learning as found in the literature. One of the most thoughtful and comprehensive is Hoover's (1977): "Experiential learning exists when a personally responsible participant(s) cognitively, affectively, and behaviorally processes knowledge, skills, and/or attitudes in a learning situation characterized by a high level of active involvement" (p. 116). In common with most such definitions, this one emphasizes (1) that the student has a personal responsibility for the learning he or she is to achieve, (2) that more than just cognitive processes are involved, (3) that the learning goals include skills and attitudes as well as the traditional goal of developing knowledge, and (4) that somehow the participant is active, both physically and psychologically, in the learning process. Presumably, then, traditional strategies tend to feature contrasting assumptions and attributes, for example, (1) the teacher holds major responsibility for bringing about learning and (2) produces such learning mainly with cognitive processes (3) that emphasize the analysis of facts and abstract concepts (4) in a manner that requires minimal personal involvement and active participation on the part of the student. Let's explore more closely each of these four distinctions between experiential and traditional learning.

Dimension 1: Locus of Responsibility

Somebody once observed that many of our students—not to mention their parents, deans and other college officials, state legislators, boards of trustees, and other salient pressure groups—seem to be devotees of the "filling-station" theory of education. That is to say, a college is a place where an empty (ignorant) student pulls up and pays to have his or her head filled up. The responsibility for the quality of the knowledge pumped belongs to the operator of the filling station—the faculty member.

Surely, no one involved in higher education would verbally subscribe to this approach. But does the metaphor hold a grain of truth in describing the behavior of teachers and students in traditional teaching strategies? Although many would so contend, I believe that the student's responsibility for his or her learning is just as great in a lecture course as it is in a t-group, although, it is true, the student may tend to be less aware of the fact in the former situation. T-groups can make the learner painfully and immediately aware of the personal responsibility for one's own learning, but changing the format of the course does not shift the responsibility. As any teacher knows, what a student gets from a class is basically a question of what the student chooses to put in to it.

Lundberg and Motamedi (1978), like most commentators, link the teacher's role and locus of responsibility. They observe that a teacher can choose as in traditional strategies to adopt the role of an authority figure or the role of a facilitator. A third possibility, for which students rely entirely on themselves for learning, is also identified: "taking responsibility for their own learning with minimal interference from the teacher" (pp. 15-16). The authors point out that the different teacher roles will tend to elicit behavior in pupils ranging from dependence to autonomy.

Most experienced teachers will readily recognize the phenomena described by Lundberg and Motamedi. Certainly there is a tendency for students to assume, usually unconsciously, that the instructor should accept responsibility for the student's learning, and I suspect that all too often we teachers allow ourselves to be seduced into accepting this definition. If this is so, we may be jeopardizing the development of both ourselves and our pupils.

Speculation over how to apportion the responsibility for learning between teacher and student misses the point that the student's responsibility for *learning* is always total. It must be, because this is an obligation the student owes himself or herself, and the teacher's responsibility to teach is just as complete to do the best job of teaching possible. As with any teaching technique, the experiential mode can be done well or badly. If the instructor is ill-prepared, does not give an adequate introduction, is not available for coaching or support, and so forth, students will find it more difficult to learn. As Filley, Foster, and Herbert (1979) note,

> it is possible that such group-centered methods are used merely to increase student satisfaction. . . . To provide a "meaningful" experience without tying it to a cognitive map can be self-defeating, since it does little to provide obvious employment skills or to establish contingencies for application. (p. 16)

I suspect that the process of education will be best served when teachers define their responsibility as teaching well, when students define theirs as learning well, and both parties recognize that the problem is to manage the relationship in as satisfying a manner as possible.

Dimension 2: The Processes Involved

Hoover's definition, like that of most others (e.g., Bradford & Strauss, 1975; Kolb, Rubin, & McIntyre, 1979), suggests that the unique feature of experiential learning is that it requires the student to become involved affectively and behaviorally with the material. In other words, students are to *actively do something,* and as a consequence, *experience their feelings* about what happens. Indeed, it is this experiencing that distinguishes experiential teaching in both name and process.

But aren't most students in traditional, cognitive classes also doing and feeling something with the materials when they are taking notes, reading about the ideas, and manipulating the ideas in term papers and exams? Aren't they feeling and reacting to the teacher's style, the course structure, and the classroom procedures? True, *what* students do and feel is probably different in the traditional course, yet it cannot be denied that ideas obtained from the readings and lectures do become part of the attitude toward the material (and are central to whether one is inclined to use the ideas presented). More important, I strongly suspect that students' attitudes and predisposition toward practicing the skills being taught are often as much a function of *how* the material is presented as they are to *what* is presented. One of the important learnings that students may develop if they find a course dry, uninteresting, or beyond their abilities is an aversion for the material. The best example may be the widespread block many students have developed in regard to quantitative subjects. Incidentally, there is some evidence that management education tends to reward behavior (Daft, 1979) and inculcate values (Akin, 1979) that are *contrary* to those sought by the designers of the programs.

The central point here is simply this: *All learning involves some kind of an experience,* for being passive and dependent is, after all, an experience of sorts. I think that those of us who have been exploring experiential approaches like to claim that we attempt to manage this experience a bit more consciously so that the learning of our students is facilitated by experiences of personal growth, confirmation, and enhanced self-esteem.

Moreover, not only does the presence or absence of experience fail to distinguish experiential from traditional teaching but it is also clear that the two modes are not differentiated in terms of the positive or negative qualities of the experience. Some highly skilled lecturers generate high levels of satisfaction in their audiences, and some students are threatened by experiential techniques.

Dimension 3: Teaching Skills and Values Versus Knowledge

Experiential teaching is usually assumed to have a goal of teaching skills and attitudes and values as well as knowledge. Even though the attitudes and values learned under different forms of pedagogy may vary, it seems fatuous to assume that students do not acquire attitudes and values in traditional courses. Nevertheless, one of the most frequently encountered concerns of traditional teachers is a misgiving that experiential modes of teaching may inflict a system of values on students. Mezoff voices his concern as follows (see Mezoff et al., 1979): "There is, also, an ethical implication to the decision to innovate in a required course, especially if the instructor's agenda ('hidden' or otherwise) includes a focus on personal growth and change (overlaps the values-attitudes area?)" (p. 33). Cohen's rejoinder is worth repeating, because he raises the question of whether there is ever such a thing as a value-free pedagogy (see Mezoff et al., 1979):

> Fundamentally, I believe that all education implies change—by definition—and . . . in OB we have an obligation to address the change consciously rather than inadvertently. Even straight content affects values, attitudes, feelings and self-esteem; at conventional non-innovative colleges students change in these areas as a result of their experiences in and out of the classroom. (p. 35)

My own observations are similar to Cohen's; it is clear to me that many of my more cognitively oriented colleagues are just as dedicated as I am to modifying student's attitudes and skills in addition to teaching concepts. For example, our traditional colleagues stress students' gaining an appreciation for the research and theoretical basis of management and organizational behavior and acquiring the skills of being able to apply these ideas in a rigorously analytical fashion. For me, these are also important, although not primary, goals for my students who tend to be present or future practitioners of management rather than Ph.D. candidates. Thus I would argue that students learn skills under both methods—it is merely the nature of the skills and the degree of their transferability from one setting to another that is presumed to differ. Nor is the choice really one between knowledge and skills, because neither approach advocates one without the other. They *do* differ in the nature of the knowledge they seek because they differ in their vision of how knowledge informs practice, as Lundberg and Motamedi (1978) argue:

> "Knowledge about" refers to secondhand knowledge and consists of the information derived from others, e.g., from lectures and books. "Knowledge of acquaintance" refers to information obtained firsthand from one's own experience. Those educators or learners who are concerned with efficiency of transmission and accuracy of general truths clearly favor the former. Those concerned about the effectiveness of knowledge, particularly the ability to put knowledge into practice, tend to favor knowledge of acquaintance (Kelly, 1947; Lynton, 1960). (p. 18)

Is there any empirical evidence that either approach achieves its aims? My conclusion is that rigorous research is badly needed. However, until we employ longitudinal research designs assessing the ability and inclination of students to use skills learned in the classroom 5 or more years after graduation, statements about the relative efficacy of one teaching method compared with another should be treated with skepticism.

Dimension 4: Level of Student Involvement

By now, the reader may share the belief that I have been developing for some time that the ideology of experiential teaching is overburdened with vague buzz words and imprecise clichés. When examined closely, many of the truisms on which advocates build the case for experiential learning simply do not hold. Nowhere, I think, is this more true than in the oft-repeated statement that the objective of experiential learning is to promote student involvement. What is meant by *involvement?*

Lau (1979) uses the term in the sense of psychological and physical activity required of students: "It places primary emphasis on the processes of interaction and thinking rather than on the factual content of the area being studies" (p.17). Posner and Randolph (1978) similarly describe the nature of student participation in terms of whether learning tasks require students to be active or reflective in their learning. House (1979) suggests that one purpose in increasing student participation is to make the lesson more meaningful; to get students to both create supportive data of their own and to give them firsthand experience of the central concepts under study.

To others (e.g., Senger, 1975, p. 8), involvement appears to be simply good feelings, excitement, and fun. Students themselves, indeed, often use the term in this fashion. Senger is, legitimately I think, critical of experiential teaching if its only objective is to make students happier without regard for their learning.

It is clear that being active, participating, enjoying, thinking, and doing are invariable highly correlated behaviors that lead to accepting concepts and finding them more meaningful? Just a little reflection indicates that it is presumptuous to overgeneralize on this issue. For example,

1. The management and organizational studies literature is filled with studies of workers in routine jobs for which a high degree of physical activity and participation is accompanied by *low* levels of psychological participation and task meaningfulness.

2. The invitation to participate is not seen by all students as enjoyable, nor does it always lead to greater acceptance of learning points.

3. The emphasis on enjoyment of the learning process in much of the experiential teaching literature runs counter to an important aspect of my own learning experience—and I suspect that of others, too. For me, many of my most important and meaningful personal learning experiences have been occasions of great pain and discomfort. *Brutally frank feedback, personal insecurity and uncertainty,* and *sustained turmoil and hardship* are the words that may best describe deeper experiences of learning (most former Ph.D. candidates will relate to this I'm sure). To emphasize the fun 'n' games of experiential learning may be unwittingly to confirm that the lessons are not always as important as they should be. This point is an ancient one: As Aristotle said, learning is not child's play, for we cannot learn without pain. A real learning experience may ultimately be deeply satisfying, even though the process of getting there may be difficult. I have been intrigued that several of my students seem to appreciate this point when they say, "You're tougher [than other instructors], but I like you better because I get more from your course."

The students' comments suggests another meaning for *student involvement;* perhaps one intended in the writings of others but seldom explicitly proposed. *Involvement,* as in the concept of job involvement (Lodahl & Kejner, 1965), means a willingness to commit energy and time to a task. A similar concept of student involvement would seem to provide a useful starting point for research; this might in turn lead to an empirically based distinction between different teaching styles that would be of real import for both theory and practice.

Do students work harder in experiential than in traditional courses? I am not presently aware of any convincing evidence one way or the other on this issue.

TABLE 13.1.
Analysis of the Arguments For and Against Experiential
and Traditional Teaching

Proponents of Experiential Teaching Tend to Claim:	*Close Comparison of Experiential and Traditional Teaching Suggests:*
Dimension 1: Locus of responsibility	
Traditional teaching makes the teacher responsible for learning; experiential teaching makes the student responsible	The student is the only person who can be responsible for his or her learning, no matter what form of pedagogy is involved
Dimension 2: The processes involved	
Traditional teaching draws on cognitive processes only; experiential teaching involves affective and behavioral processes as well	All learning involves some kind of an experience; students in traditional courses also do something with and develop feelings about the course materials—and the feelings generated are often pleasant
Dimension 3: Teaching skills and values versus knowledge	
Traditional teaching deals only with the cognitive and conceptual; experiential teaching aims at teaching skills and changing attitudes and values as well	Both experiential and traditional teaching teach skills, attitudes, and values as well as a cognitive understanding of the material; whatever differences exist are issues of degree of emphasis and qualitative differences in values, skills, and so on
Dimension 4: Level of student involvement	
Experiential teaching encourages higher levels of student involvement	*Involvement* is a vague term in the literature, used with several different meanings; it might be productive to focus on the issue of which types of teaching styles elicit the most commitments of time and energy from students (there is no evidence on this topic at present)

Recapitulating

As we have seen, advocates of both experiential and traditional teaching tend to differentiate the two strategies on four major dimensions as summarized in Table 13.1. I have argued that many of the most commonly alleged differences between them do not hold up under close scrutiny. If these are the dimensions that distinguish between two major teaching strategies in management education, the actual differences are more illusive than commonly believed. To the extent that real differences do exist, they tend to be qualitative and perhaps relatively minor. For example, both strategies appear to aim at imparting skills; traditional teaching may emphasize conceptual/analytical skills, whereas experiential teaching may stress interpersonal skills.

If the present debate over experiential and traditional teaching has, as I suggest, centered on relatively minor or phony issues, it should not be surprising that we learn relatively little from it. Perhaps it is time that we reformulate the questions to move on to something more productive.

Refocusing the Argument

Because traditional versus experiential appears to be an oversimplification and given that most management and organizational behavior instructors now use mixtures of several strategies, isn't it time that we dismiss these misleading labels? If we do, we can be much more specific about discussing different types of teaching strategies. One set of questions would deal with the conditions (types of students, learning goals, and educational climate) one encounters; a second set, with methods (e.g., lecture, cases, experiential case discussion, structured exercise, and library research term papers).

The problem is to employ an optimal mix of teaching techniques. The lack of solid criteria and empirical evidence on the outcomes of various instructional strategies is only one of several reasons for the difficulty in specifying optimality for the management teacher. Fundamental to one's position on this issue is a wide range of questions about what one sees as the purpose of management education. Here are some examples.

1. Who are the students? What do we want them to get from the course? To what extent do we weigh their needs and expectations in making pedagogical decisions? Teachers seem to vary widely in the degree to which they recognize differences between undergraduates, MBAs, doctoral students, and executive program participants. The skills versus knowledge argument is frequently waged on this basis, but other questions, such as the role of the instructor's style and one's view of the purpose of teaching management, are also relevant.

2. What is the purpose of management and organizational studies in the curriculum? Over the years, several philosophical positions on this issue seem to have arisen. Occasionally one meets the zealot for one particular stance, but most of us seem to have in mind some combination of the following:

- *Management and organizational theory as liberal education:* Proponents of this view emphasize an academic approach and question the advisability, respectability, and/or possibility of teaching skills and applications in management education.
- *Management education as a bag of tricks:* In this view, skills and techniques are emphasized with virtually no reference to theory, research, or internal logical consistency; consulting fees are often the mark of success here.

- *Management education as personal growth:* Self-awareness, self-exploration, authentic communication, joy, and other good feelings are stressed here.
- *Management education as survival training:* This is a fairly recent perspective, which has the objective of teaching students how to survive and prosper in an unstable, unpredictable, even hostile world of bastards and uncaring bureaucrats.
- *Management education as managerial finishing school:* This is a hybrid approach for which the attempt is both to sharpen students' managerial skills and simultaneously to give them enough knowledge to impress their future boss, co-workers, and cocktail-party acquaintances.
- *The study of management and organizational behavior as rabble-rousing:* A sociological perspective, it blames all the unhappiness of the world on either a grasping power elite or a self-maintaining hierarchical structure; this school argues that the individual doesn't stand a chance against the system.

3. What are the needs and style of the instructor? Although the foregoing list of management education philosophies was admittedly something of a caricature, it should help to make the point that our instructional objectives must undoubtedly reflect our own preferences as teachers. Despite our frequent claims that our teaching strategies are unselfishly based on student needs, it seems unlikely to me that a teacher can be effective in a strategy that requires a style the instructor is not comfortable with or that fails to satisfy important needs he or she may have. We need to develop a philosophy that legitimizes the consideration of the instructor's preferences while recognizing that there must be responsible limits of self-indulgence.

None of these points is really new, but if one had to identify the bedrock issues, the above are the ones that have been most central in helping me to think about my teaching. I am not suggesting that all teachers will come to the same conclusions, but I do think it is difficult to go far in developing one's theory of teaching without confronting these questions. I do suggest these are the questions we need to address in terms of specific instructional techniques rather than oversimplified dichotomies such as experiential versus traditional. Rather than locking in on these or other polarizations, what we need is a much more exploratory attitude until we begin to amass solid data for the effects of different approaches on teaching. Perhaps we need to be willing to admit that we know a lot less than we would like about our teaching.

References

Akin, G. (1979). On getting back to learning. *Exchange: The Organizational Behavior Teaching Journal, 4*(2), 22-25.

Bradford, D. L., & Strauss, G. (1975). OB of the present and future—Reflections from the S.M.U. Conference. *The Teaching of Organization Behavior, 1*(4), 3-8.

Daft, R. L. (1979). MBA admission criteria, communication skill and academic success: An unexpected finding. *Proceedings of the Annual Meeting of the Academy of Management* (pp. 48-52).

Filley, A. C., Foster, L. W., & Herbert, T. T. (1979). Teaching organizational behavior: Current patterns and implications. *Exchange: The Organizational Behavior Teaching Journal, 4*(2), 13-18.

Green, S. G., & Taber, T. D. (1978). Structuring experiential learning through experimentation. *Academy of Management Review, 3,* 889-895.

Hoover, D. J. (1977). Experiential learning: Conceptualization and definition. In R. E. Horn (Ed.), *The guide to simulations/games for education and training. Vol. 2: Business* (3rd ed., pp. 115-116). Cranford, NJ: Didactic Systems.

House, R. J. (1979). Experiential learning: A sad passing fad? *Exchange: The Organizational Behavior Teaching Journal, 4*(3), 8-12.

Kelly, E. C. (1947). *Education for what is real.* New York: Harper.

Kolb, D. A., Rubin, I. M., & McIntyre, J. M. (1979). *Organizational psychology: An experiential approach* (3rd ed.). Englewood Cliffs, NJ: Prentice-Hall.

Lau, J. B. (1979). *Behavior in organizations: An experiential approach* (rev. ed.). Homewood, IL: Irwin.

Lodahl, T., & Kejner, M. (1965). The definition and measurement of job involvement. *Journal of Applied Psychology, 49,* 24-33.

Lundberg, C. C., & Motamedi, K. K. (1978). Toward extending the teaching of organizational behavior. *Exchange: The Organizational Behavior Teaching Journal, 3*(1), 14-20.

Lynton, R. P. (1960). *The tide of learning: The Aoka experience.* London: Routledge & Kegan Paul.

Mezoff, R. M., Cohen, A. R., & Bradford, D. L. (1979). A dialogue on treating the classroom as an organization. *Exchange: The Organizational Behavior Teaching Journal, 4*(1), 25-36.

Posner, B. Z., & Randolph, W. A. (1975). A decision tree approach to decide when to use different pedagogical techniques. *Exchange: The Organizational Behavior Teaching Journal, 3*(2), 16-17.

Senger, J. (1975). Let's hear it for the cognitive aspect! *The Teaching of Organization Behavior, 1*(2), 7-9.

Fourteen

A Model for Teaching Management Skills

KIM S. CAMERON
*National Center for Higher Education
Management Systems*

DAVID A. WHETTEN
University of Illinois

Criticism of the preparation students receive in American business schools for management positions has become widespread in the business community. For example, Mandt (1982), vice president of Mutual Life Insurance Co., observed, "The business school graduate is adequately trained to get the first job but often has difficulty holding it and advancing. To be blunt, the typical business school curriculum fails to prepare students properly" (p. 49). Endicott (1982), director of placement, emeritus, at Northwestern University, summarized the problems of new business school graduates this way:

"The graduates lacked a practical, disciplined understanding of themselves and their environment . . . they didn't know how to use knowledge effectively. In short, they weren't educated" (p. 48). Livingston's (1971) indictment of business school preparation is well known:

Many highly intelligent and ambitious men are not learning from either their formal education or their own experience what they most want to know to build successful careers in management. Their failure is due, in part, to the

This chapter originally appeared in *Exchange: The Organizational Behavior Teaching Journal,*
Volume 8, Issue 2.

fact that many crucial managerial tasks are not taught in management education programs (p. 88).

A common suggestion among critics is to incorporate management skill training into the business school curriculum, so that students are better prepared to use their knowledge rather than just regurgitate it. Making a distinction between teaching *about* management and teaching *to* manage is a prerequisite pointed out by a variety of writers (e.g., Miner, 1973; Mintzberg, 1975; Pfeffer, 1981).

Our intent in this article is to describe a model for teaching students to manage rather than just about management. This model is based on the assumption that individuals will become more competent managers by developing critical management skills in the classroom rather than by waiting until they are on the job. We have developed and refined this model over the last several years in our teaching of undergraduate, graduate, and executive development courses in business schools and in public and private sector organizations. We don't claim our approach to be the only appropriate way to teach management skills, but we are convinced that it provides a useful alternative to traditional management and organizational behavior classroom approaches.

Our discussion begins with a brief treatment of what we mean by management skills and a description of a set of skills particularly relevant for effective managers. Our discussion then turns to a model for helping students develop and improve their competency in these skills. We conclude by reviewing a variety of issues connected with teaching management skills, giving particular attention to the evaluation of skill development in the college classroom.

Identifying Critical Management Skills

To develop an approach to helping students develop management skills, we first had to be clear about what was meant by the term *management skill*. Skills differ from inherent personality traits (e.g., being aggressive), motives (e.g., need for security), roles (e.g., supervisor), and functions (e.g., planning). On the one hand, they encompass more than single managerial actions such as writing one's name or smiling at an employee. On the other hand, they encompass less than the multiple behaviors involved in the classic management functions (e.g., POSDCORB). Skills include cognitive knowledge or how to perform an action, but they involve more than just knowledge itself.

Although it is difficult, and somewhat arbitrary, to establish the boundaries for what is and what isn't to be considered a skill, we feel comfortable in adopting the following definition of management skills: A management skill involves a sequential pattern of behaviors performed to achieve a desired outcome.[1] This definition eliminates traits such as honesty and loyalty, because these concepts are not defined by a specific, sequential set of behaviors. It also eliminates roles or functions such as leading and controlling as skills, because they involve a variety of patterns of behaviors.

With an idea of what constitutes a management skill, our next step was to identify the skills that are performed by effective managers. First, we conducted a study in which more than 400 managers at various hierarchical levels of both public and private organizations were asked to identify the skills they used in their work on a regular basis.[2] Our results were then compared with the characteristics of effective managers proposed by others (Boyatsis, 1982; Flanders, 1981; Ghiselli, 1963; Livingston, 1971; Miner, 1973; Mintzberg, 1975). A summary list was formed that fit the following criteria: (1) the list contained a combination of both personal and interpersonal skills, (2) it focused on proven characteristics of high-performing managers, (3) it contained only characteristics that have trainable behavioral components, and (4) it avoided highly situational specific techniques that are best suited for on-the-job training. The final summary list is given in Table 14.1.

Social Learning Theory as an Approach to Teaching Management Skills

To integrate effectively management skills training into the curriculum requires modifying pedagogical approaches as well as the course content. Staying with the traditional lecture-discussion format might teach students *about* the skills they need to acquire, but it would not provide an opportunity for them to *develop* these skills. The use of traditional approaches would also give the erroneous impression that these skills are simply techniques to be recalled from memory and applied when the need arises and then returned to storage (similar to cost accounting or cash flow analysis techniques). Katz (1974) points out the error in thinking about management skills in this manner.

> Real skill in working with others must become a natural, continuous activity, since it involves sensitivity not only at times of decision making, but also in the day-to-day behavior of the individual. Human skills cannot be a "sometime thing." Techniques cannot be randomly applied, nor can personality traits be put on or removed like an overcoat. Because everything which an executive says and does (or leaves unsaid or undone) has an effect on his associates, his true self will, in

TABLE 14.1.
Characteristics of Effective Managers: Management Skill Topics

1. Self-awareness
   - Personality
   - Values
   - Needs
   - Cognitive style
2. Managing personal stress
   - Time management
   - Goals
   - Activity balance
3. Creative problem solving
   - Divergent thinking
   - Conceptual blocks
   - Redefining problems
4. Establishing supportive communication
   - Listening
   - Empathy
   - Counseling
5. Improving employee performance, motivating others
   - Needs/expectations
   - Rewards
   - Timing

6. Effective delegation and joint decision making
   - Assigning tasks
   - Evaluating performance
   - Autonomous versus joint decision making
7. Gaining power and influence
   - Sources of power
   - Converting power to influence
   - Beneficial use, not abuse, of power
8. Managing conflict
   - Sources of conflict
   - Assertiveness and sensitivity
   - Handling criticism
9. Improving group decision making
   - Chairing meetings
   - Avoiding pitfalls of bad meetings
   - Making effective presentations

turn, show through. Thus, to be effective, the skill must be naturally developed, and unconsciously as well as consistently demonstrated in the individual's every action. It must become an integral part of his whole being. (p. 92)

If students are to learn managerial skills, a new approach to classroom learning is needed. The approach we suggest relies heavily on social learning theory (Bandura, 1977; Davis & Luthans, 1980) that has been used widely in supervisory training programs in industry (Goldstein & Sorcher, 1974) as well as in allied professional education classroom settings such as teacher education and social work (Rose, Cayner, & Edleson, 1977; Singleton, Spurgeon, & Stammers, 1980). Social learning theory focuses on changing behavior through the modeling process. By focusing on shaping behaviors directly, social learning theory differs from traditional approaches to education by relying less on the power of intellectual persuasion to induce changes in behavior and more on observing role models and adopting their behaviors.

The reason we are advocating the use of a modified form of social learning theory in this article is that there is substantial evidence that management effectiveness can be significantly improved by using it in skill training (see Burnaska, 1976; Latham & Saari, 1979; Moses & Ritchie, 1976; Porras & Anderson, 1981; Smith, 1976). Extrapolating from the impressive track record of this approach to management training in applied settings, we are confident that students who do well in a course on management skills using this learning model will significantly increase the probability of their doing well as managers on the job.

The approach used most widely for skill training in industry usually consists of four steps (Goldstein & Sorcher, 1974): (1) the presentation of principles (sometimes called behavioral guidelines or key action steps) that are based on data collected from successful practicing managers or derived from general theories of human behavior; (2) demonstration of the principles to participants by the instructor, a videotaped incident, or written scripts; (3) opportunities to practice the principles in role-plays or exercises; and (4) feedback on personal performance received from the instructor, experts, and/or peers.

Our suggestion for teaching management skills follows these four activities, but we also have made two additions. First, because most students do not have extensive managerial experience in organizations, it is difficult for them to know their current level of competence in management skills. Moreover, because of this lack of experience, the importance of developing some of the skills may not be immediately apparent. Therefore, we suggest the addition of a preassessment activity at the beginning of the learning experience that serves both to let students know how well they can perform the skill (because it is impossible to improve unless one knows where one is starting) and to motivate them to improve their skill performance. Second, we have added an application activity at the end of the learning experience. This activity is designed to help students apply the skills in a setting similar to one they will face on the job. Its purpose is to provide an opportunity to practice the skill in an environment more similar to an actual managerial environment than the college classroom. Most application activities require that students record their experiences in a journal or an essay so as to analyze their degree of success or failure.

Based on these modifications, our suggested approach to teaching management skills follows the format in Table 14.2. At the beginning of each skill learning experience, students are given an opportunity to assess their current level of understanding and competence in each skill topic before engaging in any learning activities. This skill preassessment takes the form of a questionnaire, questions about a brief case, or a role-play or other experiential activity. The purpose of the preassessment is to increase the efficiency of the learning process by focusing attention on deficiencies in knowledge or performance.

TABLE 14.2
Suggested Skill Learning Approach

Components	Contents	Objectives
Skill preassessment	Survey, instruments, role-plays	Assess current level of skill competence and knowledge
Skill learning	Written text, behavioral guidelines	Teach correct principles and present rationale for the behavioral guidelines
Skill analysis	Cases	Provide examples of appropriate and inappropriate skill performance; analyze behavioral guidelines and why they work
Skill practice	Exercises, simulations, role-plays	Practice behavioral guidelines; adapt general prescriptions to personal style; receive feedback and assistance
Skill application	Assignments (behavioral and written)	Transfer classroom learning to real-life situations; foster ongoing personal development

The second step is skill learning through the presentation of conceptual material based on the most essential and relevant theory and research. That is, need to know takes priority over nice to know and empirically tested principles take precedence over anecdotal or opinion data. The specific objective is to provide a sound rationale for the behavioral principles that are summarized and enumerated by the instructor. It is important that behavioral guidelines are specified by the instructor rather than just descriptions of theories, cases, or examples. This set of guidelines serves as the foundation for subsequent practice and application activities, and it is generally presented best in a lecture-discussion format.

Third, a skill analysis activity should be presented wherein students are asked to analyze one or two brief cases. These cases serve both a modeling function (showing competent and/or incompetent skill performance) and a cognitive function, allowing students to analyze how the behavioral principles apply in real-world situations. The intent of this section is to bridge the gap between intellectual assimilation and behavioral application. Critiquing the performance of managers in these cases provides students with an opportunity to check comprehension of the skill learning material before practicing it themselves and to analyze a model of the skill being performed. We have used written cases for this activity as well as videotapes, audio recordings, and movies.

Fourth, the skill practice activity allows students to begin trying out and experimenting with the behavioral guidelines in the supportive atmosphere of the classroom. It is important that they avoid the trap of simply mimicking the style or particular mannerisms of a role model (either written or visual). Instead, they are encouraged to experiment, adapting each set of behavioral principles to their particular personality and interpersonal style. Feedback from peers and the instructor performs an important function during this activity by allowing students the opportunity to correct mistakes, rehearse various alternatives, and find out with little risk how well they are doing. Student observers sharpen their observation, perception, and feedback skills as they help one another, and the new skill behaviors begin to become internalized and habitual. Skill practice activities generally take the form of exercises, role-plays, and group activities, all of which are accompanied by observation and feedback.

Fifth, the skill application activity contains specific assignments to facilitate the transfer of classroom learning to everyday practice. These assignments may ask students to teach the skill to someone else (an excellent test of understanding), to report on the impact that friends and associates have on others when they succeed or fail in using the behavioral principles, to report on a personal effort to apply the principles in an appropriate setting, to confront a problem for which skill performance is required, and so on. The intent of these activities is to provide the opportunity to perform the skill in a real-world setting while still maintaining a close monitoring relationship with the instructor. Opportunities for self-analysis and feedback from others during this activity can help refine and improve skill performance.

Combining these five activities in teaching skill development has advantages over other common approaches to teaching. For example, it incorporates the lecture-discussion technique, but goes beyond that method by allowing for personal diagnosis and skill practice. This approach also uses case analysis to help students analyze problems and apply concepts to new situations, but the addition of preassessment, presentation of behavioral guidelines, practice, and application/help overcome the limitations of a traditional case approach. Similarly, experiential exercises and group participation have their place; however, they are not included merely to illustrate concepts or theories but are designed as practice opportunities and evaluation activities through which competencies can be improved.[3]

Issues in Teaching Management Skills

Introducing management skills into the business school curriculum is not a straightforward or unencumbered endeavor. A variety of issues are associated with teaching management skills, and they must be addressed.

For example, fewer subjects can be covered in a skills course than in a traditional organizational behavior or management course. Extra time is required for students to analyze and practice new behaviors. Faculty must be prepared to model some of the behaviors associated with effective skill performance, because students often look to them to see whether they can practice what they preach. Large class sizes are more difficult to handle than small classes when teaching skills; the logistics of video-taping each student's performance, for example, is often prohibitive. Because teaching management skills is seldom directly connected to faculty members' research, trade-offs between spending extra time in teaching versus research become an issue. Alternative class schedules may need to be considered. Traditional 50-minute time slots may not always be appropriate. The level at which the skill course is taught is an important consideration. It generally should not be the first management or organizational behavior class students take, because the theory and management principles taught in most introductory courses serve as a good foundation for students' skill and development. (Conversely, we have found that the closer students are to graduation and the job market, the more motivated they are to develop skill competencies.) Care must be taken to maintain students' sense of self-worth; derogatory or insensitively given feedback can be more damaging than helpful as students try to improve their behavioral skills.

Aside from these issues, probably the most important issue associated with teaching management skills is how to evaluate and grade skill competency. Rose et al. (1977) pointed out:

> The development of professional interpersonal skills is of paramount concern. . . . However, few of these [skill training] programs have been evaluated to determine their effectiveness or their relevance to interpersonal activities. At best, participants are asked to indicate their satisfaction with programs or are given some form of paper-and-pencil test to measure what they have learned. (p. 125)

The cognitive component of skill development can be assessed relatively easily using traditional paper-and-pencil tests, but other methods are also required if behavioral competency is to evaluated. Evaluating the behavioral component of skills often raises issues of the criteria to be included, who will do the evaluating, whether an equitable standard can be established, and the amount of time it will take. We have derived several guidelines that have proven useful to us in addressing these issues in our own skill development classes.

First, behavioral guidelines must be clearly specified. It is difficult to assess skill competency unless it is clear what constitutes effective performance. That is why the skill learning activities must be more than a review of theory and examples. Instructors must help students learn what behaviors are to be performed (see, e.g., Whetten & Cameron, 1991).

Second, multiple assessment sources are needed. Because there is always some subjectivity in evaluating skill competency, instructors may be accused of being biased, arbitrary, or stylistic in rating students' performance. Having multiple rating sources guards against the accusation that "it's your opinion against mine." We use four sources of ratings to assess the extent to which students perform a skill competently: (1) the student's own self-assessments after viewing a video or audio recording of his or her performance, (2) peer assessments of performance, which are always guided by an assessment or observer's form (i.e., a form outlining the appropriate behaviors to be performed), (3) instructor's ratings, and (4) outside observers' ratings (frequently business executives or practicing managers who are invited into the class). Evaluation from these four sources is usually done in the context of a role-play, in-basket exercise, interview, formal presentation, or group problem-solving session.

Third, multiple assessment devices are needed. Because traditional tests are inadequate by themselves, we have relied on at least four different devices to grade skill competency. They are not listed in priority order, because depending on the skill being assessed, the weighting of importance given to each assessment device may change: (1) paper-and-pencil examinations, which assess the cognitive component of the skill (e.g., reading material); (2) rater evaluations of behavior from the four sources mentioned above; (3) a personal journal kept by each student; and (4) written essays by students, which address issues, solve problems, discuss when particular skills are relevant, point out conditions for which the behavioral guidelines are not appropriate, and so on. These essays differ from journal entries in that they are much longer and they generally involve library research.

The journal is used by students to analyze their own skill performance and skill application; frequently, we have asked students to respond to certain questions or problem situations in their journals. Students write in journals regularly and the written material is evaluated several times during the skill course. Our experience with requiring students to keep journals has been much the same as Kaiser (1981), Progoff (1975), and others: "The journal was a vehicle that led to greater creativity. But I found that a good many journals were just diaries: without a project to be done, people's diaries just went around in circles" (Kaiser, 1981, p. 76). When kept in connection with attempts to improve skill competency, journals become powerful tools for personal growth for students as well as a device for evaluation by the instructor.

The fourth evaluation guideline is that presence-absence or frequency-type rating scales are often better than are good-bad rating scales in evaluating skills. It frequently is easier, less controversial, and more helpful to students to record whether or not they performed a behavior, or how many times they displayed an action, than to judge how well they did or how good they are. Presence-absence evaluations are more objective than are good-bad evaluations, and reliable ratings are less dependent on prior experience by the rater (i.e., untrained students can serve as raters). Moreover, suggestions for how to improve skill performance can be more easily provided by suggesting what behaviors to include in skill performance than to simply suggest that they do it better. This type of evaluation requires that the behavioral guidelines associated with each skill are specified in a presence-absence format, so that just doing certain behaviors is sufficient to indicate effective skill performance. For example, performing effective delegation requires specifying a time to report back, indicating the level of initiative to be taken by subordinates, informing those to be affected by the delegated task, and so on. In other words, ask "Was the behavior performed?" not, "How well was it performed?"

Differences in the quality of skill performance always exist among students, of course, but those quality differences are more reliably assessed by experts such as the instructor or the outside raters than by student peers. Previous experience in management is generally a prerequisite to differentiating reliably among qualitative differences in performances.

We have discovered that evaluating students is much more time-consuming in management skill courses than in regular organizational behavior or management courses. This is mainly because of the necessity of rating behavioral performance and providing feedback in addition to reading papers and grading tests. This extra time commitment is one of the major inhibitors to management skill training being widely practiced in business schools. We have tried to reduce the extra time required of instructors by having multiple rating exercises going on simultaneously (when multiple sets of peers or outside raters are present) and by instituting several structural changes in the format of the class itself. For example, we have used lab sessions (similar to a biology lab) conducted by teaching assistants for the skill practice and the evaluation activities. Students receive a lab grade from the teaching assistant. We have divided large classes into smaller sections and had teaching assistants conduct the sections independently. We have had students go to the media center on their own time to be videotaped in certain evaluation exercises. Tapes were analyzed later by the instructor or in class. We have limited the number of students permitted in the course so that the workload was less burdensome. Each of these formats has advantages and disadvantages, and some may be more practical than others in certain institutions. Despite these time-conservation methods, however, instructors in management skill courses must still recognize that evaluation and feedback play central roles in helping students develop competencies. Therefore, the time required to perform these activities properly is greater than in most other types of classes.

Conclusion

We have suggested in this article that including management skills in the business school curriculum will be a positive step in helping students prepare for successful management careers. It is important first, however, to identify the skills required by effective managers and to teach them in a way that moves beyond mere cognitive awareness to behavioral change. Evaluating skill competency in students also requires methods that are different from traditional college classes. In response to these requirements, we have presented an approach to teaching and evaluating management skills that we have found to be successful in college classrooms and executive training seminars. That approach relies on social learning theory, and it prescribes that five distinct learning activities be present in teaching each skill.

There are some faculty and administrators who still argue that teaching management skills is inappropriate in a university setting. Education should be separated from training, they claim. Education belongs in the university; training belongs in the technical school or on the job. Our feeling is that not only are management skills a prerequisite for making students better prepared to be successful managers but skill competencies are a critical requirement for any educated person. A quotation from Holt (1964) summarizes our point of view succinctly:

> When we talk about intelligence, we do not mean the ability to get a good score on a certain kind of test or even the ability to do well in school; these are at best only indicators of something larger, deeper and far more important. By intelligence we mean a style of life, a way of behaving in various situations. The true test of intelligence is not how much we know how to do, but how we behave when we don't know what to do. (p. 165)

Developing such intelligence is the goal of management skills courses.

Notes

1. See Boyatzis (1982) and Katz (1974) for a more thorough discussion of what constitutes management skills.
2. The specific results are reported in Whetten and Cameron (1991).

3. Preassessment instruments, behavioral guidelines, cases, practice exercises, and application assignments are provided for the nine skills listed in Table 1 in Whetten and Cameron (1991).

References

Bandura, A. (1977). *Social learning theory.* Englewood Cliffs, NJ: Prentice-Hall.

Boyatzis, R. E. (1982). *The competent manager.* New York: Wiley.

Burnaska, R. F. (1976). The effects of behavior modeling training upon managers' behavior and employees' perceptions. *Personnel Psychology, 29,* 329-335.

Davis, T. W., & Luthans, F. A. (1980). A social learning approach to organizational behavior. *Academy of Management Review, 5,* 281-290.

Endicott, F. S. (1982). The 1977 Endicott report. In E. J. Mandt, Ed., Failure of business education—And what to do about it. *Management Review,* 47-52. (Original work published 1977)

Flanders, L. R. (1981). *Report 1 from the federal manager's job and role survey: Analysis of responses by SES and mid-management levels executive and management development division.* Washington, DC: U.S. Office of Personnel Management.

Ghiselli, E. E. (1963). Managerial talent. *American Psychologist, 18,* 631-642.

Goldstein, A. P., & Sorcher, M. (1974). *Changing supervisor behavior.* New York: Pergamon.

Holt, J. (1964). *How children fail.* New York: Pitman.

Katz, R. L. (1974). Skills of an effective administrator. *Harvard Business Review, 51,* 90-102.

Kaiser, R. B. (1981). The way of the journal. *Psychology Today, 15*(3), 64-76.

Latham, G. P., & Saari, L. M. (1979). Application of social-learning theory to training supervisors through behavioral modeling. *Journal of Applied Psychology, 64,* 239-246.

Livingston, J. W. (1971). Myth of the well educated manager. *Harvard Business Review, 49,* 79-89.

Mandt, E. J., Ed. (1982, August). The failure of business education—And what to do about it. *Management Review,* 47-52.

Miner, J. B. (1973). The real crunch in managerial manpower. *Harvard Business Review, 51,* 146-158.

Mintzberg, H. (1975). The manager's job: Folklore and fact. *Harvard Business Review, 53,* 49-71.

Moses, J. L., & Ritchie, R. J. (1976). Supervisory relationships training: A behavioral evaluation of a behavior modeling program. *Personnel Psychology, 29,* 337-343.

Pfeffer, J. (1981). *Power in Organizations.* Marshfield, MA: Pitman.

Porras, J. I., & Anderson, B. (1981). Improving managerial effectiveness through modeling-based training. *Organizational Dynamics, 9,* 60-77.

Progoff, I. (1975). *At a journal workshop.* New York: Dialogue House.

Rose, S. D., Cayner, J. J., & Edleson, J. L. (1977). Measuring interpersonal competence. *Social Work, 22,* 125-129.

Singleton, W. T., Spurgeon, P., & Stammers, R. B. (1980).*The analysis of social skill.* New York: Plenum.

Smith, P. E. (1976). Management modeling training to improve morale and customer satisfaction. *Personnel Psychology, 29,* 351-359.

Whetten, D. A., & Cameron, K. S. (1991). *Developing management skills* (2nd ed.). New York: HarperCollins.

Suggested Readings

Jennerich, E. J. (1981). Competencies for department chairpersons: Myths and realities. *Liberal Education, 67,* 46-70.
Sayles, L. R. (1979). *Leadership.* New York: McGraw-Hill.

Learning in Groups

DAVID L. BRADFORD
Stanford University

In the 11th century, the first universities were established in Italy. The format was quite simple: An instructor was hired to lecture to a group of students who sat around gathering in his words. Disturbing, isn't it, how little has changed in the subsequent 900 years? The basic structure in the majority of university classrooms continues as before. Unfortunately, all too often, this form of education could be described as "knowledge passing from the notes of the teacher to the notes of the students, without passing through the minds of either."

This traditional form of teaching continues to dominate, even though abundant research has demonstrated the superiority of group-centered methods (summarized in Johnson & Johnson, 1984). Student teams, when properly structured, produce greater learning, higher student motivation, and fewer failures. These results are not limited to courses in the behavioral sciences but occur over a wide range of subject matter, including math and the physical sciences. Furthermore, group-centered teaching should be especially relevant in the management area given the emphasis in organizations on working in teams. Such courses offer two for the price of one in increasing students' content knowledge while also improving group and interpersonal competencies.

The first decision to be made is, "How extensively do I want to use groups in this course?" As a minimum, one could just encourage students to form (self-selected) study groups to prepare for class and the exams. Or student teams could be an integral part of the course, meeting outside of class to work on assigned problems or to conduct a field project. Still more extensive would be to build the entire course around student groups. Two exciting examples of the latter is the work that Michaelsen, Watson,

Cragin, and Fink (1982) have done with large classes, and the University of New Hampshire faculty team that developed the notion of the "classroom as an organization" (see Cohen, Chapter 8, this volume).

Irrespective of the centrality of groups, there are four principal areas that serve as barriers to effective use of student teams. This section introduction will briefly explore the factors that cause faculty to underuse (or misuse) teams. Although not insurmountable barriers, they tend to discourage any but the most committed from achieving the full potential that student groups can bring. To conclude, I will examine how the four articles in this section speak to these constraints.

Barrier 1: Issues of Structure

Most academic institutions have developed rigid structures around the educational process. Courses are confined within a set number of weeks and meet a certain number of days per week in a prescribed time period (usually 50 or 90 minutes). There are often physical constraints in how the classroom itself is designed. Except for a few seminar rooms, too often chairs are bolted to the floor and in a layered amphitheater format. Almost unknown is a layout of small group breakout rooms around the parameter of one larger meeting room. Thus one has to move mountains (and administrators!) to establish the appropriate time and space to truly have a group-centered learning environment.

A third structural barrier is the lack of support material for group-centered teaching. Although there are now many more books of group exercises since the classic *Organizational Psychology: An Experiential Approach,* by Kolb, Rubin, and McIntyre, came out in 1971, the instructor who uses student teams as the focus of the course is likely to have to make an initial time investment developing support materials (such as instructions to the groups).

The common practice of most instructors is not to build the course totally around groups, since that is such a major departure from traditional methods, but to see groups as a valuable adjunct to a traditional class format. Although having groups meet outside of the scheduled class hour removes some of the structural limitations discussed above, it can pose scheduling problems for evening programs, commuter colleges, or for students who also work (as is the case with an increasing percentage of management students).

Barrier 2: Expectations of Students
and Instructor (and One's Peers)

All parties hold (often unstated) expectations about what the educational process should be like, the role of the instructor and the (limited) responsibilities of the student. The value of a class is often judged by the number of pages of notes taken (students) and getting through all the material (faculty). Group meetings, which need time for startup, often are felt by all as not a good use of contact time.

The expectations about the instructor usually center around being the direct dispenser of knowledge. A premium is placed on classroom performance (interesting that schools may have *teaching* awards but rarely have *educator* awards). One day when my students were meeting in their groups, I was wandering the halls to stay out of their way. A colleague, with just a touch of sarcasm, said, "Ah, I see you are hard at work teaching again, Bradford." (The only rejoinder I could muster was, "I don't believe that teaching should get in the way of learning.") But insofar as we are concerned about acceptance from peers (and students), we may be hesitant to deviate too far from traditional approaches.

There are also expectations as to the (very limited) student's role. Most commonly that role involves doing the homework, coming prepared to class and making useful comments (not talking for the sake of talking). Students rarely feel responsible for each other's performance and none for the success of the course itself.

There are also expectations that students bring to a specific class on the basis of their past experience. Many international students believe firmly in the (active) expert-(passive) learner split. Students may walk through the door with negative experiences from other group courses that were poorly structured and unrewarding (see Bowen & Jackson, 1986, for an interesting discussion of this issue). Thus, even if our course is new to them, students come with expectations that must be handled.

These expectations reinforce the traditional teaching format. Thus to add out-of-class group meetings to the course requirement is often thought of as an excessive demand. Even more, to be held responsible for the learning (and, God forbid, the evaluation) of one's peers is seen as unconscionable! If this is an elective course, the instructor has a greater chance to set new expectations, but there can be severe limitations with a required course (especially if the other sections are taught in a more traditional manner).

Barrier 3: Issues of Group Formation and Development

Even when the instructor has set appropriate expectations, group-centered courses can fail because insufficient attention has been paid to the format and development of the groups. One crucial dimension is gaining clarity as to the purpose of the team. Are their tasks central to course objectives or are groups assigned because "it's a good thing to do"? Group tasks need to be meaningful, demand interdependency for successful accomplishment, and pull on the varied competencies of the members. Just forming teams and telling them to study the material is unlikely to produce successful collaboration.

Group composition is also crucial for team success. Letting students self-select is rarely advisable because the choice is likely to be made on the basis of comfort (usually past friendships and/or similar demographic characteristics). But if the instructor determines membership, thought must be given to deciding exactly what are the most relevant criteria for this particular course with its unique goals.

Even though groups go through relatively predictable stages of development, this process is neither easy nor problem free (Bradford, 1993). Students vary in their interpersonal and group competencies. Also, even those with extensive group experience will still find difficulties, because members have different expectations, work styles, interests, and abilities. Even if they have the skills to process such issues, there can be reluctance to raise the problems in the first place, as there usually are student norms against directly confronting each other.

What support should the instructor give in assisting the groups to develop into effective teams (and helping them learn from their experiences)? The answer, of course, depends on the competence of students and their need for structure. But some of the dimensions the instructor should consider are

- How explicit should the expectations be as the role of the group and responsibilities of members?
- Should some initial classes be spent dealing with issues of a group's dynamics and its development? Should there be skill training on raising and resolving interpersonal and group issues?
- To what extent should the group's meeting time be structured (with assigned cases, role-plays, and discussion topics) as opposed to unstructured with team members deciding their own task and structure?
- How much direct support and resources should be allocated to consult with teams as difficulties arise (e.g., the instructor or teaching assistants available as process consultants)?
- And because students will be reluctant to process interpersonal and group issues with their classmates, should a structure be given that all groups are to follow (e.g., a group diagnostic questionnaire assigned and set time and format for processing)?

Barrier 4: Issues of Control and Equity

For better or for worse, one of the advantages of the traditional classroom is that the instructor knows what is going on. But what is occurring in the teams? Are they doing work of value? Keeping on schedule? Experiencing any difficulties (internally or externally to the team)? There are various ways for the instructor to keep abreast, such as with assigned group leaders (or meeting weekly with group representatives), ongoing progress reports, individual journals, and the like. But whatever the form, most instructors want to have some progress check so that problems can be corrected in time.

Assigning grades can also be a problem. Does one give one grade to the entire group (and is that equitable given the likelihood of differential work among the members)? But if a variable grade, how does one collect accurate information? Is self-report accurate enough, and how does one deal with students' resistance to grading each other? If the option is to have the work be in discrete parts, does that cut down on the interdependency of the task?

Summary

These barriers individually are not that major, and they can be overcome with forethought. But they do take conscious attention, because collectively, they can seriously impair the benefit from a group-centered course. The four articles in this section provide additional guidance in the use of groups.

Curtis Cook's article (Chapter 15) takes a slant on the use of groups that is different from the other three articles. He describes how one of the advantages of groups (joint problem solving) can be used within a traditional classroom format through the nominal group technique (NGT) and the Delphi method. Chapter 16, by David Johnson and Roger Johnson, provides a useful overview of cooperative learning and spells out how such learning groups need to be structured. Although Chapter 17, by Larry Michaelsen, Warren Watson, and Charles Shrader, deals with the very innovative way they have modified the testing procedure, it also gives a good picture of their group-centered classroom. David Jalajas and Robert Sutton's article (Chapter 18) will speak to the heart of every instructor who has ever used groups and suffered through students who seem intent on undermining the process! Especially useful are their recommendations for minimizing (and dealing with) such problem students.

In terms of other resources, one will find within back issues of *The Journal of Management Education* (and its previous incarnations, *The Organizational Behavior Teaching Review* and *Exchange: The Organizational Behavior Teaching Journal*) a rich source of ideas and suggestions. Of the several books containing group exercises, especially recommended is *Experiences in Management and Organizational Behavior* by Hall, Bowen, Lewicki, and Hall (1982). An invaluable storehouse of exercises and suggestions about how to use student teams is the very extensive instructor's manual to the introductory text *Effective Behavior in Organizations,* by Cohen, Fink, Gaden, and Willits (1992). Their manual also describes in detail their model of the classroom as an organization.

References

Bowen, D. D., & Jackson, C. N. (1986). Curing those ol' omigod-not-another-group-class blues. *The Organizational Behavior Teaching Review, 10*(4), 21-31.

Bradford, D. L. (1993). Building high performance teams. In A. R. Cohen (Ed.), *The portable MBA in management, organization and leadership* (pp. 38-70). New York: Wiley.

Cohen, A. R., Fink, S. L., Gaden, H., & Willits, R. D. (1992). *Effective behavior in organizations* (5th ed.). Homewood, IL: Irwin.

Hall, D. T., Bowen, D. D., Lewicki, R. J., & Hall, F. S. (1982). *Experiences in management and organizational behavior* (2nd ed.). New York: Wiley.

Kolb, D. A., Rubin, I. M., & McIntyre, J. M. (1971). *Organizational psychology: An experiential approach.* Englewood Cliffs, NJ: Prentice-Hall.

Johnson, D. W., & Johnson, R. (1984). *Cooperative learning.* New Brighton, MN: Interaction.

Michaelsen, L. K., Watson, W. E., Cragin, J. P., & Fink, L. D. (1982). Team learning: A potential solution to the problems of large classes. *Exchange: The Organizational Behavior Teaching Journal, 7*(1), 13-22.

Fifteen

Nominal Group Methods Enrich Classroom Learning

CURTIS W. COOK
San Jose State University

Murphy's Law is not infallible. However, for teachers of management and organizational behavior courses, events often seem to go wrong when attempting to involve students in the learning process. Whether using discussions, case analyses, role-plays, or experiential exercises, instructors who use discovery-based learning approaches experience occasional disappointment, if not failure. Many factors contribute to the shortfall between intended learning and actual outcomes when students are allowed to take learning into their own hands.

Among the variables that singularly or interactively can reduce the educational value of class discussion and experimentation, several critical ones include (1) disproportionate levels of student involvement, (2) quantity overrides quality of discussion, (3) students attempt to guess the instructor's favored answer (Argyris, 1980), (4) groupthink and unimaginative solutions, (5) moving too quickly through decision stages, (6) overshadowing substantive learning with entertainment (Filley, Foster, & Herbert, 1979), and (7) underplaying experiential behaviors because of the instructor's weak clinical or debriefing skills (House, 1979).

Basics of the Nominal Group Technique and Delphi Method

Two methods to overcome these potential inhibitors of learning are the nominal group technique (NGT) and Delphi method. Both (1) draw on a

This chapter originally appeared in *Exchange: The Organizational Behavior Teaching Journal*, Volume 5, Issue 3.

diverse pool of human knowledge, (2) ensure involvement and equality of participation, and (3) systematically evaluate ideas generated by participants. Both employ nominal groups in the sense that procedures deliberately are structured to limit participant interaction—or even prevent it in the case of many Delphi applications.

Although similar in purpose and behavior premise, there are distinct procedural differences between the two. Also the types of tasks for which these techniques are best suited differ. As subsequently explained, classroom use of nominal group methods helps students not only learn techniques for utilizing group ideas but also develop more fully their comprehension or understanding of other issues pertinent to the course material.

NOMINAL GROUP TECHNIQUE

NGT was developed about 1968 by Delbecq and Van de Ven to aid in creative problem focusing, idea generation, and collective decisions. NGT is useful whenever a wide variety of creative individual judgments (ideas, opinion, and knowledge) needs to be combined to resolve a multifaceted problem too complicated for individual resolution. Furthermore, NGT restricts patterns of member interaction so that the potential drawbacks of group dynamics are minimized. This is done through (1) involvement of every participant, (2) equality of member influence, and (3) breadth and variety of problem coverage.

Delbecq, Van de Ven, and Gustafson (1975) extensively describe the sequential phases that provide the uniqueness of the NGT process. In adapting their technique to the classroom, I find the following eight-stage process useful.

1. *Public Orientation.* Formation of five- to eight-person groups and presentation of a clear statement of the task, worded to invite an extensive listing of ideas or alternatives (10 minutes).
2. *Private Brainstorming.* Participants write their own personal ideas about the problem, usually as themes or brief phrases (5 minutes).
3. *Public Round-Robin Sharing (Procedural).* Each person in turn contributes one idea, which is listed on a flip-chart, with rotational sharing continued until all ideas are publicly recorded (10 to 15 minutes).
4. *Public Discussion (Interactive).* When necessary, each idea is briefly clarified by means of examples and explanations but not debated for relative merits. Obvious duplicates are eliminated and global ideas are refined into two or more specific items (10 to 25 minutes).
5. *Private Evaluation.* Individuals rank or classify all ideas in writing according to criteria specified by the instructor (5 to 15 minutes).

6. *Public Pooling (Procedural).* The group tabulates and summarizes all individual evaluations to produce a mathematically derived group decision (10 to 15 minutes).
7. *Public Debriefing (Interactive).* Instructor debriefs for insight into factors that affected group functioning, learning, and quality—with comparisons to other group and individual experiences (15 to 30 minutes).
8. *Public Planning (Interactive).* Discussion and action planning of how to implement the results, with Delphi extensions and refinements under some circumstances (open ended).

DELPHI METHOD

The Delphi method was developed at the Rand Corporation for technological forecasting and predates NGT by about 20 years. Unlike NGT, Delphi normally works with a panel of experts that can be dispersed geographically rather than assembled (although not relevant for classroom use). Participant anonymity is valued and preserved by collecting written individual responses to one or more questions. When conducted within the classroom, Delphi essentially involves the following six steps:

1. Select the panel of experts, the members of which are diversely informed about the focal task (usually everyone in the class).
2. Submit a question or questionnaire to the class and obtain their written responses, possibly including supportive reasons.
3. Anonymously tabulate and summarize the responses.
4. Feedback and discuss the summarized data.
5. Request a second data response (with the same or a modified question), which allows participants to reconsider their original personal responses.
6. Repeat steps two to five until results stabilize or a predetermined schedule (i.e., three iterations) has been completed.

Within the classroom, NGT and Delphi may be used separately to investigate independent issues, or linked sequentially under special circumstances. Because NGT for a class of 40 students typically involves five or six groups, there is more verbal interaction and therefore usually a greater investment in class time than for Delphi. Also, because several NGT groups may explore the same issue, topic, or problem, the ideas produced by each are likely to be somewhat diverse. For some investigations this diversity may be valued and emphasized; for others, refinement may be preferable. In the latter case, the themes produced by the NGT technique can be evaluated via Delphi participation of the total class. The two techniques may thus be used in tandem and build on each other, as described later.

Applications: To Explore Course Issues

I have used nominal group decision-focusing techniques in more than 20 courses—undergraduate and graduate, required as well as elective. Usually, I find that both techniques lead students to explore issues more fully than do general class discussions of the what-do-you-think variety. Nominal group methods not only enhance the quantity and quality of expressed ideas but also lead to higher general involvement and result in a decision about the relevance of generated possibilities. Students thus experience closure about a subject rather than the frustration of being left up in the air.

The flexibility of purpose and application in regard to NGT or Delphi is limited only by the imagination of the instructor and students. But to illustrate how they can be put into practice within the classroom, let us take three examples. Afterward, several specific suggestions are offered about how to avoid pitfalls of the nominal group technique.

EXAMPLE 1—NGT

Consider the question, "What dehumanizing experiences do people have in organizations?" This formulation is sufficiently complex so that it enables every student to express personal experiences (phase 1). Then, after assembling groups of five to eight people and outlining the NGT phases, students begin a personal brainstorming session around the idea of what experiences they had as students, customers, employees, and citizens that were stressful, humiliating, frustrating, or anger producing (phase 2). By drawing from the personally familiar rather than theoretical, and by expressing ideas in their own words, most groups generate lengthy lists of richly descriptive abuses (phase 3). These usually range from those that stem from organizational policy to those that are interpersonal.

During clarification and group discussion (phase 4), I encourage students to share briefly with each other whether they have experienced each identified abuse. When only one person is familiar with the problem, he or she explains quickly the circumstances under which it occurred. The idea is to sensitize those who are naive about organizational behavior to the imperfections that humans create for themselves and others. This means that I devote more time to sharing experiences than I might for discussion of a more straightforward question, such as, "In what ways can a manager reward others for helpful performances?"

When it comes time for personally evaluating the list of abuses (phase 5), I have used two methods: simple ranking of the 10 most common, and assigning abuses to classifications according to "most offensive" and "most correctable" criteria. Evaluations according to two sets of criteria are useful with this task because tabulated pooling (phase 6) usually shows that those abuses that rank high in one factor may not in another.

During debriefing and applications (phases 7 and 8), I encourage undergraduate students to apply the concepts of the course to personal coping strategies for navigating organizations. Not only does this make the course material more relevant but the different applications highlight individual differences of perceptions and values. Finally, for present and future managers, this task yields spin-offs about organizational ethics and the manager's role in preventing abuses in their organizations.

EXAMPLE 2—NGT

Alternatively, NGT can be used to decide on course procedures, for example, "What should be the behavioral objectives of this course?" Such a question is very appropriate for advanced or elective courses. (It should not be explored the 1st week of class, because it is necessary for students to develop a feel for the subject matter and the instructor; otherwise this task becomes little more than a make-work exercise.)

When I use this task, I normally put it in the 2nd or 3rd week and then ask students in the preceding session to scan the text and to think about specific objectives for which they may be held accountable. An explanation of why and how to specify testable behavioral objectives should precede this process. By not specifying objectives in the syllabus, students who usually rely on external directives may become anxious, and this anxiety may be an interesting subject to discuss during debriefing. Especially for undergraduates, such a task dramatizes both the difficulty of specifying objectives and the fact that objectives can seldom be meaningfully developed until action has begun—an idea that is glossed over in most introductory management texts.

EXAMPLE 3—DELPHI

The above NGT task about course objectives may produce (1) themes that are not operationally stated in behavioral terms, and (2) differences in opinion among groups. Therefore, it is natural to use the NGT weighted lists (phase 6) as a starting point for Delphi application. Each NGT task group refines its most valued objectives, then sends a representative to a staff group. This group eliminates duplicates, pools items into a questionnaire, and develops an evaluation system (usually a Likert scale). Copies of this questionnaire are produced, administered to all students, tabulated by the staff group, then fed back to the class for general discussion of supporting reasons for certain objectives. The narrowed field of items is individually readministered, tabulated, and so on to produce a final ordering of course objectives.

Such a task can then be discussed around such themes as a sense of helplessness versus being in control, acceptance of responsibility with accountability, and the use of objectives. A simple variation applicable to undergraduates would involve the instructor listing possible tasks for which they could be evaluated (exams, cases, team project, etc.). Then, after discussion, each participant would write on a piece of paper not only what percentage of the final grade should depend on these separate things but also how many exams there should be and so on. In Delphi tradition, responses are collected, tabulated, fed back, and a second or even a third balloting is conducted if necessary. Obviously, for an instructor to maintain credibility with students, the results generally have to be incorporated into the course.

Potential Pitfalls of NGT

It takes little imagination to envision other creative in-class uses of NGT and Delphi. However, nominal group methods are not without their potential pitfalls, most of which can be easily avoided by taking precautions at the planning stage. I offer these insights from my own "surprise" experiences as guidance for others.

PROBLEM SELECTION

Two notes of caution apply to problem selection: First, the problem must be amenable to the technique. NGT in particular requires that the task provoke a rich outpouring of ideas that can be succinctly listed in short phrases. Normally I expect a five- to eight-person group to generate between 20 and 30 separate ideas. If the problem appears to have few answers, then the Delphi (or a freely interacting group) is preferred.

Second, the task has to be appropriate to the knowledge and experience of the participants. Consider the following NGT task: "What organization development (OD) methods are widely used in attempting to bring about change in organization?" Such a problem might be very useful as a mid-course review for a graduate seminar specializing in OD (where I have used it) but would be out of the question for the undergraduate introductory management course.

PROBLEM SPECIFICATION

In all NGT tasks, it is desirable to allow students to raise questions and offer examples to clarify the central task (phase 1). Often what emerges is the need to define terms more precisely before nominal groups begin to generate ideas. Recently, I used the OD methods problem (noted above) but failed to distinguish adequately between techniques, tools, concepts, and philosophies. This oversight produced lists that included mixes such as "confrontation meeting, role analysis technique, action research interviewing, and unfreezing/changing/refreezing." To prevent ambiguity, a statement of the task with terms defined should be written on a flip chart, chalkboard, and/or distributed as a handout.

EVALUATION CRITERIA TO ASSESS ITEMS

An impulsive leap into a nominal group task may lead the instructor to select hastily an inappropriate criterion for evaluating the ideas generated by the group. Even when the criterion selected is relevant, that may not be the only appropriate one. And picking only one dimension overlooks the possibility of evaluating the group data from multiple viewpoints. Possible criteria include most frequent, most critical, most satisfying, and easiest to change or implement. Often by making two separate sortings (but not more than two), students may realize, for example, that those factors that have the most far-reaching consequences are among the most difficult to alter. By anticipating different uses of the data before engaging the class, synergy is achieved from a single data bank of ideas.

DATA SORTING METHODS

As part of the decision in regard to the appropriate criteria, the instructor should plan the method of evaluation (NGT phase 5 or as part of many Delphi second iterations). Although simple ranking appears to be the most straightforward method, few people are capable of making meaningful differentiations among 20 to 30 items. Whenever there are a large number of factors, consider the purpose of the task and alternative methods of assigning values to the data. Three alternatives to ranking the total list of items are (1) Arbitrarily instruct students to select the 7 (or 10) items most congruent with the criterion. These items can then be ranked. A method that compensates for the fact that not all students will have selected the same 7 items is to have them assign a value of 7 to the most salient, 6 to the next most, and so forth. (2) Participants begin with a fixed number of points (i.e., 25) that they can distribute among favored ideas, subject to the constraint that a minimum number of items must be included (i.e., 7). (3) A modified Q-sort could be used whereby students divide the items into a predetermined number of categories (3 to 5).

Benefits of NGT

Students can be taught about group processes, nominal techniques, and decision making by reading, listening to lectures, discussing issues, and analyzing cases. But as Harvey (1979) suggests, why try to teach when students can so easily learn through direct involvement? Unlike contrived exercises in which the tasks themselves have little or no direct learning value but only stimulate personal and interactive behaviors, NGT and Delphi achieve synergistic learning by producing outcomes on at least two levels.

On one level, every student experiences a strong grasp of the course-related material that is explored by NGT and/or Delphi. Specifically, (1) everyone has to become cognitively if not emotionally involved in the focal question(s), (2) the array of viewpoints is broadly defined because of the systematic processing of alternative possibilities, (3) everyone has equal responsibility for thinking about and acting evaluatively on the question-related data, and (4) interpretation and closure is forced through the evaluative decision process. Thus students usually come away from the investigation with a substantive understanding that is broader, more penetrating, and more personalized than typically occurs in freely interactive case or topic discussions.

On the second level, students actually experience two group decision techniques rather than simply hear about them. By living through each phase of NGT and Delphi methodology, students leave the course with an operational skill rather than a rapidly fading memory of two concepts once mentioned in a management course. After using the techniques to explore problems of direct relevance to their learning or lives, most students understand the practical circumstances within which NGT and/or Delphi are applicable. They feel competent to administer the processes in future organizational experiences.

References

Argyris, C., (1980). Some limitations of the case method: Experiences in a management development program. *Academy of Management Review, 5*(2), 291-298.

Delbecq, A. L., Van de Ven, A. H., & Gustafson, D. H. (1975). *Group techniques for program planning: A guide to nominal group and Delphi processes.* Glenview, IL: Scott, Foresman.

Filley, A. C., Foster, L. W., & Herbert, T. T. (1979). Teaching organization behavior: Current patterns and implications. *Exchange: The Organizational Behavior Teaching Journal, 4*(2), 13-18.

Harvey, J. B. (1979). Learning to not teach. *Exchange: The Organizational Behavior Teaching Journal, 4*(2), 19-21.

House, R. J. (1979). Experiential learning: A sad passing fad? *Exchange: The Organizational Behavior Teaching Journal, 4*(2), 8-12.

Sixteen

Structuring Groups for Cooperative Learning

DAVID W. JOHNSON
ROGER T. JOHNSON
University of Minnesota

The college classroom is first and foremost a scene of recurrent interpersonal interactions where an instructor and 30 to 50 or more students all interact with one another. College faculty have traditionally viewed the interaction between the instructor and student and between the student and materials as the two most important sources of subject matter mastery, professional socialization, and intellectual and social development. As a result, considerable attention has been focused on the effects of the instructor's behavior on student learning. For example, studies have investigated such things as instructors' expectations of students' ability to perform on academic tasks, warmth, empathy, and democraticness in dealing with students, distribution of reinforcers to students for achievement and appropriate social behavior, and feedback to the student concerning achievement and appropriate behavior. Similarly, a great deal of attention has been directed toward constructing instructional materials that promote learning, for example, effective instructional materials are attractive in appearance; are illustrated with figures, graphs, and even cartoons; take the student through a series of text and questions in a linear step-by-step manner; provide feedback and reinforcement either through showing the student he or she has gotten the right answer or through direct compliments ("you're

This chapter originally appeared in *The Organizational Behavior Teaching Review*, Volume 9, Issue 4.

right!"); and contain pretests and posttests to determine level of entry into the material and assess how well the material has been mastered.

Student-Student Interaction: Ignored But Powerful

By contrast, it has most often been assumed that the infrequent and minor peer interaction that does exist in the classroom is either irrelevant or an unhealthy and bothersome influence aimed at discouraging academic achievement and encouraging off-task or disruptive behavior. The role of the "good" student has been defined as listening attentively to the instructor and working quietly and alone to get the work done "better" than one's classmates. How students interact with each other is a neglected aspect of most college instruction. It should not be. How instructors structure student-student interaction patterns will have a great deal of influence on how well students learn, their attitudes toward the class and subject area, their attitudes toward each other, their self-esteem and psychological health, and their ability to work collaboratively with others in career, family, and community settings.

Competitive, Individualistic, and Cooperative Interaction

Any course requirement or learning task may be structured competitively, individualistically, or cooperatively (Johnson & Johnson, 1975). Of the three interaction patterns, competition is presently the most dominant in college classmates (e.g., many classes involve a midterm and final exam that are graded on a curve). In a *competitive* learning situation, students' goal achievements are negatively correlated; when one student achieves his or her goal, all others with whom he or she is competitively linked are more likely to fail to achieve their goals. Students seek outcomes that are personally beneficial but also are detrimental to the others with whom they are competitively linked. Any course requirement that is evaluated on a norm-referenced basis is inherently competitive. The pattern of individual responsibility to attend lectures and complete course requirements while competing with classmates for grades is an example.

In an *individualistic* learning situation, students' goal achievements are independent; the goal achievement of one student is unrelated to the goal achievement of others. Students seek outcomes that are personally beneficial and they ignore as irrelevant the goal achievement of their classmates. Keller's (1968) system of self-paced instruction that uses criterion-referenced evaluation as part of a competency-based instructional program is an example. Other examples of individualistic learning that have grown in popularity during the past 15 years include programmed learning and computer-assisted programs for which students meet preset criteria as they work their way through course content.

In a *cooperative* learning situation, students' goal achievements are positively correlated; students perceive that they can reach their learning goals if and only if the other students in the learning group also reach their goals. Thus students seek outcomes that are beneficial to all those with whom they are cooperatively linked. Students discuss the material with each other, help one another understand it, and encourage each other to work hard. Unfortunately, cooperation among students, within which students work together to complete the course requirements, discuss the material being learned, and support each other's learning, is rare despite the fact that extensive research validates its effectiveness (Johnson & Johnson, 1983; Sharan, 1980; Slavin, 1977).

In the ideal course, all three goal structures would be appropriately used. All students would learn how to collaborate with other students, compete for fun and enjoyment, and work autonomously. Instructors should carefully structure learning within the goal structure that is the most productive for the type of task to be done and for the cognitive and affective outcomes desired. It is the instructor who decides which goal structure to implement within each instructional activity. The way in which instructors structure learning goals determines how students interact with each other and with the instructor. The interaction patterns, in turn, determine the cognitive and affective outcomes of instruction. There is no aspect of teaching more important than the appropriate use of goal structures.

Groups and Cooperative Learning

There is a difference between having students work in a group and structuring students to work cooperatively. It is important that when learning groups are used that they be carefully structured to promote cooperative interaction among students. There are a number of basic differences between the typical use of learning groups and cooperative learning groups (Table 16.1). These are

1. *Positive Interdependence.* Cooperative learning goals are structured so that they are positively interdependent and students need to be concerned about the performance of other group members as well as their own; this can be accomplished through goal, task, role, reward, and resource interdependence.

TABLE 16.1
Differences Between Groups and Cooperative Learning

Cooperative Learning Groups	*Typical Learning Groups*
Positive interdependence	Minimal interdependence
Individual accountability	No individual accountability
Heterogeneous	Homogeneous
Shared leadership	One appointed leader
Shared responsibility for each other	Responsibility only for self
Task and maintenance emphasized	Only task emphasized
Social skills directly taught	Social skills assumed and ignored
Instructor observes and intervenes	Instructor ignores group functioning
Groups process their effectiveness	Generally no group processing

2. *Individual Accountability.* Instructors must provide a method to assess student's mastery of assigned material and give feedback on his or her progress; in addition, the group must have feedback on how each member is progressing so that members know who needs assistance, support, and encouragement.

3. *Responsibility for Each Other's Learning Is Shared.* Group members are expected to provide help and encouragement to each other to ensure that all members do the assigned work; in traditional learning groups, members are seldom held responsible for each other's learning.

4. *Collaborative Skills.* Students are taught and encouraged to use the collaborative skills such as leadership, communication, trust building, decision making, and conflict management.

5. *The Instructor Observes the Groups.* In cooperative learning, the instructor analyzes the problems students have in working together and gives each group feedback on its effectiveness; instructor observation and intervention seldom take place in traditional learning groups.

6. *Group Processing.* The instructor structures procedures and time for students to process how effectively they are working together; students must then analyze how their group functions and how effectively they are using their collaborative skills (Johnson & Johnson, 1975, 1984b; Johnson, Johnson, Holubec & Roy, 1984).

Positive Instructional Outcomes
From Cooperative Learning

Extensive research comparing cooperative, competitive, and individualistic learning situations dates back to the late 1800s (Johnson & Johnson, 1975, 1978, 1983; Johnson, Johnson, & Maruyama, 1983; Johnson, Maruyama,

Johnson, Nelson & Skon, 1981; Sharan, 1980; Slavin, 1977). The hundreds of studies that have been conducted indicate that a wide range of positive outcomes can be expected when the conditions for cooperative learning are met.

ACHIEVEMENT

Students achieve more in cooperative than in competitive or individual-istic learning situations. A metaanalysis of all the research studies that compared cooperative, competitive, and individualistic learning (122 stud-ies from 1924 to 1981) clearly indicated that cooperative learning experi-ences result in higher achievement and greater retention of learning than do competitive or individualistic learning (Johnson, Maruyama, et al., 1981). The average student in a cooperative learning situation performed at approximately the 80th percentile of students in competitive and indi-vidualistic learning situations. This finding held for all age groups, ability levels, subject areas, and learning tasks. The more the learning task involved problem solving, divergent thinking, decision making, and con-ceptual learning, the greater the superiority of cooperation. Students in cooperative learning situations tend to use higher-level thought processes, engage in more higher-level oral rehearsal, and discover higher-level strategies more frequently than do students in competitive and individual-istic learning situations.

MOTIVATION

Cooperative learning experiences, compared with competitive and indi-vidualistic ones, promoted greater achievement motivation, more intrinsic motivation, more persistence in completing tasks, and greater continuing motivation to learn (Johnson & Johnson, 1985).

ATTITUDES TOWARD SUBJECT AREA
AND PROFESSOR

Cooperative learning experiences resulted in more positive attitudes toward the subject area and instructor than did competitive and individu-alistic learning experiences (Johnson & Johnson, 1983). In addition, after collaborating to complete joint tasks, most students perceive a system in which group members are jointly rewarded as being fairer than a competi-tive or individualistic reward system.

RELATIONSHIPS WITH OTHER STUDENTS

Cooperative learning experiences, compared with competitive and indi-vidualistic ones, resulted in more positive relationships among students, characterized by mutual liking and perceptions that students care about one's academic progress and about one as a person. A metaanalysis (Johnson, Johnson & Maruyama, 1983) that reviewed all the studies comparing the three goal structures on attitudes toward other students (98 studies conducted between 1944 and 1982) found that these results held among homogeneous students, students from different ethnic groups, and handicapped and nonhandicapped students. Cooperative experiences typically resulted in a reduction of stereotyping and a more differentiated, dynamic, and realistic view of other students. As academics we frequently talk about wanting to reduce racial, ethnic, and other prejudice; cooperative learning provides an effective and practical means of doing something about it.

SELF-ESTEEM AND PSYCHOLOGICAL HEALTH

Cooperative learning experiences resulted in higher levels of self-esteem, healthier processes for deriving conclusions about one's self-worth, and greater psychological health than did competitive and individualistic learning experiences (Johnson & Johnson, 1983, 1985).

PERSPECTIVE TAKING

Cooperative learning experiences, compared with competitive and individualistic ones, promoted greater cognitive and emotional perspective taking (Johnson & Johnson, 1983). Competitiveness has been found to be related to egocentrism.

COLLABORATIVE COMPETENCIES

Employability rests to a great extent on the ability to work collaboratively with superiors, colleagues, subordinates, and clients. Obviously, students who have had extensive cooperative learning experiences have been found to have more interpersonal and small group skills than did students who have primarily experienced competitive and individualistic learning experiences (Johnson & Johnson, 1983). The ability to utilize one's knowledge and resources in collaborative activities with other people in career, family, community, and societal settings was found to be promoted by cooperative learning experiences.

Cooperative Goal Structures

During the past few years the use of groups for instructional purposes has increased rather dramatically. Groups are now being successfully used in many different academic disciplines (Bouton & Garth, 1983); for a wide range of instructional objectives including the development of interpersonal skills (Johnson, 1981), the interpersonal and small group skills needed to function as an effective employee (Johnson, 1978), and the small group skills needed in management and decision-making situations (Johnson & Johnson, 1982); and in a variety of ways including short-focused discussions during lectures, structured learning activities, long-term groups within courses, and even a support base for entire degree programs.

There is increasing recognition of the potential of learning groups. Instructors, program directors, and other faculty members, however, have all too often naively assumed that simply placing students in groups will ensure the success of the learning experience. Careful structuring of group learning experiences is required whether the specific application consists of an activity that lasts a few minutes or is intended to support students as they progress through a degree program. Failures occur, however, with considerable frequency (Fiechtner & Davis, 1984) and often have the unfortunate effect of souring both faculty members and students on what can be an extremely powerful learning aid.

In our opinion, most of the failures with learning groups at every level can be avoided if the instructors or administrators involved ensure that a cooperative goal structure is established for the course or program in which the groups are used. The four most basic elements of a cooperative goal structure will be outlined below along with specific examples of how they apply to the design of group learning activities (see Johnson & Johnson, 1975, 1984a, 1984b; Johnson, Johnson, Holubec & Roy, 1984, for a more detailed discussion). These are *positive interdependence, individual accountability, collaborative skills training,* and *group processing.*

POSITIVE INTERDEPENDENCE

Positive interdependence is the perception that one is linked with others in such a way that one cannot succeed unless the others do (and vice versa), so that their work benefits one and one's work benefits them. It is a sense of mutuality, mutual causation, and common fate that is the essence of organizations, small groups, families, communities, and societies.

The degree of positive interdependence that is built into learning activities is a function of the parameters in five different aspects of group assignments: goals, rewards, resources, roles, and tasks. As a result, instructors can control the degree of positive interdependence by establishing or removing different kinds of constraints within each of these areas. Several of the most frequently effective mechanisms for ensuring a high degree of positive interdependence in the different aspects of group assignments are as follows:

1. *Positive goal interdependence* is enhanced by requiring one product from the group, having all students complete a project with the understanding that the instructor will randomly select one to evaluate the entire group or by giving each student an individual test and taking a group average.

2. The instructor can establish *positive reward interdependence* by giving a single grade for the group's efforts, adding bonus points to each member's individual score when all the group members achieve a certain standard, or giving nonacademic rewards such as free time or a trip to the local pizza parlor when everyone in the group masters a designated academic task.

3. *Positive resource interdependence* is likely to be high in heterogeneous groups because the information or skills needed for task completion will generally be broadly distributed within the group. In addition, instructors can ensure a high degree of positive resource interdependence for specific activities by limiting the resources given to the group (only one pencil, book, dictionary, etc.), or by distributing material or information so that each member only has a part of what is needed to complete the assignment.

4. Group members are likely to experience *positive role interdependence* when each person is given a specific role to play within the group.

5. *Positive task interdependence* will be high when the group is operating under a division of labor that requires the actions of one group member to be completed if the next team member is to complete his or her assigned responsibilities.

INDIVIDUAL ACCOUNTABILITY

Individual accountability exists when the performance of each individual student is assessed so that the group knows who needs more assistance in completing the assignment and so that each member perceives that he or she must fulfill particular responsibilities for him or her and the group to be successful. Giving individual tests on the material that the group is responsible for learning and then averaging the group members' scores or randomly selecting one student's product to represent the entire group are both common ways to ensure that individual accountability exists.

COLLABORATIVE SKILLS

Groups cannot function effectively if students do not have and use the needed collaborative skills. These skills have to be taught just as purposefully and precisely as academic skills. Many college students have never been required to collaborate in learning situations and, therefore, lack the needed social skills for doing so. Instructors may have to supplement the academic experiential learning experiences with experiences directly aimed at teaching the leadership, decision-making, trust-building, communication, and conflict-management skills needed to function effectively in cooperative learning groups.

GROUP PROCESSING

Groups need specific time to discuss how well they are achieving their goals and maintaining effective working relationships among members. Groups need to describe what member actions were helpful and unhelpful and make decisions about what member actions to continue or change. Such processing enables task groups to focus on group maintenance, facilitates the learning of collaborative skills, ensures that members receive feedback on their participation, and reminds students to practice collaborative skills consistently. Some of the keys to successful processing are allowing sufficient time for it to take place, making specific rather than vague generalities, maintaining student involvement in processing, lack of consistent use of collaborative skills during processing, and ensuring that clear expectations as to the purpose of processing have been communicated (Johnson & Johnson, 1984b).

PROBLEM BEHAVIORS

When students are working in cooperative learning groups, they sometimes engage in unproductive or potentially disruptive behaviors. Careful attention to positive interdependence, individual accountability, collaborative skills, and group processing usually solve such problems. Four of the most common problem behavior patterns are passive uninvolvement, active uninvolvement, independence, and taking charge (Johnson & Johnson, 1984b). Some suggestions for dealing with such problems are as follows.

Passive Uninvolvement. Passive uninvolvement would include such behaviors as turning away from the group, not participating, not paying attention to the group's work, saying little or nothing, showing no enthusiasm, or not bringing assigned work or materials. When these behaviors occur, instructors can minimize their impact by taking steps to increase the level of positive interdependence that will stimulate other group members to involve the passive student. This can be done by dividing up responsibilities and assigning the passive student a role that is essential to the group's success, or by rewarding the group on the basis of their average performance.

Active Uninvolvement. Occasionally a student will engage in behavior that clearly disrupts the functioning of the group. Some of the most frequent manifestations of active uninvolvement are talking about everything but the assignment, leaving the group without the group's permission, attempting to sabotage the group's work by giving wrong answers or destroying the group's product, refusing to do work, or refusing to work with another group member. When these behaviors occur, instructors can often solve the problem by assigning the student a specific role to fulfill, or making the student a group observer with high accountability to collect data about group functioning. Other possibilities include sitting in on group processing sessions and confronting the student and offering a reward that this student or group finds especially attractive and structuring the task so that all members must work steadily and contribute for the group to succeed and attain the reward.

Independence. Given the typical competitive structure of the majority of university classes, probably the most common problem involves a student actively but independently working on the assigned task. When this occurs, instructors can generally solve the problem by limiting the resources of the group. For example, if there is only one answer sheet, the members will be unable to work independently. Another effective strategy is jigsawing materials so that the student cannot do the work without the other members' information.

Taking Charge. Occasionally a student will become overly assertive and simply attempt to take charge of the group. Typically this involves such behavior as doing all the work, refusing to let other members participate, ordering other members around, bullying other members, or making decisions for the group without checking to see if the other members agree. Two of the most effective strategies for dealing with these problems are reducing the offender's ability to influence the group by jigsawing resources or structuring tasks so that other group members have the most powerful and dominant roles. Another effective method is rewarding the group on the basis of the lowest two scores by group members. This will place pressure on the student taking charge to encourage and help other members learn the material and complete the task.

Summary and Conclusions

Although considerable attention has been focused on instructor-student and student-materials interaction, instructors are typically given little guidance concerning student-student interaction. There are three ways in which interaction among students may be structured: competitively, individualistically, and cooperatively. While all three types of interaction are appropriate under certain conditions, cooperative learning is by far the most important in terms of promoting desirable instructional outcomes and is the least used in most American colleges and universities. Cooperative, compared with competitive and individualistic learning situations, tend to promote higher achievement, greater motivation, more positive attitudes toward the professor and the subject area being studied, more positive relationships among students (regardless of the heterogeneity represented), higher self-esteem and psychological health, greater interpersonal competence, and greater perspective-taking ability.

Given the overwhelmingly positive outcomes that result from the use of cooperative learning, it is surprising that classroom practice is not more consistent with research findings. Current estimates of the use of small group learning indicate that students in American schools are working together only 7% to 20% of the time. In addition, even in those instances in which small groups are used, we suspect that the basic elements of cooperation (positive interdependence, individual accountability, collaborative skills, and group processing) are all too often being ignored. It is time to reduce the discrepancy between what research indicates is effective and what instructors actually do.

References

Bouton, C., & Garth, R. Y. (1983). Students in learning groups: Active learning through conversation. In C. Bouton & R. Y. Garth (Eds.), *Learning in groups* (pp. 73-82). San Francisco: Jossey-Bass.

Fiechtner, S. B., & Davis, E. A. (1984). Why some groups fail: A survey of students' experiences with learning groups. *The Organizational Behavior Teaching Review, 9*(4), 58-73.

Johnson, D. W. (1978). *Human relations and your career: A guide to interpersonal skills.* Englewood Cliffs, NJ: Prentice-Hall.

Johnson, D. W. (1981). *Reaching out: Interpersonal effectiveness and self-actualization* (2nd ed.). Englewood Cliffs, NJ: Prentice-Hall, 1981.

Johnson, D. W., & Johnson, F. *Joining together: Group theory and group skills* (2nd ed.). Englewood Cliffs, NJ: Prentice-Hall.

Johnson, D. W., & Johnson, R. (1975). *Learning together and alone: Cooperation, competition, and individualization.* Englewood Cliffs, NJ: Prentice-Hall.

Johnson, D. W., & Johnson, R. (1978). Cooperative, competitive and individualistic learning. *Journal of Research and Development in Education, 12,* 3-15.

Johnson, D. W., & Johnson, R. (1983). The socialization and achievement crisis: Are cooperative learning experiences the solution? In L. Bickman (Ed.), *Applied social psychology annual, 4* (pp. 119-164). Beverly Hills, CA: Sage.

Johnson, D. W., & Johnson, R. (Eds.) (1984a). *Structuring cooperative learning: Lesson plans for teachers.* New Brighton, MN: Interaction.

Johnson, D. W., & Johnson, R. (1984b). *Cooperative learning.* New Brighton, MN: Interaction.

Johnson, D. W., & Johnson, R. (1985). Motivational processes in cooperative, competitive, and individualistic learning situations. In C. Ames & R. Ames (Eds.), *Attitudes and attitude change in special education: Its theory and practice.* Berkeley, CA: McCutchen.

Johnson, D. W., Johnson, R., Holubec, E., & Roy, P. (1984). *Circles of learning: Cooperation in the classroom.* Alexandria, VA: Association for Supervision and Curriculum Development.

Johnson, D. W., Johnson, R., & Maruyama, G. Interdependence and interpersonal attraction among heterogeneous and homogeneous individuals: A theoretical formulation and meta-analysis of the research. *Review of Educational Research, 53,* 5-54.

Johnson, D. W., Maruyama, G., Johnson, R., Nelson, D., & Skon, L. The effects of cooperative, competitive, and individualistic goal structures on achievement: A meta-analysis. *Psychological Bulletin, 89,* 47-62.

Keller, F. S. (1968). Good-bye teacher. . . . *Journal of Applied Behavioral Analysis, 1,* 78-79.

Sharan, S. (1980). Cooperative learning in small groups: Recent methods and effects on achievement, attitudes and ethnic relations. *Review of Educational Research, 50,* 241-271.

Slavin, R. E. (1977). A student team approach to teaching adolescents with special emotional and behavioral needs. *Psychology in the Schools, 14*(1), 77-84.

Seventeen

Informative Testing
A Practical Approach for Tutoring With Groups

LARRY K. MICHAELSEN
University of Oklahoma

WARREN E. WATSON
North Texas State University

CHARLES B. SHRADER
Iowa State University

Most educators would agree that the ideal learning situation would be one in which each student had his or her own personal instructor. In fact, achievement test scores of the average student in a one-to-one tutoring situation are typically about two standard deviations higher than the average student in a conventional class with an instructor and 30 or so students (see Bloom, 1984, for a review of the relevant empirical research). In other words, *the average student who is exposed to the feedback and individualized corrective instruction that is characteristic of a one-to-one tutor situation is likely to outperform 98% of the students in conventional classes.* These findings suggest two important conclusions: (1) the vast majority of students are capable of high levels of achievement when they receive sufficient personal attention, feedback, and individualized corrective instruction and (2) the tremendous challenge that faces educators

This chapter originally appeared in *The Organizational Behavior Teaching Review,* Volume 9, Issue 4.

today is the development of instructional formats that are as cost-effective as classroom instruction but that, nonetheless, produce the informational and motivational conditions that naturally occur in a one-to-one tutorial situation.

The purposes of this article are to: (1) outline the key characteristics that promote learning in a one-to-one tutoring situation, (2) compare these with the interpersonal and informational process that are produced by three widely used instructional formats: conventional classroom instruction, mastery learning, and cooperative learning (i.e., permanent small groups within the classroom) and, (3) describe a recently developed instructional process that produces a learning situation similar to one-to-one tutoring by using the activity sequence of mastery learning, heterogeneous learning teams, and a unique testing/feedback system that employs both individual and group exams.

Tutoring

The tutorial process, which has its roots in the apprenticeship process through which skilled craftspeople have received their training for literally thousands of years, is ideally suited for the transfer of information as well as the development of high levels of learner motivation. The three key elements of the information transfer process are illustrated by Brubacher and Rudy (1976) in the following description of the apprenticeship approach to professional education before the advent of professional schools in the United States:

> The professional candidate placed himself under an able and mature minister, lawyer, or doctor and hoped by observation and imitation to be admitted subsequently to professional status. . . . Through assisting a practitioner in the performance of his professional duties, the novice had an opportunity not only to learn professional skills himself but also to repay his benefactor in some degree for both the opportunity to learn and for the direction given to his learning. . . . The would-be physician started making himself useful by washing bottles, later mixing drugs and perhaps at a still later stage progressing to such routine matters as bloodletting. By being present in the doctor's office and accompanying him on calls he picked up much of the lore of diagnosis and therapy. (p. 198-199)

The result of an ongoing tutorial relationship is that (1) the learner is exposed to a set of concepts, (2) the tutor can directly observe the behavior of the learner to determine whether or not the concepts have been mastered, and (3) the tutor can give immediate corrective instruction if the learner's performance reveals deficiencies in his or her understanding of the concepts in question.

The tutorial process is also ideally suited for promoting the development of high levels of student motivation. The ongoing interaction ensures that the tutor will be able to provide the kind of assistance that students need to make rapid progress on learning tasks. Being allowed to progress to increasingly complex tasks provides the learner both recognition and positive reinforcement. Finally, the process often results in the development of a positive interpersonal relationship with the tutor that in turn increases the student's commitment to the learning task. Indeed performing in a way that is pleasing to the tutor frequently becomes a more important source of motivation than any longer term outcomes such as a grade and/or some other form of certification.

In spite of these advantages, the tutorial approach is simply too costly to employ in most instructional settings. As a result, most instruction takes place in a classroom with 20 to 30 or more students and an instructor who has a limited set of options for presenting new material, monitoring student progress, and providing corrective instruction.

Conventional Classroom Instruction and Summative Testing

In contrast to the typical tutoring situation in which instruction, testing, and corrective feedback are an ongoing process, in conventional classrooms the flow of information is much more formal and primarily from the instructor to the students. The only time that this information flow pattern is reversed is the two or three times per term when summative exams are given to rate students' progress and provide a basis for awarding grades (Bloom, Madous, & Hastings, 1981) (Fig. 17.1). This combination of formal presentations and summative testing places severe restrictions on two of the key instructional activities that are characteristic of the tutorial process: monitoring students' progress and providing individualized corrective instruction. As a result, instructors are often forced to plan their presentations with, at best, a partial understanding of what students already know. In addition, students are often unaware of errors in their understanding of foundational concepts until they experience difficulty comprehending later presentations or, worse yet, until the errors have been compounded in further misinterpretations of subsequent material (Bloom et al., 1981).

Except in very small classes, these disadvantages of the conventional classroom instruction are inherent in the process. For example, even

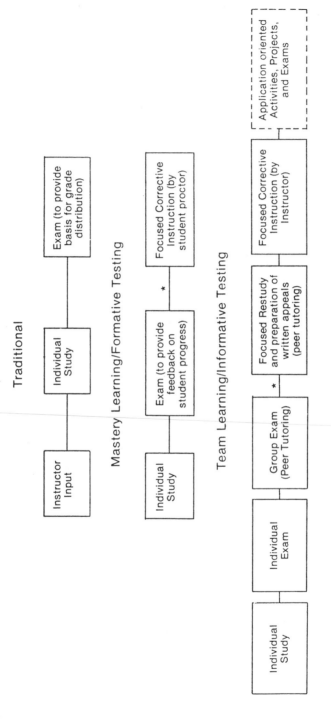

Traditional

Mastery Learning/Formative Testing

Team Learning/Informative Testing

*Preliminary Scoring of exams.

Figure 17.1. Comparison of instructional activity sequences.

though the use of individual homework problems has proven to be one of the most effective methods identified to date (Bloom, 1984), the instructor's ability to monitor students' progress and provide individualized corrective instruction is limited by several factors. It is extremely difficult to design problems that are as effective as direct observation for revealing why students are unable to develop a correct solution. Another is the time and effort required for correcting students' work and preparing individualized feedback. Finally, from the students' perspective, the ideal time to have individual help is while they are actually working on the assignment, as would be the case in a tutorial situation, and not one or two class periods later.

Students may become frustrated when they are unable to obtain individual help or have to struggle to overcome misunderstandings that could be avoided. Probably the most detrimental consequence of conventional classroom instruction is that it eliminates many of the sources of student motivation that are inherent in one-to-one tutoring. Overall, students progress at a much slower pace and are less likely to obtain a feeling of accomplishment from their own progress or to receive positive reinforcement from the instructor (Bloom, 1984). Finally, students seldom have the opportunity to develop personal relationships with the instructor that have the potential of increasing their desire to excel at the learning tasks.

Mastery Learning and Formative Testing

One of the most promising alternatives to conventional classroom instruction that has been developed in the last 20 years is mastery learning. Based on evidence from a wide variety of settings, achievement test scores increase by approximately a full standard deviation when mastery learning is employed. The average student taught in classes using mastery learning progresses to a level that is above 84% of the students in the conventional classes (e.g., see Bloom, 1976; Bloom et al., 1981; Kulick, Kulick, & Smith, 1976; McKeachie, 1978 for summaries of empirical studies).

Probably the greatest reason for the success of mastery learning is its unique testing format, which differs from the more conventional summative testing in three important ways. First, the main purpose of testing is to monitor student progress rather than to provide a basis for grades; second, test items are designed to reveal specific difficulties or misunderstandings; third, the tests are given both more frequently and much earlier in the instruction process (see Fig. 17.1) so that misunderstandings can be detected before students experience the frustration of trying to assimilate concepts for which they are unprepared (Bloom et al., 1981, p. 156). As a result, they are referred to as *formative tests* (Bloom, 1971) because they provide data to assist students while understanding is still in a formative stage.

A second reason for the success of mastery learning is that it provides two alternative mechanisms for using the information from formative tests in the learning process. One approach, which has been widely used in the physical sciences, is abandoning the notion of classes per se and allowing students to progress at their own rate (Keller, 1968). This is accomplished by providing students with materials to guide their individual study and allowing them to go to a testing center and take an exam whenever they feel they have mastered each unit of instruction. If they pass the exam they are then eligible to progress to the next learning unit; if not, they typically have the opportunity to discuss troublesome concepts with a student proctor who will also direct them to remedial instructional materials as needed. The other method, which maintains the concept of classes, involves providing students with alternative sources of individual help in overcoming misunderstandings identified by the formative tests. These would include the instructor discussing particularly troublesome concepts with the class as a whole, providing study guides that link formative test items with specific references in the test and/or other enrichment materials that could include lecture notes or even audio/video tapes, offering individual tutorial help, and/or encouraging students to form study groups with one or two other members of the class (Bloom et al., 1981, p. 64).

One way of illustrating the significance of providing mechanisms for individualized corrective instruction is the contrast between mastery learning and using a pretest in a conventional class. The basic problem in the conventional class is that even if the pretest precisely reveals the learning needs of individual students, the instructor will still have to develop mechanisms to provide feedback and corrective instruction to *each member of the class.* Otherwise, much of the instructional value of a pretest would be lost. Alternatively, the instructor could choose the less desirable strategy of using the pretest to focus class presentations at the level of the "typical" student in a conventional class, but he or she would still be faced with the problem of what to do about those who were either above or below the norm. If they focused class presentations to meet the needs of least-prepared students they would do so at the expense of the better-prepared students. On the other hand, if they presented material geared toward the advanced students and let the other students sink or swim they would be likely to produce a different set of undesirable outcomes. These would include the possibility of placing a premium on passing exams at the expense of mastering concepts; failing a significant proportion of the students in the class (irrespective of the reasons for either their inherent capability or their lack of initial preparation); and for generating frustration, anxiety, and hostility even among those whose complete the course work.

From the standpoint of students' motivation, the procedures used in mastery learning produces many of the positive aspects of one-to-one tutoring. Formative testing minimizes the negative impact of misconceptions by increasing the likelihood that they will be detected and corrected. The test results provide benchmarks that both stimulate the use of positive reinforcement by instructors, and students have the opportunity to build confidence and gain a sense of accomplishment when they successfully complete a series of instructional units. Finally, some of the methods for providing corrective instruction also allow students to develop interpersonal relationships as they perform the learning tasks (Bloom et al., 1981).

In spite of its impressive accomplishments, however, the mastery learning approach is also subject to a number of problems. The investment necessary for the development of study guides and multiple forms of each exam is much greater than with conventional instruction. The others vary depending on the mechanisms that are used to provide corrective instruction. When the process is self-paced, students sometimes delay studying for mastery classes each time they are faced with an evaluation exam in a concurrent traditional course (see Green, 1974) to the point that they are sometimes forced to drop out of the mastery classes or complete them in a later term. Also locating, training, managing, and compensating tutors and proctors to provide individual help when the students need it can be expensive (Bloom, 1976). When the integrity of the class is maintained, the problems center around planning for and providing alternative sources of corrective instruction and motivating students to take advantage of the opportunities that are available.

Cooperative Learning

Another promising alternative to conventional classroom instruction that approaches mastery learning in its effectiveness is cooperative learning (Johnson & Johnson, 1983; Slavin & Karweit, 1981). Based on data from a variety of settings, achievement test scores increase nearly 0.8 of a standard deviation when cooperative learning is employed. In other words, the average student in a cooperative learning situation will out perform approximately 79% of the students from conventional classes

Although the term cooperative learning has been used to describe a fairly wide range of instructional activities the key elements of the process are illustrated by Johnson and Johnson (1983):

> In a cooperatively structural math class, heterogeneous small groups would
> be formed. The students would be given three tasks: to learn how to solve each
> assigned math problem, to make sure that the other members of their group
> know how to solve each problem, and to make sure that everyone in the class
> knows how to solve each problem. While the students work on the math
> problems, they discuss the solution of each with the other members of their
> group, explaining how to solve each problem, listening to each other's expla-
> nations, encouraging each other to try to understand the solutions, and pro-
> viding academic help and assistance. When everyone in their group has
> mastered the solutions, they go look for another group to help until everyone
> in the class understands how to work the problems. (p. 122)

Classes are subdivided into small heterogeneous teams, the grading structure is deliberately designed to reward students for providing assistance to
other members of their group, and students work in the learning teams
during a significant proportion of their time in class.

Much of the success of cooperative learning is the result of the high level
of interaction that naturally occurs within the learning teams. In fact, the
major difference between cooperative learning and one-to-one tutoring is
that the interaction is with peers rather than instructors. As a result,
students in a cooperative learning class are exposed to feedback and
corrective instruction on an ongoing basis and are also likely to develop
personal relationships that will enhance their desire to excel at the learning
tasks. In addition, working in teams also provides several bonuses. These
include the development of (1) interpersonal and group interaction skills,
(2) increased self-esteem and psychological health, and (3) a more differentiated view of others, which in turn reduces tendencies toward racial and
other prejudices (Johnson & Johnson, 1983).

Most of the problems with cooperative learning are related to monitoring instructional processes to enable the instructor to provide corrective
feedback when learning errors occur within groups, designing activities
that are appropriate for learning teams, and/or guiding the groups to ensure
that they function effectively. Unfortunately, failure to address any one of
these aspects of the cooperative learning process can make the use of
learning teams both frustrating and educationally unproductive.

Team Learning and Informative Testing

The team learning process was developed by us to provide the immediate feedback and personal attention of one-to-one tutoring without sacrificing the motivational and cost advantages of instructor-paced classroom

instruction. This is accomplished by using the steps employed by the formative testing process of mastery learning in conjunction with a grading system and classroom activities that are characteristic of cooperative learning.

BACKGROUND

The informative testing process was originally developed in conjunction with the team learning instructional format used in a course in organizational behavior (Michaelsen, Watson, Cragin, & Fink 1982). Subsequently, informative testing has been modified for a wide variety of business, humanities, physical science, and social science courses, including accounting, business policy, chemistry, communication, engineering finance, English, geography, and zoology as well as for classes of up to 225 students. Prominent features of informative testing process include (1) permanent and purposefully heterogeneous work groups; (2) reduced reliance on instructor input (i.e., lectures); and (3) grading based on a combination of individual performance, group performance, and peer evaluation. An additional feature of most courses is the frequent use of application-oriented classroom activities (e.g., cases in business policy and problems in accounting, engineering, and statistics).

The activity sequence followed in informative testing is (1) individual study, (2) individual exam,[1] (3) group exam (with immediate scoring of both individual and group exams), (4) preparation of "appeals," (5) corrective instructor input, and (6) application-oriented projects or activities (see Fig. 17.1).

Steps one, two and five, which are the same as in formative testing, furnish data that allow the instructor to monitor student progress as would be the case in mastery learning and ensure that students will have an adequate understanding of basic concepts before engaging in later application oriented activities.

Steps three and four, which involve group interaction, add a number of dimensions that may not be present in formative testing but are typical of one-to-one tutoring. For example, the discussions during the group exams routinely require students to reveal both how they answered each question and the rationale on which their answer was based. This aids learning in two ways. One is that students have access to individualized corrective instruction from their peers on an ongoing basis. The other is that the process of articulating the rationale for a particular answer by itself promotes learning (e.g., Slavin & Karweit, 1981).

Steps four and five provide corrective instruction in case the dominant view within the groups is in error. During the preparation of the appeals, students are highly motivated to reexamine the relevant sections of their assigned readings and also have the other members of their group as a resource. In fact, with an entire group of students scanning the material, it is a rare instance when they are unable to locate the needed reference material in just a minute or two. Thus by the time the instructor's input is called for in step five, the vast majority of basic questions have been answered and students have just aided each other in completing a review of the troublesome concepts. Thus this testing process is formative in the same sense as with mastery learning but, in addition, has a number of features that provide both students and the instructor with additional sources of information. As a result, we have chosen to call this process *informative* testing.

The high level of interpersonal interaction that naturally occurs during informative tests provides benefits that extend beyond the classroom. Students are highly motivated to complete out-of-class work so that they can contribute to their team. Friendships that develop naturally provide a strong incentive for regular class attendance and also provides a base of social support to students in coping with problems that arise in other courses and in dealing with the university bureaucracy. Working on the group projects and exams develops students' capacity for functioning as contributing members of project teams in the classroom and job settings.

OPERATIONAL PROCEDURES

As part of the introduction to a course in which the informative exams are used, students are assigned to groups and told that (1) the major vehicle for achieving familiarity with basic concepts is through completion of the homework assignments, (2) informative exams and subsequent application-oriented assignments will provide them with feedback on their understanding of the concepts and will help the instructor identify topics requiring clarification, and (3) exams will be given very early in the instruction process of each major topic area. (In instances in which good written material is available we give the informative tests before *any* coverage of the material in class. Thus we typically schedule the first test for the *beginning* of the second class meeting.)

On the days when the informative exams are given, we distribute test forms and answer sheets to groups in a manila folder and give the following instructions (Fig. 17.2):

1. Students should complete their individual tests (usually 15 to 20 in true-false and multiple-choice questions, short-answer essay questions, or problems that require 10 to 25 minutes to complete).
2. As soon as all members of a group complete their exams, a representative should turn in the individual answer sheets in a designated folder and pick up

	Time Schedule		
Activity	Determined by "5-5" Rule	5 Min.	As Needed
1. Work on individual exam	———— — — — —		
2. Work on group exam*	— — — ———— — —		
3. Turn in and score group exam and pick-up individual exams	— — — — ⊣		
4. Work on "appeals"**	— — — — — ⊣		
5. Turn in "appeals" and discuss Mini-test***			

——— Entire class working on same activity
— — Groups working on different activities

*May begin as soon as packet of individual answer sheets has been turned in
**Books and notes may be used in preparing appeals
***We refer to the informative exams as mini-tests or chapter quizzes

Figure 17.2. Informative testing activity sequence and time schedule.

a group answer sheet. Groups should then reach a consensus on the answer to each question. The time available for the individual *and* group exams will be determined by a "5-5" rule (i.e., when 5 out of 20 groups have completed their exams, the remaining groups have a maximum of 5 minutes to complete the exam). (We also use a "2-5," "3-5," and "4-5," rule, depending on the number of groups in the class.)

3. When the exam is completed, a representative should turn in the group answer sheet, score the exam, post the group score, and pick up the individual answer sheets for his or her group (which generally will have been scored).

4. As soon as the group exam has been turned in, group members are free to use their books and notes to prepare written appeals for any question they have answered incorrectly.[2] All appeals must be turned within 5 minutes after the group test period has ended.

5. The instructor will then list troublesome questions on the board and discuss the reasoning behind both the question and the answer.

Time Requirements. The time required for the entire informative exam process (i.e., test administration, scoring, feedback, and discussion) is approximately 45 to 50 minutes for a 15 to 20 question test. The 5-5 rule automatically adjusts the time available for variations in the length or difficulty of the test but nonetheless provides a substantial incentive for students to work quickly during the individual portion of the test process (to avoid using too much of their group's discussion time). In addition, intergroup competition inevitably develops to the point that some groups adopt the strategy of working quickly to place pressure on groups that have trouble reaching a consensus.

Individual Preparation. One reason for the success of the informative testing process is that it measurably stimulates student preparation before class. In fact, scores on the individual exams generally given *before* either instructor input or in-class peer tutoring[3] have averaged between 65% and 70%, which is only 10% to 15% below scores on similar questions in midterm and final exams in previous courses taught by the same instructors. One reason for the diligent individual preparation is that the level of each member's preparation is apparent to his or her peers and helps determine the quality of the group's performance. As a result, students' relationship with their group often becomes more important than grades in determining whether or not they complete the reading assignments. (In course evaluations nearly 40% of the students rank either feelings of responsibility for their group or expectations of their group as a main determinant of whether or not they studied the reading assignments.)

Feedback. Probably the most valuable aspect of the informative testing process is that it provides immediate feedback to both the students and the instructor. Most of the individual feedback comes from peers and occurs as the groups are working on the exams. Additional feedback is provided by (1) the initial scoring of the exam, (2) the focused restudy that occurs during the preparation of appeals, and (3) the subsequent focused corrective instruction by the instructor.

Peer Tutoring. Group scores on the informative tests consistently average between 90% and 95% in every discipline in which the process has been used. In addition, most group discussions clarify concepts to the point that the major barrier to a perfect score is the ambiguity of the questions not a lack of mastery of the concepts. Furthermore, group scores have been higher than the highest individual score in the group more than 95% of the time. This indicates even the best students are learning from their peers. The process through which this kind of peer tutoring occurs has been described by Bruffe (1978) as follows:

Students do not tend, as we might expect, to reinforce a single, perhaps incorrect interpretation of the problems presented. Instead they begin their discussion of each problem by trying to force their preconceptions upon each other. The result of this attempt, however, is that contradictory inferences emerge which the group cannot leave unresolved. Through the process of struggling toward a consensus in order to resolve the problem, the students first uncover the biases and limitations others bring to the judgmental task, only to discover, second and most importantly, the biases and limitations which they bring to it themselves. (p. 454)

OTHER POSITIVE RESULTS

Informative testing also has other benefits. One of the most important is that it can be used to facilitate the development of application, analysis, and synthesis skills (Bloom, 1956). In part, this is possible because the thorough and consistent individual study and the ongoing availability of peer tutoring reduce the amount of class time that must be devoted to coverage of basic material. In addition, the informative testing process generally develops groups to the point that group discussions are an extremely rich source of information, feedback, and intellectual stimulation (Fandt & White, 1985). As a result, groups readily and enthusiastically tackle application analysis and synthesis-oriented activities, projects, and exams at a level of competence exceeding that of the vast majority of the students working on their own.

The intensive interaction in the project teams also yields a variety of positive outcomes such as greater student involvement, interest, acceptance, trust, realism, academic rigor, division of labor, knowledge, and less stress and test anxiety (Shrader & Henderson, 1984). Additional benefits include reduced absenteeism, the development of friendships that provide social support and often lead to the spontaneous development of peer learning groups in subsequent courses, and the opportunity to gain experience working in groups—a bonus to students who will eventually find employment in settings in which group problem solving and project team skills are important to job success.

Concept Mastery. Probably the best evidence of the effectiveness of the informative exam process is that in virtually every course in which it has been used there has been improved performance on comprehensive exams, fewer withdrawals, fewer failing grades, *and* better performance in subsequent course work.[4] In addition, instructors using informative testing consistently report that a higher proportion of students are conversant with course terminology, active in class discussion, and able to complete application-oriented assignments. Also students are less likely to request individual help from the instructor in completing their assigned work.[5]

Data from the large (120-plus students) management classes in which informative tests were first used also provide evidence that the process is effective. Scores on identical true-false and multiple-choice minitests have been virtually the same in large undergraduate classes as in graduate classes of 20 to 35 students. Scores on a summative exam covering the same material as the informative tests have been impressive (82% average for individuals and 92% for groups).[6] In addition, students' evaluations of their progress on a number of learning objectives have been at or above the 19th percentile of courses rated using the IDEA course-evaluation instrument.[7] These objectives include mastery of the basic concepts on which the informative tests focused (i.e., learning fundamental principles, generalizations and theories) and higher-order conceptual skills (e.g, learning to apply course material to improve rational thinking, problem solving, and decision making).

Student Attitudes. Overall, students have been positive about the informative testing process. Students frequently comment in course evaluations that this was the first time they ever enjoyed taking exams. Some reasons cited for students' positive reactions to informative testing are (1) having an incentive to keep up with the class, (2) receiving immediate feedback on how well one is doing, (3) experiencing a sense of accomplishment from the group exam if one misses several questions on the individual test, (4) being rewarded for work outside of class (instead of being bored while the instructor goes over the same material), (5) learning that group discussions can be a reliable source of information, and (6) developing friendships with class members.

POTENTIAL DISADVANTAGES

One factor that should be considered before making a decision to use informative exams is the instructor's ability to handle questions on a wide range of topics (the focus of the instructor's input is determined by the results of the testing process) and cope with the student-instructor conflict that frequently results from giving immediate feedback on group exams.[8] Instructors who are comfortable with being confronted about their responses and able to channel students' emotional energy into further study are likely to be successful in using this method.

Another potential disadvantage of the informative testing process is necessity of preparing frequent examinations and providing immediate feedback. As with formative testing, exam preparation is a challenge because the tests are (1) more frequent, (2) given at the beginning rather than the end of major units of instruction, and (3) the primary means the instructor has for ensuring that students develop an understanding of foundational concepts.

Providing for immediate feedback is challenging in technical courses in which the exam requires problem solving (e.g., in statistics, engineering, and accounting).[9] With exams of this type it is necessary to prepare and duplicate solutions so that they can be distributed to each of the groups as they hand in their group exam.

Another consideration in deciding whether or not to use the informative exam process is whether or not a classroom is available in which project teams can (1) work as a group with a reasonable degree of comfort and (2) be readily identified. The ideal classroom is one in which team members can sit at a table or in appropriately arranged individual chairs. Less desirable, but workable nevertheless, is a tiered amphitheater-style classroom in which team members in adjacent rows can interact by temporarily standing or turning their chairs around. Once the groups have been assigned to a work area, an inexpensive yet effective means of identification is to mount numbered plastic cups on top of "flagpoles" (made from a dowel inserted in a hole in a wooden block) placed on the tables around which the teams work or suspended from the ceiling (in rooms with chairs having individual table arms).

A final consideration in deciding whether or not to use the informative testing process is the fact that generally it produces initial resistance from students and long-term resistance from fellow faculty members. Most student resistance stems one of two sources; one is the fear that they might have to carry less motivated or less able peers, the other is anxiety about having part of their grade determined by exams over material that has not been covered in class. However, these concerns are largely alleviated by involving students in determining the actual weights for each of the performance criteria employed in the grading system (Michaelsen, Cragin, & Watson, 1981). Beyond that, a few students (usually well below 5%) continue to have negative feelings about the informative testing process because (1) they want more input and direction from the instructor, (2) they feel that they are guinea pigs in an experiment, or (3) they feel that they are being coerced into preparing on a daily basis.

Fellow faculty members' resistance to the informative testing process also stems largely from a concern about grades. The problem arises because, student attitudes and performance being substantially improved, instructors tend to give fewer low grades. In traditional settings, this is often interpreted as sacrificing academic rigor in favor of increased popularity. A variety of strategies can help reduce the severity of the problem.

These include grading on a modified curve (see Michaelsen et al., 1981), documenting the effects of the process, and involving fellow faculty members in the evaluation process. Unfortunately, however, in many settings innovative instructors are continuously on trial, and the jury can be particularly hostile when instructors use groups and assign fewer low grades and when students appear to enjoy the process.

Summary and Conclusion

One great asset of the informative testing is that it can be used in a wide range of academic disciplines and class sizes. Another advantage is that everyone involved benefits from the process: Students receive personalized tutorial help and gain experience in a teaching role (a role many will perform in later employment) while increasing their own understanding of the material, instructors perform their teaching role more effectively, and administrators are pleased with the potential for increased efficiency. A final benefit of the informative testing is that it promotes the development of cohesive student work groups, which in turn reduce absenteeism, facilitate the formation of friendships, and offset many of the impersonal aspects of the instructional process.

In summary, instructors using informative testing become much less dispensers of information and much more managers of a learning process by using resources that are available in every classroom—the students themselves.

Notes

1. The grading system should be structured so that these exams count enough so that students will not be tempted to let the other guy do all the work. We generally use the "Grade Weight Setting" exercise (Michaelsen et al., 1981) through which students establish grading system in which the individual portion of the formative exam (which we refer to as a minitest) typically counts for a total of 10% to 15% and the group portion for 15% to 18% of the course grade.

2. We accept appeals from groups only, but if an appeal is granted, it counts for the group members' individual exams as well. (We recognize that students occasionally get a free ride on a group appeal but believe that is outweighted by the advantage of removing the possibility that our incentive system might place individual and group needs in direct conflict.)

3. Groups often meet voluntarily outside of class to prepare for upcoming minitests.

4. Comparisons from which these conclusions are derived are for the most part based on data from previous semesters with the same course and instructor. Two exceptions are controlled experiments conducted in 16 sections of an introductory zoology course (Jones, 1982) and in six sections of an introductory accounting course (Wilson, 1982).

5. Most students apparently get the individual help they need from their peers. In the few instances in which no one has the answer, the students often come in *as a group* to seek additional help.

6. The test has not counted toward the final grade and has been given immediately following a major group project; the scores probably reflected student knowledge *before* their review of course material in preparation for the final exam.

7. The norms for the percentile scores on the IDEA course-evaluation instrument are based on data from approximately 50,000 courses at 250 schools nationwide (Cashin & Perrin, 1978).

8. The magnitude of this potential problem is, however, greatly reduced by allowing groups to prepare written appeals. This process appears to help in three ways: first, students often discover that they (not the instructor) were wrong as they prepare their appeal; second, writing the appeal reduces the need to let off steam; and third, the appeals can be used to improve the questions themselves (see also Miner, 1978).

9. With multiple-choice exams in smaller classes (40 or fewer), we generally score the exams by preparing an overlay or by using a transparency with a series of brightly colored dots corresponding to the correct answers. With larger classes, we generally score the test on Datronics 550 portable marked-sense scoring machine. An equally acceptable solution is retaining the answer sheets to be scored on the computer and providing each group with a list of correct answers when they turn in their group exam.

References

Bloom, B. S. (1956). *Taxonomy of educational objectives: The classification of educational goals.* New York: McKay.

Bloom, B. S., (Ed.). (1971). Mastery learning. In J. H. Block (Ed.), *Mastery learning: Theory and practice* (pp. 47-63). New York: Holt, Rinehart & Winston.

Bloom, B. S. (1976). *Human characteristics and social learning.* New York: McGraw-Hill.

Bloom, B. S. (1984). The 2 sigma problem: The search for methods of group instruction as effective as one-to-one tutoring. *Educational Researcher, 13*(6), 4-16.

Bloom, B. S., Madous, Hastings, G. F., & Thomas, J. (1981). *Evaluation to improve learning.* New York: McGraw-Hill.

Brubacher, J. S., & Willis, R. (1976). *Higher education in transition.* New York: Harper & Row.

Bruffee, K. H. (1978). The Brooklyn plan: Attaining intellectual growth through peer-group tutoring. *Liberal Education, 64,* 447-486.

Cashin, W. E., & Perrin, B. M. (1978). *Description of IDEA Standard Form Data Base* (IDEA Technical Report No. 4). Manhattan, KS: Center for Faculty Education and Development.

Fandt, P. M., & White, M. A. (1985). Classroom team learning experiences: A study of results. In *Proceedings of the Southwest Division of the Academy of Management's 27th Annual Meeting* (pp. 191-194).

Jones, C. A. (1982). *Peer tutoring in project teams.* Unpublished doctoral dissertation, University of Oklahoma.

Johnson, D. W., & Johnson, R. T. (1983). The socialization and achievement crisis: Are cooperative learning experiences the solution? In L. Bickman (Ed.), *Applied social psychology annual, 4* (pp. 119-164). Beverly Hills, CA: Sage.

Keller, F. S. (1968). Good-bye teacher. . . . *Journal of Applied Behavioral Analysis, 1,* 78-89.

Kulick, J. A., Kulick, C. L. C., & Smith, B. B. (1976). Research on personalized system of instruction. *Programmed Learning and Educational Technology, 13,* 23-30.

McKeachie, W. J. (1978). *Teaching tips: A guidebook for the beginning college teacher* (7th ed.). Boston: Heath.

Michaelsen, L. K., Cragin, J. P., & Watson, W. E. (1981). Grading and anxiety: A strategy for coping. *Exchange: The Organizational Behavior Teaching Journal, 6,*(1), 8-14.

Michaelsen, L. K., Watson, W. E., Cragin, J. P., & Fink, L. D. (1982). Team learning: A potential solution to the problems of large classes. *Exchange: The Organizational Behavior Teaching Journal, 7,*(1), 13-22.

Miner, F. C., Jr. (1978). An alternative test return procedure. *Exchange: The Organizational Behavior Teaching Journal, 3*(1), 38-39.

Shrader, C. B., & Henderson, D. W. (1984). A strategy for using group examinations to teach OB principles. In *Proceedings of the Southwest Division of the Academy of Management's 26th Annual Meeting* (pp. 70-73).

Slavin, R. E., Karweit, N. L. (1981). Cognitive and affective outcomes of an intensive student team learning experience. *Journal of Experimental Education, 50*(1), 29-35.

Suggested Readings

Green, B. A. (1974). *Workshop on the personalized system of instruction ("PSI by PSI").* Washington, DC: Georgetown University, Center for Personalized Instruction.

Michaelsen, L. K. (1992). Team learning: A comprehensive approach for harnessing the power of small groups in higher education. In D. H. Wulff & J. D. Nyquist (Eds.), *To improve the academy* (pp. 107-122). Stillwater, OK: New Forums.

Michaelsen, L. K. (in press). Classroom organization and management: Making a case for the small-group option. In K. W. Pichard & R. M. Sawyer (Eds.), *Handbook of college teaching: Theory and applications.* Westport, CT: Greenwood.

Michaelsen, L. K., Fink, L. D., & Watson, W. E. (in press). Effective minitests: An efficient solution to covering content. *Journal of Management Education.*

Wilson, W. R. (1982). *The use of permanent learning groups in teaching introductory accounting.* Unpublished doctoral dissertation, University of Oklahoma.

Eighteen

Feuds in Student Groups
Coping With Whiners, Martyrs, Saboteurs, Bullies, and Deadbeats

DAVID S. JALAJAS
Clarkson University

ROBERT I. SUTTON
Stanford University

Freud (1921/1959) was right about human groups: They bring out the best and the worst of the species. At best, groups are superior to individuals because they can accomplish more work, are more creative, have more information, and offer more pleasure through the process of task accomplishment. At worst, groups waste time insidiously, accomplish little work, and create an arena in which interpersonal conflict can rage.

We focus here on conflict within student groups. Group projects are used frequently in the organizational behavior classes that we teach in Stanford's department of industrial engineering and engineering management. To illustrate, student groups in our undergraduate organizational behavior class write a case description of a local company. Other groups in a master's-level class (organizational transitions) recently studied the use of blame and secrecy in bankrupt Silicon Valley firms. Our (sometimes unpleasant) experiences with such groups have forced us to learn about conflict development in student groups and to devise strategies for handling such feuds.

This chapter originally appeared in *The Organizational Behavior Teaching Review*, Volume 9, Issue 4.

A trio of structural aspects set the stage for feuds in student groups: interdependence, reward systems, and the mix of educational backgrounds and demographic characteristics among students. The enhanced interdependence of group tasks (compared with individual tasks) creates a setting in which conflict can take place. Students working on a group project often have diverse and opposing ideas about the best way to approach the assignment. As Pfeffer and Salancik (1978) write, "Interdependence is the reason why nothing comes out quite the way one wants it to" (p. 40) The strain of such interdependence is evident when students are conducting field research. One member may be responsible for obtaining contacts with say, a business, whereas another may be responsible for obtaining interviews with members of that business. The pressure of interdependence is also evident when students must contribute to the production of a single essay. The performance of one student may have little bearing on the grade he or she receives if others do not have sufficient skill or involvement. Individual students sometimes complain, "I would have done better by myself than I did with this group."

The reward system instituted by the teacher can also lead to conflict among students. Students work hard to discover how grades are allocated, and they are keenly perceptive about how the cookies are divided. Students focus their efforts elsewhere when they learn that group performance has little influence on their grade. Furthermore, members of a group may vary in how much they believe group work is rewarded. Such perceptions can lead (initially) to inequitable effort and (later) to feuding. A student of dubious initiative, or one who has more pressing concerns in other classes, may not carry out his or her responsibilities to the group. The group's grade may suffer, or feelings of inequity may arise.

Finally, we have found that the composition of a student team can generate conflict among members. A group composed of males and females and students of various ethnic, religious, and academic backgrounds may use such diversity to its advantage. To illustrate, imagine that a group composed of a sociology major, an engineering major, and an English major is writing a case study about a high-technology firm. A superior case could be written if the sociology major contributes special knowledge about the organization's structure, the engineer helps the other members understand the software program produced by the firm, and the English major carefully edits the final report.

Unfortunately, groups composed of members with diverse backgrounds can feud so much that it interferes with performance. In one of our classes, a group included a female master's student in engineering, a male undergraduate in engineering, and two female liberal arts majors. They fought constantly. After the group's paper had been turned in, the male engineering undergraduate tried to convince Sutton to allow him to repair the "errors" made by the master's student. He complained, "She thinks she can push me around just because she's a graduate student."

Whiners, Martyrs, Saboteurs, Bullies, and Deadbeats

Interdependence creates an arena in which students with different perspectives and a common assignment may fight. The reward system employed by the instructor may enhance the conflict if cooperative effort is not sufficiently rewarded. Students with diverse backgrounds may also feud because of differences in worldview and language. Nevertheless, as teachers, we rarely hear about such structural factors from feuding students. Rather, we hear complaints about troublesome individuals.

We have noticed that such troublesome characters fall into distinguishable categories. We have identified five types of students that are associated with conflict in student groups. We are not attributing fault to these people, but we have observed that conflict tends to be more common in groups that don't manage them well. The characters we have identified are The Whiner, The Martyr, The Saboteur, The Bully, and The Deadbeat. After describing the attributes of each of these characters, we will suggest methods for managing them.

THE WHINER

The group project is one hassle after another for The Whiner. The Whiner feels that the group meets on the most inconvenient day and time, the paper is turning out to be too long, and nobody else is contributing as much to the project. The Whiner can't see how the project will be any good or be done on time. Our experience suggests that this person was snake bitten during prior group projects and is resigned to the inevitable failure and antiintellectualism of group endeavors. The focus of the group may become diverted from the project to mollifying The Whiner. Such activity can often lead to an inordinate weighting of The Whiner's input at the expense of more valuable, but less vociferous, contributions by others in the group. Moreover, the unnecessary anxiety of approaching a group meeting containing The Whiner can be unpleasant, lead to fewer meetings than might be necessary, and hamper the effectiveness in meetings that are held.

THE MARTYR

The Martyr is certain that he or she is getting the worst assignment, the worst chores to perform, and has the dumbest partners for group members.

The Martyr may complain to other group members or to the instructor about the burden. Yet, in contrast to The Whiner, The Martyr doesn't seem to want anything to change; he or she just wants others to feel guilty. The Martyr tells the other group members, "It's okay, go skiing, I don't mind doing the paper."

One martyr who Sutton spoke with said that she had done 75% of the work on a group paper. The student didn't want any change in her grade or the grade of other group members; she just wanted Sutton to appreciate her burden. The Martyr can create conflict in a variety of ways, members may tire of the constant complaining or they may spend too much time trying to appease The Martyr. In one of our groups, the members simply scheduled meetings without The Martyr.

THE SABOTEUR

In contrast to The Martyr and The Whiner, The Saboteur takes an active role in the disruption of the group. Such disruption is often unintentional; the student may only be trying to enhance the quality of the group's work. The Saboteur's trademark is that these "enhancements" are implemented without the knowledge of the other group members. Unfortunately for the group, the altered work may be of lower quality than the original. In one of our classes, for example, a student had the task of typing the group's report. All group members had agreed that no other work was needed on the manuscript. The typist turned Saboteur: he changed the manuscript drastically and these "improvements" damaged the quality of the paper. A nasty fight took place between The Saboteur and the other group members after the changes had been discovered. A second feud broke out after the paper received a poor grade.

THE BULLY

This character also takes an active role in the disruption of the group, but unlike The Saboteur, The Bully isn't shy about letting the group know how things should be done. The Bully's special talent is making others in the group feel inadequate or dumb. This problem is accentuated if The Bully is either brighter or better prepared than the others in the group. If the superior ability of The Bully is clear to the other members, they may be unwilling to contribute anything to the project. Alternately, a backlash may develop within the group; other members may choose to ignore The Bully or argue with everything The Bully says. In an extreme case we encountered two members of a group ganged up on the remaining two members. The two Bullies withheld critical project-related material and excluded the outcasts from their secret meetings. Phone calls by the two victims were not returned and appointments were ignored. The Bullies thought they could do better work without the victims and only included the outcasts in the final stages of the project.

A variation on The Bully is the The Lazy Bully. The Lazy Bully plays no active role in the group until some critical decision must be made. At this juncture, The Lazy Bully tries to force his or her will on the other members of the group. This character is disruptive because coworkers resent The Lazy Bully's newfound interest in the group task. Concerns are expressed such as, "Where were you during the last five meetings?" The potential for backlash against The Lazy Bully is more pronounced here than for The Bully. The Lazy Bully lacks even the pretense of having contributed to the group.

THE DEADBEAT

The Whiner, The Martyr, The Saboteur, and The Bully each take actions that disrupt the group. The Deadbeat doesn't necessarily disrupt anything. Yet The Deadbeat can evoke feuds when other group members refuse to carry an unproductive member. Members may decide that something must be done about The Deadbeat and spend an inordinate amount of time deciding how to cope with their idle coworker They may even spend time fighting with The Deadbeat. During the beginning weeks of one class, we had a group that could not locate a member. We told the group members to do their work without him. The missing member approached Jalajas on the day the first project was due and said that he didn't know a group project had been assigned. This identified him as a Deadbeat. The group was plagued by The Deadbeat throughout the term. The group found themselves rescheduling meetings in an attempt to accommodate him and bad feelings among the group members arose.

Coping With Troublesome Characters

The Whiner, Martyr, Saboteur, Bully, and Deadbeat were described above as if they were fully developed personality types. Under the right set of circumstances, however, the majority of the students in our classes would probably behave in ways that would be typical of one or more of these troublesome characters. Thus, in our opinion, we should do all we can to create conditions that discourage the emergence of these troublesome characters and minimize the extent to which they have a negative impact on their groups when they do appear.

Some of the most helpful ideas for minimizing the negative impact of feuds in student groups that we have identified to date are summarized in

TABLE 18.1
Coping Strategies for Conflicts in Student Groups

Strategy	Available to Teachers	Available to Students
Preventive	1. Develop an appropriate reward system	1. Make the division of responsibilities clear
	2. Address the issue of teacher- versus student-assigned groups	2. Don't blindly accept problems
	3. Remind students of the three truths	3. Don't take responsibility for the happiness of others
Corrective	1. Discuss the problem with group members	1. Reopen discussions about responsibilities
		2. Confront the troublesome character
		3. Reduce contact with the character
		4. Don't let The Saboteur be responsible for editing or typing papers
		5. Do all editing and typing together

Table 18.1. These include both preventive and corrective strategies and alternatives that are available to students as well as instructors.

PREVENTIVE STRATEGIES AVAILABLE TO TEACHERS

The preventive strategies available to teachers that are listed in Table 18.1 can help instructors reduce the potential for feuds. First, teachers can structure the rewards for group assignments so that students are more likely to cooperate with each other and to work hard. The emergence of Martyrs and Deadbeats will be discouraged if all students believe that the group assignment has a strong influence on the final grade. Thus teachers should ensure that each group assignment constitutes a significant portion of the final grade. We recommend, for example, that group papers constitute at least 20% of the course grade.

One hazard of group projects is that no single person is responsible for the completion of the task; each member may expect the others to carry the load. The rewards allocated for group projects can be used to stem diffusion of responsibility among group members. We have found that a useful method for reducing conflict is to build in some sort of accountability for individual students. This minimizes the possibility that students who wish to coast through the project have the opportunity to do so. A professor in our department addresses this problem by requiring that members of a group indicate on the first page of the paper the percentage of effort contributed by each member to the final project.

Teachers should also be aware that the composition of the student groups may also be a potential source of conflict. As we mentioned earlier, groups that are composed of diverse members are more likely to feud. Yet a dilemma arises; although heterogeneous groups are more susceptible to conflict, the complementary skills of their members are likely to lead to high performance. Our experience suggests that if students form their own groups, then homogeneity is often so high that it interferes with perform-ance. We have noticed, for example, that in classes where students are asked to form groups, students whose first language is not English will tend to form groups with those of a similar nationality. They appear to seek the comfort, security, and convenience of others who speak the same language. This is a common problem in Stanford's Engineering School. In one case, we observed a group of Japanese nationals who formed their own group and seemed to enjoy the experience. Unfortunately, when members of this group interviewed outsiders (who only spoke English), the language barrier prevented them from writing a high-quality report. Although con-flict in such groups may be lower, performance may also be lower when a group lacks members with key skills.

Although the case of the Japanese nationals is an extreme example, we have encountered similar problems in other homogeneous groups such as those composed of students who are all members of the same fraternity. As a result, despite the potential for greater conflict, we usually place students in heterogeneous groups that we have designed. Typically, we seek to assemble groups that are composed of both men and women, and that have members who are majoring in a variety of subjects. We suggest, however, that heterogeneous groups only be used if steps are taken to manage the enhanced conflict. One strategy that we use allows for a longer "storming stage" in the development of such groups (Tuckman, 1965). We give student groups at least two assignments. The first is a simple exercise that accounts for only 5% of the course grade. We warn students, however, that they will work with the same groups on a subsequent assignment that constitutes 30% of the course grade. We suggest that students use the initial assignment to develop norms and a role structure so that they can reach Tuckman's "performing stage" by the time that they must write the major paper.

The final strategy sets the stage for preventive strategies available to students. We contend that teachers should take an active role in making a few truths known to their students. In other words, teachers can give students a few tips about actions that can be taken to stem the emergence of troublesome characters. Some of these insights may seem obvious, but our experience reveals that the obvious may evaporate in the heat of the semester.

PREVENTIVE STRATEGIES AVAILABLE TO STUDENTS

We remind students of three truths at the outset of each group assignment (see Table 18.1). Our first suggestion is to remind students to make the division of responsibilities explicit. Students should decide in advance who will type the final draft, which areas of the project will be covered by whom and who will drive to off-campus sites. They should also decide when and where meetings will be held, who will be responsible for editing drafts and how much latitude each member should have in making changes. Clear distribution of responsibility will give The Whiner less to whine about and provide The Martyr with less cause to claim martyrdom. Furthermore, if the distribution of tasks is done with skill, The Saboteur may have less reason (or less opportunity) for altering the work of others and The Bully may have a few less topics to be a bully about. Research has shown that commitments that are made in public (the group, in this case) are more difficult to revoke (Salancik & Pfeffer, 1978). Hence, after stating their responsibilities, members of the group will be more likely to comply with their assignments and members who don't perform as promised (e.g., Deadbeats) can be easily identified.

A second suggestion is to encourage students not to accept blindly the problems that they find in their groups. If a student doesn't approve of a decision or a procedure proposed by another in the group, that person has an obligation to say so. Such encouragement may reduce the disruptive opportunities available to The Whiner and The Martyr. Although this gives The Whiner license to complain, the complaints are often more constructive and incite thought rather than rattle nerves. Also, when The Bully is a problem, the other members are encouraged not to let him or her run roughshod over them. In addition, we encourage students to get further advice about their problem if conflicts escalate beyond the point they can be handled within the group.

Our third suggestion is to explain to the students that, individually, they are not responsible for the happiness of the other members of their group They are responsible for behaving ethically and for treating other group members with respect, but the purpose of the group is not to develop lifelong friendships. We have found that members of groups often form social groups that last beyond the due date of the group project. This is great. Yet, when a group is experiencing high levels of conflict, the desire not to hurt feelings only compounds the pressure already on the group from their project-related problems. We have encountered many cases in which students have told us that they have not suggested alternatives to the ideas presented in group discussions for fear of stepping on another group member's toes.

We suspect that The Bully, The Saboteur, and The Deadbeat are aware of the norms for peaceful coexistence and are able to play off of these norms to their benefit. The Whiner and The Martyr, on the other hand, are able to avoid confrontations with other students by evoking feelings of sympathy or pity. Members of groups with these troublesome characters, however, must not be shy about asking them to contribute their fair share of effort.

CORRECTIVE STRATEGIES AVAILABLE TO INSTRUCTORS

When a feud has already occurred, the teacher may be able to help the students repair the problem. A modest level of conflict within a group is desirable because it prevents the dangerous unanimity of opinion associated with groupthink (Janis, 1982). The heightened emotions also may inspire members to develop better ideas. Concern by the teacher, however, is justified when conflict within a group has become upsetting to some members. One reliable indicator of destructive conflict is when a student approaches a teacher about a feud in his or her group. At this stage a teacher has the option of using two problem-solving styles. The first style is an advisory role; the teacher acts more like a counselor than a boss. The suggestions a teacher may provide in this situation are listed in Table 18.1 under the heading "Corrective Strategies Available to Students." The second style is a more authoritarian stance. There are, however, many dilemmas associated with the use of authority in the classroom (Berg, 1984). We suggest that the instructor behave this way in only the most extreme cases of discord.

The corrective technique we have found most useful in reducing the negative impact of conflict within groups is meeting with the entire group and helping members to clarify the problem. We generally encourage students to solve problems of conflict among themselves. Occasionally, however, we have also had private talks with the disruptive member of the group. Such a conversation typically helps to clarify the cause of the conflict and makes it clear to the student that he or she needs to reevaluate the seriousness of the problem.

CORRECTIVE STRATEGIES AVAILABLE TO STUDENTS

Once the projects have begun, students are in a far better position than the instructor to correct problems that arise, and they should be aware of the strategies they can use to cope with troublesome characters (see Table 18.1). One of the most promising ways to handle The Whiner or The Martyr is to reopen discussions about the responsibilities of group members. Another, and somewhat stronger, approach is for distraught group members to confront the offending member with their concerns. If these measures prove to be inadequate, students can attenuate The Bully's influence by reducing the amount of contact with that person. For example, one of our groups was having a problem with a Bully during its meetings. The other group members discovered that The Bully worked a part-time job on campus and surreptitiously constructed The Bully's schedule. The group then scheduled meetings at the times when The Bully was working. We should emphasize, however, that this technique should only be used when all other attempts at reasoning with The Bully have failed, because it generally results in hard feelings and doesn't really solve the problem.

In dealing with a Saboteur, making responsibilities of group members clear and confronting The Saboteur as early as possible, usually solves the problem. In addition, students can reduce opportunities for sabotage by structuring responsibilities so that this character has less opportunity to change the work of others. One obvious example is to not let a Saboteur be responsible for editing or typing group papers. Another solution is for the group to do all the editing and typing together.

Conclusions

Structural characteristics of student projects often give rise to the emergence of five troublesome characters: Whiners, Martyrs, Saboteurs, Bullies, and Deadbeats. These people can cause conflict and endanger the effectiveness of student work groups. Although extreme conflict is destructive, the groupthink literature suggests that moderate conflict is a characteristic of high-performing groups. We maintain that we can and should design our projects so that enough conflict will emerge to push our students to make the most of their collective talents. In addition, we should take steps to ensure that the conflict does not escalate to the point that it destroys students' learning opportunities. As a result, we have suggested a number of measures that are effective in preventing or controlling the troublesome characters that could otherwise compromise the value of student project teams.

References

Berg, D. N. (1984). Authority and experiential methods. *The Organizational Behavior Teaching Review, 9,* 36-41.

Freud, S. (1959) *Group psychology and the analysis of the ego.* New York: Norton. (Original work published 1921)

Janis, I. L. (1982). *Groupthink.* Boston: Houghton Mifflin.

Pfeffer, J., & Salancik, G. R. (1978). *The external control of organizations.* New York: Harper & Row.

Salancik, G. R., & Pfeffer, J. (1978). A social information processing approach to job attitudes and task design. *Administrative Science Quarterly, 23,* 224-253.
Tuckman, B. W. (1965). Development sequence in small groups. *Psychological Bulletin, 63,* 384-399.

Suggested Reading

Lott, A. J., & Lott, B. E. (1965). Group cohesiveness as interpersonal attraction: A review of relationships with antecedent and consequent variables. *Psychological Bulletin, 63,* 259-309.

Participative Course Management

FRANCINE S. HALL
University of New Hampshire

When General Foods initiated participative management at its Topeka, Kansas Pet Food plant, it focused on changing the roles of employees as well as the culture of the organization. In time it became clear, however, that participative management dramatically altered the roles of both employees and managers, not to mention support functions. Employees had to learn to work in new, often collaborative ways, taking on responsibilities that previously had been within the purview of their managers and/or support staff. Managers in turn had to learn to delegate and relinquish many of their previous responsibilities. They also had to learn to lead through coaching, counseling, and developing others.

Participative management in the classroom is but one organizational application of what began as the *industrial democracy* movement, evolved through the empowerment movement, and is today heralded as part of total quality management. Yes, classrooms are organizations. Those of us who assume the facilitator role have the unique opportunity to reconfigure our classroom structures just as our corporate counterparts might reconfigure their organizations. As I write this, I am struck with how clear the parallel is. We are leaders—our classroom is a learning organization. Yet how seldom does each of us stop and think of himself or herself in that way. Most of us continue to view ourselves as teachers, and to define that role in terms of fairly traditional models of instructor-student relations, classroom conduct, and course design.

Come! Venture out of the traditional classroom as organization. Forget for a moment the role of instructor as authority figure. Put aside the emphasis on the transmittal of facts and information. Think of student participation as going beyond merely responding to instructors' questions. It also involves students providing inputs and making decisions that directly affect course design and management. This section of the book offers an opportunity to encounter new teacher-student relationships, and to discover models for redefining both participation and power relations in the classroom.

Creating Conditions for Success

There are many reasons for choosing participative management as a model for accomplishing one's learning-teaching objectives. Let us consider some of these reasons.

WHY TRY PARTICIPATION?

When I recently broke my class into groups and assigned each group a different type of organization design to research, analyze, illustrate, and report on to the class as a whole, my motive was to get each person involved with the concept of structure. As I listened to the reports, however, I was dramatically taken by the rich mixture of ideas. I was especially taken by the examples that each group contributed. I thought back to my notes on the advantages of group decision making versus individual decision making—the group usually outperforms even the best individual on a complex task. It is not clear that the teacher is necessarily the "best," but as I listened to my student groups' presentations, I felt that they had outperformed me that day through the rich and diverse illustrations that they had brought to our discussion of a difficult topic. Thus I would argue that one reason for using participative management is that it enhances problem solving in learning and brings a broader, richer mix of resources into the lecture-discussion learning experience.

A second reason for a participative approach is that students tend to own the learning that they have helped to create. By this I mean that they take it more seriously. They develop a commitment to becoming more skilled or knowledgeable. Participation also generally contributes to higher learning and performance standards, a possible third reason for adopting a participative management model. I have found that undergraduate students and executives are two groups that are concerned with looking good before their peers. Peer evaluations are important to them, whether formal or informal. I have never seen a bad final group presentation in a class. Some may be better than others, but no group has ever come into class unprepared or even poorly prepared on a task for which they will be seen in comparison with others and evaluated by fellow peers.

The foregoing reasons suggest that through participation students enhance the teaching environment for us as instructors. I firmly believe that this is true. There are, however, clear benefits for the students as well. Let us consider these.

One of the most beneficial aspects of participation is that process (how the class is run) becomes a content in itself, apart from whatever subject matter is taught. In a human resources course, for example, a colleague and I divided the class into several task forces, each of which corresponded to a human resourse management (HRM) subfunction: training and development, professional development, and career development. We then assigned tasks: lining up HRM professionals as speakers, assisting with facilitating experiential exercises, setting up liaisons with professional organizations, and so on. These activities provided professional human resources experience and helped students work on skills that they would need later. All of this, of course, was in addition to the core content of the course. It was also experience that the students could not obtain from a textbook. As the example above illustrates, the secondary content that the participation process provides is often a process content through which one learns methodology, skills, and judgment. It is the application of learning by doing.

ANTICIPATING ISSUES

A core issue in participative management is power. This holds whether we are in the corporate or classroom realm. Authority is the right to influence. Power is the capacity to do so. As our students develop, their power increases. To educate a person is, in effect, to empower that person. We do so not at the expense of our power, but as a result of it. As many authors have noted, by sharing power we can *increase* it. We have the opportunity to increase a student's individual power base through increasing his or her skills, knowledge, capacity to be assertive, and ability to create. We also have the unique opportunity to increase the power of the group through the synergy that is generated by facilitating interaction among the members of the class.

In many industries, empowerment may be questioned or constrained. For those of us in the learning industry, empowerment is the *essence* of our role. Our goal is not to bind our students to us but rather to enable them to become independent and to teach themselves. Although sharing power has its demands as well as its consequences, the real issue for me is not whether I should teach participatively. I cannot function in a learning environment any other way. The real issue for me is discovering under what conditions and how I can best accomplish this.

In the remainder of this introduction I shall discuss some of the generic issues that need to be addressed to ensure the success of any participative approach. The articles that follow this introduction provide specific examples and techniques for participative ways of handling classroom issues.

DELEGATION ISSUES

Participative management in the classroom requires that the teacher share decision making as well as control over the means of carrying out the learning process. This can apply to what is learned as well as to the methods for evaluating learning outcomes. In so doing we create accountability. It is, therefore, the educational equivalent of delegation.

Delegation requires several conditions. People need to know what is expected—what the assigned task or duties entail. We need to ensure there is ample opportunity for communication and feedback. Students need an opportunity to participate in planning the event, activity, or task not just in carrying it out. Finally, we need to ensure that the support, facilities, and access to equipment, supplies, and people are sufficient for students to complete their work successfully.

Caveat: Expect to spend at least as much and probably more preparation time when delegating to students, and anticipate that the time you spend will be primarily in the role of a coach or counselor.

TIMING, EXPECTATIONS, AND READINESS

Just as one would not delegate to an inexperienced subordinate, we need to be careful about when (in the sequence of learning) participation is introduced, and to what extent it is used. My experience is that students who have a conceptual foundation will be most comfortable entering into a shared authority situation. Novices not only lack the knowledge base from which to run a class but also bring expectations about what the teacher will or will not do. The two different situations in which my participative style flopped were with freshmen and a group of executives that included several military leaders. Both groups came into the classroom expecting me to function as an authority figure, to present an established learning content, and to deliver it as the gospel. The autonomy and inclusion in decision making that I set up were interpreted by the freshmen as lack of preparation. The executives considered me flaky. In comparison, juniors and especially seniors come to my office to tell me how much they enjoy the chance to become involved. Both examples point out the need for *fit*. The use of participative techniques will only be effective if they fit the abilities and developmental stage of the group.

Caveat: Assess the readiness of the group. Are the members ready to assume a participative role? Try to provide a stretching experience but watch out for loading on any more than one person or group can handle alone.

CLASSROOM VALUES AND CULTURE

Our knowledge of when group decision making works invariably leads us back to the culture of the organization. Is it competitive? Is it collaborative? We as teachers have a unique opportunity. We can shape and manage the culture of each class with whom we work. In effect we develop a new organization and a new culture. We know that a collaborative culture or climate facilitates group participation. How do we establish this?

My experience leads me to several conclusions and, hence, suggestions. The first is to be open and honest. This does not mean relegating one's position, authority, or power. It means, simply, to be honest about (1) not being perfect (this giving students the permission to make mistakes and learn from them), (2) sharing values and biases (thus inviting students to be up front about who they are and what they believe), and (3) one's own humanness and learning (thus creating a we-are-all-in-this-together climate).

A second suggestion is to discuss values around learning and education. I, for one, really have never liked multiple-choice exams. I also don't like having grades drive the course. I talk about these personal feelings and elicit students' own feelings.

A third suggestion involves feedback. My research in industry, my knowledge of management and organizational behavior, and my personal teaching experiences have all led me to the conclusion that the effective use of feedback is one of the most powerful tools we have for motivating students.

Participative management allows us to use feedback in a variety of ways—from us to our students, from students to students, from students to us. The effective use of feedback can contribute more to the development of a collaborative culture than any other single variable. To have both positive and constructive feedback, people must have trust. They must also share a common value-based goal: Enhancing the development of each individual is the purpose of the course.

Illustrative Articles

The articles that follow introduce us to specific participative approaches in the classroom. They also offer concrete techniques and advice, while illustrating one or more issues that arise when we manage participation.

Mike McCaskey (Chapter 19) reminds us of the timing and modeling issues. Feedback as participative input from students needs to occur at several points in a course. What we receive at the end, as in any performance appraisal, should summarize what has been communicated in an ongoing manner. To accomplish ongoing feedback in the classroom, the teacher needs to model two-way communication and to cultivate a culture of openness.

Nick Maddox (Chapter 20) reinforces the need to examine the culture and values that we cultivate through our methods of developing evaluation procedures. Maddox both argues for and demonstrates how to involve students in generating exams. A key point that he makes is that the ideals we often espouse (e.g., the importance of experiential and collaborative learning) and those that guide classroom behavior (autocratic, teacher-generated evaluation procedures) are often incongruous. The Maddox article is particularly useful in that it contains a healthy and helpful dose of how-to.

Kenneth Murrell (Chapter 21) provides an example of delegating the traditional instructor responsibility of student performance evaluation. In his system, work groups learn to develop their own system for evaluating student performance. In the process, not only do they develop group skills but they also learn about giving feedback and performance appraisal. Murrell points out that the success of this participative management approach depends, among other things, on factors such as clear guidelines and prior expectations. All of these reinforce the need for each of us to recognize and assume our roles as leaders-managers in the classroom.

Overarching Themes: A Conclusion

The role of the teacher-trainer is evolving. The evolution parallels the evolution of the role of the manager. We are all, in the end, leaders whose task it is to influence both the development and the performance of others.

There was a time when only performance was considered important and even that was measured in narrow and rigid ways. Today, the shift is increasingly toward active learning and the development of process skills that parallel the assimilation of content. *The Wall Street Journal* (1992) recognized this when it announced in an article on active learning that "classes follow a difficult rule: student as worker, teacher as coach." In passive learning, students submit to authority. In active learning, the student is in the process of becoming an authority.

The participation of students, like factory workers, is only as effective as the management style of the leader. Leaders we know are most effective when they provide both personal support and task accomplishment guidance. It is, I like to think, an analogy to effective parenting: give them "tough love." We need to care, we need to communicate, and we need to clarify what is expected on both sides.

Many years ago, Argyris (1957) told us that we need to address the incongruence between the needs of healthy individuals and the demands of formal organizations. Argyris outlined the conditions that led to personal development, maturity, and the full utilization of the individual. He suggested that there was a "new" behavioral science field that we might call organizational behavior and that it could help us to better bring a healthy union of the individual and the organization.

Today, years later, we are still addressing that union and how to create those healthy conditions of empowerment. The factory floor appears to be far ahead of the college classroom or the corporate training session. The reason, I think, is that all too many of us have assumed and defined the role of instructor and teacher as authority figure. I would challenge all of us to reconsider, and to assume our role as a leader—open listener, coach, counselor, facilitator, and developer—and to consider the application of participative practice where appropriate.

References

Argyris, C. (1957). *Personality and organization.* New York: Harper.
The Wall Street Journal. (1992, September 11). Active learning: Special report on education. Section B, p. 1.

Suggested Readings

Beck, J., & Cox, C. (Eds.). (1980). *Advances in management education.* New York: Wiley. See especially chap. 3.
Block, P. (1991). *The Empowered manager.* San Francisco: Jossey-Bass. Places empowerment in the context of older hierarchical forms of management and addresses the issues involved in implementing changes in management style.
Brookfield, S. D. (1986). *Understanding and facilitating adult learning.* San Francisco: Jossey-Bass.
Cross, K. P. (1981). *Adults as learners: Increasing participation and facilitating learning.* San Francisco: Jossey-Bass.
Hall, F. (in press). Management education by design. *Journal of Management Education.* Presents a model that looks at the roles of teacher and student in terms of participation and power across five types of learning outcomes.
Hoberman, S., & Mailick, S. (1992). *Experiential management education: From learning to practice.* New York: Quorum. Contains useful chapters on experiential learning and addresses the issue of applying learning to practice.

Locke, R. R. (1989). *Management and higher education since 1940.* Cambridge, UK: Cambridge University Press. Examines the influence of the United States and Japan on West Germany, the United Kingdom, and France; excellent history of the development of business schools and paradigms for teaching management.
Rogers, C. R. (1969). *Freedom to learn.* Columbus, OH: Merrill.
Simmons, J., & Mares, W. (1983). *Working together.* New York: Knopf. Focuses on the need for work redesign, particularly changes that enable worker participation; the appendices provide excellent summaries of key experiments in industrial work redesign.

Nineteen

Collecting Feedback
Throughout the Course

MICHAEL B. McCASKEY
The Chicago Bears

Even those teachers who highly value feedback often wait until the end of the term to ask for student evaluation. But by that time, students' memories of the early readings, of the teacher's initial style, and of class activities are hazy or have been revised. More important, although feedback at the end of a course may help the instructor improve for next semester, it does little to help the course in process. In my past teaching experience, I began asking for and giving feedback after every major part of my course (which was about every 3 weeks). This early and frequent feedback exchange proved to be quite useful.

Feedback could be two-way because the students are eager to hear the instructor's opinion of how well they are doing. So before I passed out the questionnaire, I would offer my own oral feedback to the students for 5 to 10 minutes. I would share what I thought they were doing well, where they needed to improve and how I saw the process of the class. Sometimes I would add my feelings about working with them to that point in the course. (Although I should have known better, I was still pleasantly surprised at the value students placed on knowing my personal feelings.) My straightforward commenting on the class's work and atmosphere cleared the air, modeled giving feedback, and increased the probability that students would be candid on their feedback sheets.

This chapter originally appeared in *Exchange: The Organizational Behavior Teaching Journal,* Volume 2, Issue 3.

The way I led into handing out the feedback sheets went something like this:

> I am genuinely interested in your feelings and thoughts on how well the course is going. It is still early, and there is time to correct or make adjustments in the process of the class. I want both positive and negative feedback, since I think both are very valuable. Be specific, talk about areas that a person or the class can do something about. The feedback should be intended to be helpful.

In phrasing my request this way I tried to ask for help—for myself and for the class—without sounding as if I were turning over control of the class to the students.

The feedback sheets contain both open-ended and scaled questions. The latter asks about specific readings and cases, and the open-ended questions gather information on teaching style and the process of the class.

The other way I made feedback two-way is this: After I received their feedback sheets I would not stop with just examining them privately but would summarize their responses and feed them back at the next class session. Although many of their answers contained suggestions that an instructor could immediately implement, other comments needed to be discussed. For example, one time early in the course, several students mentioned that although they appreciated my supportive listening behavior, they wished that I would be more direct and critical with students who rambled on, argued fallaciously, or otherwise wasted class time. Not only did I use those comments to change my behavior but in the report-back session in class I pointed out that it was each person's responsibility to enforce class norms and standards, so *all* of us should work on being candidly critical of other's comments.

Discussion of the feedback can be an occasion to clear up misunderstandings. The teacher can also use this occasion to coach the student on how to give feedback. One semester someone complained that I played favorites when calling on people. I was surprised and checked it out with the total class. The general view supported my perception that I didn't call on favorites because my normal rule is to call on members who haven't yet had a chance to speak. Giving the students feedback on their feedback has the added advantage of improving their skills in giving feedback to the instructor, which should, in turn, increase their effectiveness in counseling subordinates when they are managers.

In examining the numerical ratings from the scaled questions, one has to be aware that positive or negative ratings can mean many things other than that the course is good or bad. Is a low rating due to poor teaching, poor placement or sequencing of material, or inadequate introduction of new content? Or suppose one class rates lecturing on conceptual material highly. This may indicate that not enough time has been spent so far on theory and on research findings, because the course has focused too extensively on the details of the cases. To determine the answer, the instructor must use class observations and other information to supplement the numerical ratings.

Students fill out the feedback sheets at home, and because returning them is voluntary and anonymous, the response rate varies. When I specifically indicate how important it is for me, more than 75% of the class will respond. (Otherwise, about 50% of the students hand them in.) One time, however, the response rate dropped to 36%. Wondering whether those not responding might be more negatively disposed toward the course, I asked a second and third time for the sheets. I received 16 more sheets, which brought the response rate up to 77%, and the ratings of the overall effectiveness were significantly *higher* in the second wave than in the first! So the instructor should expect the response rate to fluctuate over the term and should be leery of any simple interpretation of the number of students who do or do not return the questionnaire.

Although ongoing feedback does not substitute for adequate planning and other components of good teaching, exchanging reactions after every major part of the course takes the temperature of the class all the way through the term. Through this kind of feedback, observation of the way people behave in class, and discussions with students outside of class, an instructor should be able to read the students' responses to the course quite accurately. By being able to identify what materials students find most useful, when they feel threatened, whether some are angry with others in the classroom, and how many are dissatisfied or pleased with the direction of the class, the teacher can modify the course as it develops to provide a better learning environment for the students.

Twenty

The Use of Student-Generated Examinations
Guidelines, Benefits, and Cautions

E. NICK MADDOX
Stetson University

Introduction

Composing examinations is not my forte. This laborious task is surpassed in tedium only by grading these same exams. Conversations with other experientially oriented educators suggest to me that this is not an uncommon sentiment. In fact, many of us would like to eliminate examinations.

I have long been troubled by the negativity that testing breeds in the relationship between faculty and students. Furthermore, as an experiential educator, I have been concerned with the incongruency between experiential learning ideals and autocratic evaluation processes we often practice. In an effort to deal with these concerns, I embarked on an experiment to test the viability of student-generated exams as a testing evaluation option.

Student-generated exams are exams built from the questions that students submit for possible inclusion on a midterm or final. Although I edit and compose the final product, students are given the responsibility of building the question pool from which the exam will be drawn. In testing this method in various management and organizational behavior courses, I am satisfied that the method has reliability as an evaluative tool. Performance on student-generated exams follows a normal distribution with class

This chapter originally appeared in *The Organizational Behavior Teaching Review*, Volume 14, Issue 2.

means ranging from 70 to 84. The overall mean for the method ($N = 21$ classes) has been 74.9 with a standard deviation of 7.80. These scores compare favorably with my students' previous exam scores when using a variety of other exam methods. However, the positive behavioral and learning consequences of student-generated exams outweighs any score inflation that occurs as a result of student input.

This article provides specific guidelines for the use of student-generated exams, while specifying the benefits of the method from my experiences with and student discussions of the process. Several cautions are offered on the use of student-generated exams, although these problems can be prevented by an instructor's careful preparation of exams.

Background and Rationale for Use

As a practitioner of experiential learning, I have been troubled by students' negative attitudes toward testing. Such negativity inhibits the development of a learning community and can curtail students' active class involvement.

Traditional testing methods create distance between students and instructors. We, as educators, become the autocratic bosses who sit in judgment of students, while simultaneously attempting to build a collaborative classroom climate. This contradiction is not lost on students, and it can undermine their trust in us and in our methods. In addition, students tend to attribute their testing failures or setbacks to us, thus increasing distance in the classroom.

I began to seek student input on examinations in 1985 as a way to reduce testing pathologies. One rationale for this decision was that students could actively contribute to their own testing experience. This, to some extent, allows them to experience ownership in their learning and evaluation. Involvement and ownership seem to increase acceptance of outcomes and results in the testing process.

A second rationale for this experiment was my disdain for test banks and the poorly engineered, trivial questions that graduate students write for undergraduate consumption. In most cases, test banks are unsuitable resources for evaluation. This view is confirmed by many student complaints regarding exams that I have drawn from test banks.

A third rationale for the use of student-generated exams relates to time. In upper-division management courses where contribution grades, assignments, case analyses, team exercises, and research reports are mainstays of evaluation, time is of the essence. I have no graduate students at my disposal to prepare or grade exams. Thus I am always seeking legitimate ways to maximize the time I can devote to the learning rather than the evaluation aspects of teaching. As I share responsibility for testing with my students, I have more time to develop experientially significant dimensions of learning. This trade-off seems worthwhile and has led to a method that may be useful for others.

Guidelines for Use
of Student-Generated Exams

When I began this method, students submitted only multiple-choice questions for potential inclusion on exams. From those questions, I constructed an exam of the most relevant and appropriate questions based on the learning objectives and materials covered in a given learning unit.

Recently, I have changed this format so that students submit multiple-choice and short-answer essay questions. This approach promotes a more balanced assessment of student content knowledge and communication and problem-solving abilities as portrayed in their essay responses.

The following guidelines have evolved as my experience with the method has increased:

1. Other than specifying that exams will include short-answer essays and multiple-choice questions, the testing decision belongs to the students. Early in the semester, we discuss evaluation in a dialoguing exercise. Herein, I explain my perspective on testing and outline the method of student-generated exams. Students then share their views on testing and vote on whether they or I will write exam questions. Of the 21 classes in which I have used the method, only 1 has voted against it. After receiving their grades on the midterm, students can vote to have me write the final. All classes, to date, have voted to write their own finals.

2. To ensure continuity within the pool of questions, I provide a protocol for question composition and submission. It includes the following guidelines:

   a. All questions are submitted on 3 × 5 index cards with questions on one side of the card and the student's name on the back. Students write one question per card. This permits me to review questions quickly and my secretary to transcribe them more easily to the exam. An alternative to having students use the card system is to require that students submit their questions on a disk from a computer that is compatible with that of the instructor. This has proven to quicken question selection, editing, and transcribing.

   b. All multiple-choice questions must contain five alternatives. No "all of the above," "none of the above," or combination of response alternatives are accepted. I also discourage "which of" and "all the following except" questions. This increases the rigor of the questions that are allowed. Students identify their correct responses with an asterisk.

c. I tell students that I reserve the right to substitute or edit alternative responses within a good question when a ludicrous, illogical, or obviously irrelevant option is given. However, I will leave a humorous response in the question if the other alternatives are sound. This guideline encourages students to write better alternatives to reduce the amount of editing I contribute to an exam.

d. I counsel students against using straight definitional or rote memory questions dealing with names, dates, or obscure information. Students are informed that their questions are evaluated on their ability to use analysis and problem solving as critical activities within a question. This focuses their thinking and learning on the most salient information from content and process learnings.

e. For both a midterm and final, each student submits three to four sets of questions for review. In this case, a set is made up of 5 to 9 multiple-choice questions and 4 short-answer essays that each student writes covering materials in the learning unit. I establish the size of a set by class size and amount of information covered in a unit. Typically, I collect these questions every other week to encourage students to keep up with their work and gradually to build my pool of potential exam questions. In a class of 20 students when I ask for four sets of questions with 5 multiple-choice and 4 short-answer essay questions per set, 320 short-answer essays and 400 multiple-choice questions would be submitted for review for any given exam.

f. Students are asked to include questions drawn from cases, exercises, and class discussions as well as from texts and readings. Through class discussions and guidance as well as through topical scheduling in the class, I indicate to the students those concepts that are pivotal and peripheral to our study of course materials. This provides them with an informal context within which to write questions.

3. Because question quality varies with the aggregate pool of questions reviewed for exam inclusion, I reserve the right to allocate unequal weighting for the short-answer essay and multiple-choice components of an exam. For instance, if I receive a very poor pool of multiple-choice questions, I can weight the test so that short-answer essays account for more total points. This encourages students to write good questions in both areas.

4. I originally graded each student's question sets on a 5-point scale; 5 indicated excellent questions and 1 indicated a failure on the assignment. This grade became one-fourth of the participation grade of the student, along with attendance, quality of input, and exercise/assignment grades. More recently, I have changed to a 10-point scale to increase the variance in my ratings, although the weighting of question sets remains the same within the participation

grade. This provides tangible incentive for students to spend time and energy writing good questions.

5. After receiving a full pool of questions, I review the questions and pull those that are, in my opinion, acceptable for inclusion. I then resequence correct alternative placement so that each exam will have an equal number of a, b, c, d, e answers. The cards are then randomly shuffled and submitted for word processing. Both practices are consistent with standard test-building procedures.

6. An alternative method of question generation is to use student teams for the generation of question sets. Often this is done with the semester teams that students form for other assignments and projects. In a class of six teams, I require that each team submit approximately 15 questions per week on the various materials covered over the preceding week. I also request peer evaluations of contribution from each member of the team.

These guidelines are straightforward and easy to use. Students quickly adapt to the method and, over several testing periods, become good question writers who surpass the efforts of most test bank authors.

Benefits of this Method

As part of class dialoguing exercises, students and I have discussed the process and benefits of student-generated exams. In addition to freeing me from complete responsibility for exam preparation, the following benefits have been noted:

- Students perceive a shift of power in classes in which student-generated exams are used. Rather than "me testing them," an "us testing us" mentality evolves. This reduces hierarchical distance, especially on evaluation issues.

- A pedagogical benefit is that I never use the same exam twice in a class. Each exam has its own character and scope. This means that I stay fresh in examination preparation and that students are not tempted to go looking for old tests to use as guides for last-minute study marathons.

- In terms of experiential learning and class development, the *emergent* networking that takes place helps students get to know one another better and more quickly, while also encouraging them to deal with a complex information problem—how to get everyone's questions to all members of the class. Networking, in this case, relates to the ways in which the class goes about developing a system to accomplish this information exchange on a timely basis in advance of an exam. Although I do not tell them how to network, I do endorse the measure as a way to improve class cohesiveness and exam performance. Classes rapidly develop their own methods of networking. On occasion, classes develop norms such that everyone will submit a photocopy of their questions on the day question sets are due. Other classes have appointed one member of their work groups, to liaison with other groups so that copies of everyone's questions are circulated among groups. Regardless of the method, in classes in which aggregate exam performance has been above average, networking has become a central norm to the class. Networking also tends to downplay zealous competitiveness between students. It is a win-win situation because as everyone pulls together, everyone can benefit.

- The method indirectly allows the class to identify its marginal members and apply influence to motivate these individuals toward consistent contributions. It only takes about one episode of not living up to the class norm regarding question circulation to raise the corrective ire of assertive leaders within a class.

- The method allows students to identify the scope and parameters of their studying. With a full pool of questions, they can focus their time on familiarizing themselves with concepts in the multiple-choice items and scripting potential responses to the short-answer essays. This is a learning experience unto itself because students have no idea which questions I will choose from the pool to include on the exam. Because there is clarity of focus for the exam, frequently heard refrains of, "What should I be studying?" or "What do you want me to know?" disappear.

- Since initiating this method, I have not received a single complaint about an exam. Students have come to see and appreciate their responsibility in the learning environment. I have, on occasion, received complaints about the work entailed in writing questions for submission. When this occurs I remind the students of the class vote on the issue and open the democratic process of decision for the next exam. As noted, my classes have always rejected that option.

- Using student-generated exams helps to reduce biases I have that might affect how I compose or select questions from other sources. However, some bias remains in that I select questions that are "good and appropriate."

- Students believe that cheating becomes ludicrous because, with effective networking, they can have all potential questions available to them before an exam. They indicate that it makes more sense periodically to review the questions than to develop cheating formats when 600 to 700 questions could be used on an exam.

- Students report they adopt an incremental approach to studying because they have to keep up with both text and class information to write good questions. Rather than wait until the last minute to study, students learn incrementally before an exam. This reduces the anxiety they feel before and during an exam and may partly account for the slightly better than average performance I have noted with this method. Not surprisingly, students who do poorest on the exams tend to be the ones who try to cram for them.

- Students report that my grading their questions as part of the participation grade is appropriate and motivating. Writing good questions can increase students' contribution outcome whether they are very active or reticent about class input.

- Finally, I have noticed an entirely different attitude toward testing. Students are looser, more jocular, and more confident now than when I was the sole writer of the questions.

Overall, these benefits are consistent with and reinforce the development of a positive learning climate. If an instructor used the basic guidelines outlined herein, he or she would likely experience the same benefit.

Cautions About the Method

Ironically, my primary caution relates to the amount of time it takes to compose a good exam; it can be considerable when a lot of information is covered in a learning unit. The best way to deal with this is to have the students write questions more frequently and then to stay abreast of question review and selection before pulling the exam together.

The single bad experience I have had involved my waiting until the last minute to compose the exam and throwing together a sloppy one. That class received the highest aggregate mean score of all classes and roundly critiqued me for my sloppiness at our next dialoguing session. Waiting until the last minute can be a painful experience, especially because as many as 1000 questions can be written for an exam by a large class.

A second caution relates to using the method in large classes. It is my opinion that this is not sound practice in classes in which there are more than 35 students. The work load of managing the process exceeds the benefits that might ordinarily accrue in a smaller class.

A third consideration to be mindful of is that students must receive direct and specific feedback about their questions to improve their question-writing abilities. However, this cannot occur until after an exam because, as my students point out, advance notification of question grades cues them to study the questions of those who get the good grades. I handle this potential problem by making question set grades available to individual students on their requests after each exam.

Fourth, be prepared to accept some ribbing from more traditional colleagues who think that having students write exams is a sidestepping of duty. The consternation that others may express, directly or circuitously, is irrelevant compared with the multiple benefits that accrue from use of the method.

Finally, if examinations are the sole dimension of evaluation within a class, one should probably avoid using self-generated student exams for obvious reasons. The method works best in a balanced evaluative system in which exams are equally weighted with such things as group projects, participation, group development progress, and other criteria of performance.

Conclusion

This article has provided information and guidance on the successful use of student-generated examinations. From many years of experience with the method, I believe that it can be a credible and accurate way to measure one dimension of student performance while enhancing the overall learning climate within a classroom. The method is enthusiastically endorsed by students and may have value to educators who wish to involve students more directly in learning and evaluation.

Twenty-One

Peer Performance Evaluation
When Peers Do It,
They Do It Better

KENNETH L. MURRELL
University of West Florida

After struggling for several years to develop an effective peer evaluation format for management and organizational behavior classes, I finally gave up. I've tried simple systems of rank orderings. I've tried complicated procedures of behavioral anchored ratings and multiple and weighted criteria. The simple systems too often became "buddy" ratings, whereas the complicated systems became overwhelming as well as time-consuming.

In giving up the search for a perfect peer evaluation system, I went back to my organization development training, focused on the key issues, and asked myself who should be developing this system. As often happens in my teaching, a blinding glimpse of the obvious became apparent, and I realized I am very possibly getting in the way of the process. I've discovered that for peer evaluation-performance appraisal systems to be effective and generate results, they must be developed by those using them. In the case of teaching management and organizations, what better assignment is there than for the students to develop and write their own evaluation and appraisal systems?

Developing a Peer Evaluation System

Each semester, instead of using a ready-made form or format for peer evaluations, I require the student work groups to develop their own, based

This chapter originally appeared in *The Organizational Behavior Teaching Review,* Volume 9, Issue 4.

on what they have read about such systems and their own knowledge of the criteria for successful work in their own groups. My guiding framework for the peer evaluation begins with my stating, very clearly, that no peer evaluation system will be used until it has been approved by me. I tell the groups that it must meet the standard requirements of any system. It must be fair in evaluating more than one or two attributes of a person, it must be based on observable behaviors as much as possible, and it must be based on relevant competencies that can be shown to have an impact on the performance of the group.

I also explain that across-the-board high ratings will not be allowed and that I expect a range of ratings for the group, although I haven't found it necessary to place quotas or use forced choice ratings. My statement to the student groups is that their evaluation systems must stand up to professional scrutiny. If their forms and ratings are not professional, I will either request they redo the forms, or I will simply not credit any of the peer evaluation points available.

I have found that when I remove myself from the peer evaluation process students consistently develop a useful and acceptable evaluation system. This method serves a twofold purpose: it gives students a sense of what evaluation is all about and instills a feeling of responsibility for the system and it gives them the freedom to evaluate their peers more objectively.

1. Before developing a peer evaluation system, a *psychological contracting* phase is needed to acquaint students with the idea of group expectations and responsibilities associated with task groups.
2. Time must be devoted to developing a group and its working skills before the group can be expected to develop an effective evaluation system. Task responsibilities are necessary before a group is really aware of its capabilities. Sharing work responsibilities helps build effective teams far more quickly than any amount of talk or discussion.
3. Groups must be given some clear guidelines about what acceptable and unacceptable systems of evaluation look like but must be left with the responsibility of developing their personalized system as long as it meets professional standards and review. They are instructed that the library contains great numbers of books on performance evaluation, and that they should refer to their own management textbooks from previous classes.

Since I made the decision to have the groups develop their own peer evaluation instruments and procedures, about 90% of their systems have been both practically and conceptually sound. In addition, it has been my impression that the student-developed systems are better than any of my own at generating scores that reflect real variances in members' competencies and efforts. In at least one case, and my colleagues report similar experiences, a student on the border line between a C and a C– has had his or her grade reduced to a C– because of peer evaluation. This is very serious for our degree-seeking management majors. A C– grade in our management courses requires the student to retake the course. We have also experienced an increase in a grade when a student's contribution to his or her work group was clearly recognized by group members and rewarded.

My experience with the student-produced systems has also led to the conclusion that the peer evaluations should occur at least twice during the semester. One reason is that this simply increases the amount of feedback that students receive. Another is that poor performers have the opportunity to work on their deficiencies.

When Things Don't Work Out

The peer evaluation process generally allows students to surface and resolve conflicts and build effective problem-solving groups. Occasionally, however, as in ongoing organizations, the peer evaluations uncover problems that appear to be irresolvable. Typically, this occurs when a group member either refuses to work effectively or blocks group growth processes. In a few instances, however, the basis for the problem is that one member feels that he or she has been assigned to an unacceptable group.

In an attempt to deal with these kinds of difficult situations, we have developed a process for legally terminating a group member. This process can be initiated at any point in the semester by either a group or an individual. The termination process is also explained as a normal work issue and, if initiated, must follow prescribed guidelines parallel to those that would be in effect in most work organizations. These include documentation of both the problem and my direct involvement as a representative of management.

The Termination Process

The termination process involves three steps, each of which must be documented in writing. First, I require the group to meet at least twice in an attempt to clarify and resolve the problem on their own. Second, I meet with the group and explain the options available to the member should a termination occur. (Typically the options are either working alone or becoming a member of a group consisting of others wanting to leave their group—either way they are required to complete the same tasks as they would if they retained their group membership.) Finally, I require the group to meet and come to a consensus about the potential termination.

In most cases, this process assists the groups in solving the problem before a termination occurs. In those instances for which an individual is perceived as an offender, feedback from the process provides both the incentives and the information needed to correct his or her behavior. As a result, offenders typically respond by increasing their efforts or attempting to eliminate their disruptive actions. In those instances in which the group is at fault, the potential loss of a valuable resource is often sufficiently sobering to increase other members' commitment to the learning process.

When a member leaves a group, I make a special effort to help both the individual and the group learn as much as possible from the experience. For the individual, this typically involves coming to understand more about how he or she is perceived by others. For the groups this often involves an examination of other courses of action that it might have taken, which often brings it to the realization that firing someone may not be either the easiest or the most productive way to resolve conflict within a group.

Conclusion

The test of these design features in teaching is the learning and awareness that occurs within the students. In developing and using these procedures over several years, I have come to appreciate how well students can develop and use performance evaluations. In addition, the use of the peer evaluations and the availability of the termination process move the students from theory to practice, because they are required to take the same kind of responsibility for their actions that they will encounter in the workplace.

Teaching About Diversity Within a Diverse Learner Environment

PETER FROST
University of British Columbia

JOSEPH E. GARCIA
Western Washington University

STELLA NKOMO
University of North Carolina, Charlotte

JUDITH WHITE
Loyola Marymount University

Walls

Man is
a great wall builder
The Berlin Wall
The Wailing Wall of Jerusalem
But the wall
most impregnable
Has a moat
flowing with fright
around his heart

A wall without windows
for the spirit to breeze through

A wall
without a door
for love to walk in.

*(Used by permission
of Osward Mtshali
and Ad. Donker
[Pty] Ltd.)*

AUTHOR'S NOTE: Peter Frost is grateful to Ella Bell for her contributions to the lists of suggested readings and films.

Many of us teach about diversity. Many of us teach within a very diverse student environment. And many of us try to do both simultaneously. Of course, critical to our ability to teach effectively within a diverse classroom is our understanding of fundamental issues in managing diversity. This section will begin to examine important issues surrounding both teaching about diversity and teaching to a classroom of diverse learners.

When Charles Vance initially asked me (Peter Frost) to write an introduction to this section, I thanked him for the invitation, agreed to do so and filed the material away, to be examined and commented on closer to the deadline. On a plane to Chicago to attend a board retreat of the Organizational Behavior Teaching Society in September 1992, I opened my file. I thought about my task and the topic I was introducing. And as I read the three very fine articles by Joan Gallos Ella Bell, and Kate Kirkham, I was struck by the irony that here I was, a white male, being asked to pronounce on these pieces, in this topic area. Of course, I was honored to be asked to do so. Being a white male does not disqualify me from sharing my views on race and diversity. However, it makes for a very incomplete set of opening comments on this important challenge to management educators. On reflection, I thought it would be more meaningful to invite some other voices to the table. Charles Vance agreed. I invited Joe Garcia, Stella Nkomo, and Judith White each to share with me and with the reader their respective perspectives on the important current issues pertaining to diversity. I asked them also to identify some important ways we educators might teach about such issues. Their voices follow mine.

Peter Frost

I will speak briefly to one factor in managing learner diversity, namely, consciousness of the teacher on issues of diversity. It is a factor alluded to by all of us in this introduction. I think that the more educators have an understanding of themselves as members of a gender, an ethnic group, an age group, and so on, the better they can communicate knowledge about diversity. Part of this self-understanding about diversity for the teacher comes from scholarship (writing and research). It also comes from awareness about diversity that is available when we teach the topic in ways that leave us open to reflection on our experiences in and around the classroom. Fundamentally, however, I believe that self-knowledge relevant to issues of race and gender (and other dimensions of diversity) comes from the insights and understandings about oneself that are generated by immersion in some way into situations that are substantively different from one's own.

In my own case, I think I am potentially a better teacher on some matters of diversity because of a sense I have of my racial and ethnic identity, of what it means to be a white South African by having lived for several years away from South Africa then returning to live briefly in that country. I also gained clearer, although inevitably incomplete appreciation of how members of other ethnic groups perceived and experienced living in South Africa. In a similar way, I learned more about myself as a member of a Western country as well as learning something about people from Asia, by becoming immersed for brief periods of time in Asian countries such as China, where I was a member of a virtually invisible minority. This may enhance my competence as a teacher on dimensions of diversity that are important to Asian students.

It is the experience, the return to home base and the reflection on the experience that I believe opens the possibility for change in the way teachers can understand themselves and others from whom they differ. Of course, it is not necessary for one to engage in such extensive travels to gain an immersion experience relevant to diversity. Especially in large metropolitan areas, one can seek information nearby about the major local differences of ethnicity or gender or other aspects of diversity. However, the cultural programming that we have which conditions us to see the world in particular ways is so powerful that the change experience often requires some intensity and duration, even at times a radical change in geography, if this new understanding is to take effect. A parallel implication for us to think about is that diversity may need to be taught by teams of educators from different backgrounds if the voices that need to be heard are to be truly represented.

Joe Garcia

As teachers of organizational behavior, we face myriad challenges as we try to incorporate issues of diversity into the fabric of business education. These range from structural concerns about the nature of the field and its attraction of diverse aspiring scholars to the academy, to the development of an atmosphere where work on diversity is viewed as legitimate and not some new (perhaps reworked) social issue fad, to an understanding of what diversity is and where it should be placed in the curriculum. My purpose here is to suggest that serious attention to diversity requires a fundamental shift in our values about organizations and the people in them and to offer some recommendations about how we should be approaching the teaching of diversity.

Working with diversity requires a shift away from valuing a uniformity and consistency that reflects the worldview of those in control to a new frame of reference in which variety, flexibility and a client-driven orientation take precedence. This shift is necessary if we, in our teaching, are to move away from a context in which oppression and exclusion resulting from the top down, do-it-my-way, approach to management is allowed to exist. Why shift? First, it is consistent with the democratic principles we espouse. Second, in today's marketplace we see diversity being touted as a competitive advantage (Cox & Blake, 1991).

Translating this shift into teaching diversity requires us to rethink the curriculum with the objective of teaching our students to become effective people and organizational citizens in a world where variety and change are preeminent. How then should we proceed? I believe we ought to begin by first unfreezing existing attitudes about differences and focusing on changing student attitude orientations toward appreciating the differences that people bring to organizations. As part of this effort, I anticipate that a great deal of self-awareness will result because one needs to know oneself to recognize and appreciate difference. As a correlate, I propose that part of this learning include encounters with authentic information from and about people who are different from our students in significant ways.

Although these elements are critical, it is not enough just to value and understand differences. A caring, knowledgeable coworker who is inept is just not helpful. Ultimately, teaching about diversity must be about teaching students how to become more skilled at working with people who are different. Applying our knowledge from managerial skills education to diversity has great potential in this regard.

In sum, teaching about diversity requires a new frame of reference about organizational life, the incorporation of an appreciative attitude about differences, and the ultimate development of behavioral skills in working with people who are different. The bad news is that this is a tall order, and tackling the issue requires effort and risk taking on our part. The good news is that the technologies of organizational change, personal development, and managerial skills education are all at our disposal. Let us now apply our creative energy to furthering diversity in management education.

Stella Nkomo

There are several critical issues in the management of diversity:

HOW SHOULD DIVERSITY BE DEFINED?

What categories of difference should be addressed? Does diversity refer to all differences among people? Are all differences created equal? That is should difference owing to race, gender, class, or age be equated with difference in to education, life-style, physical attractiveness, or sexual orientation? A related issue is whether the very use of the term *diversity* obscures the essential task of dealing with the core issues of racism, sexism, and classism in organizations. There is a real danger in seeing diversity as benign variation among people. Ultimately, addressing the core issues means examining conflict, power, and domination in organizations.

RECOGNIZING THE COMPLEXITY OF IDENTITY

As we do diversity work, we are learning that people have very complex, multiple identities. So a major issue is how do we incorporate the complexity of identity into our research and practice. Our current categories are often confusing and exclusionary. For example, we tend to use terms like *women and minorities* (where do African-American women or Puerto Rican women fit?) or *Asian-Americans* (this omits the finer distinctions of Korean, Japanese, Filipina, etc.). A related point is the fact that many whites are not aware of their racial identity. Race is often viewed as something that nonwhite people have. Identity is multidimensional, but it often changes and can be affected by social, cultural, and political dynamics. It is also very much a relational concept.

SEEING DIFFERENCE NOT AS DEVIANCE

Another dilemma in diversity management is learning that difference doesn't mean deviance and that equality doesn't mean sameness. The challenge is overcoming the stereotypes we all hold about certain groups. Paradoxically, some of the training materials I have seen on diversity, instead of dispelling stereotypes and biases, actually perpetuate them. When we say Asians communicate this way or women have these kinds of skills, we often fuel preconceived notions. Diversity efforts can also wind up as an effort to fix those who are different.

SPILLOVER CONTRADICTIONS

The valuing diversity initiatives in organizations are taking place during a time when there appears to be growing polarization between races and ethnic groups and less tolerance for difference not only in the United States but around the world. This raises the following question: How do we achieve in the workplace what we have been unable to achieve in the larger society?

WHAT WORKS?

The impetus for managing diversity came out of a reaction to the Workforce 2000 report indicating that the workplace of the future will be much more racially and gender diverse than ever before. Because organizations have for so long ignored difference, we don't know what to change or how to change organizations. Our research base is woefully thin about the effects of difference in organizations or how to create an organization that values diversity. There are lots of unanswered questions: What types of interventions are best at the interpersonal level? What types are most effective at the group and organizational levels? We argue that valuing diversity will lead to more effective and efficient organizations. However, what does valuing diversity do for individuals? for traditionally excluded groups? Is there a relationship between ideological and structural understandings of power and domination and individual, psychological understandings of power in organizations? That is, does personal awareness of the issue transfer to structural changes in organizational systems?

These issues have many implications for management education on diversity. The first issue is what kinds of curriculum changes are needed. I would argue strongly against an approach that creates a course called "management of diversity" and then requires students to take this class as their only diversity education. This one-shot approach cannot effectively deal with the complex and emotional nature of the topic. Students need a safe place to do this kind of work. Also a one-shot approach can result in marginalization of the topic. Difference could be viewed as something outside of the mainstream of what organizations are really about. Ideally, all courses in the curriculum should be designed to reinforce learnings about diversity.

The second issue is the content of courses. How do we effectively address the many dimensions of diversity and at the same time help students understand their common threads? A core part of education should be to help students develop the leadership skills to take advantage of diverse talents. We have to help students confront their own identity issues and levels of awareness. Race and gender are particularly volatile components of diversity. The challenge for whites and white males is getting them to deal with the issue without fear and guilt. This is critical given the spillover effects mentioned above (e.g., whites and blacks come together in the workplace but largely live separately.)

Finally, are most faculty ready to teach about diversity? The interesting thing about diversity work is that we must confront our own identity and attitudes about difference if we're going to be effective educators. Both faculty and students will have to have a safe place to do the work.

Judith White

The mind creates the abyss, the heart crosses it.

To be without anxiety about imperfection.

These two sayings from Eastern thought capture what could be considered at the core of issues surrounding our work with diversity: moving from cognition and separation to heart and connection and accepting the nondualistic nature of human behavior. Behavior and attitudes based on fears, limited information, selective perception, and unconscious expressions of negative feelings all contribute to stereotyping and prejudices. As social animals we prefer security over instability and to be right rather than wrong. In an attempt cognitively to understand the world, the mind constructs generalizations, differentiating the self from others by labeling individuals and groups into categories. Thus the mind, through language, impacts one's attitudes and behaviors toward others. In this effort to individuate, people make judgments about what is similar and different, good and bad. The mind and its ideas are fickle; they can readily change with new information and experiences.

Although sense experience and emotions also are transitory, our hearts and bodies do not lie. One can see in the faces and bodies of others their grief, sadness, anger, joy, or excitement. Humans have the tremendous capacity to feel emotions, and feelings such as grief, hatred, love, caring, and compassion toward others are universal and commonly experienced. Fear, as one of the strongest and most prevalent feelings that people share, more often separates individuals and groups from one another rather than generates understanding and caring. The mind creates the belief that the differences among us are greater than the commonalities, resulting in the need to expend effort to learn about, understand, and appreciate the diversity among individuals and groups.

Embracing diversity with the integration of mind and emotion requires an acceptance of the myriad forms of human experience and behavior within oneself and others, and not only the ideal but also the real. Most important, individuals need to learn to tolerate ambiguity and uncertainty and approach others not solely with assumptions of total homogeneity but in a generous and sincere mode of inquiry about differences as well as similarities. One needs to examine one's assumptions concerning others, and with genuine enthusiasm inquire into the depths of individual differences along with the enhancing cultural, ethnic, racial, and gender-based group influences.

Learning and teaching about diversity can focus on two areas: awareness and understanding of self and awareness and understanding of others. In each area the work is multifaceted, investigating micro- and macrolevels of phenomena and developing perceptual, symbolic, behavioral, and affective complexity. The process of valuing, of attending to something or someone, is a model that Kolb has developed that corresponds to his four-stage model of experiential learning. Students, through new sensory and emotional experiences, reading, exposure to information and ideas, and reflective activities of writing and dialogue with others, heighten their awareness and understanding of themselves and others. To value diversity and differences requires focusing effort and attention on the variations, beginning with appreciation of one's own strengths and weaknesses and feeling a fullness or security within oneself. With an acceptance of the multiple aspects of human nature within oneself, including the light and dark sides, a person can feel comfortable enough to be generous and accepting of others, in their great many variations of human form.

If students can truly acknowledge their own aggression, hatred, or poor judgment and all that results from it, they will find greater acceptance and compassion for others. By going into the community and studying a racial, ethnic, religious, or gender group different from their own, students take in more sense experiences and discuss and reflect on new aspects of others. Through these discovery and reflective processes, students examine their hidden fears of others and see these fears as a signal of their need for security and certainty. They experience and reflect on the effort required to learn about others through an inquiry rather than an exclusively advocacy mode of relationship. For example, in learning about Latinos, a student may inquire about differences between people from Mexico, El Salvador, Argentina, and Peru, perhaps acquiring new information and understanding of social and economic class, the history of immigration, or social and military conflict in Latin America.

Through analysis and synthesis, students develop new generalizations and conceptualizations of the similarities and differences that they have seen and discussed. Following from the earlier example, students can develop a deeper understanding and respect for the hardships suffered by Latino immigrants after talking with a professionally educated, energetic, middle-aged, and unemployed Latina who is living on public assistance in central Los Angeles because of the high levels of unemployment and increased discrimination problems influenced by the economic recession.

This cycle of valuing, involving, sensing, feeling, reflecting, engaging in dialogue, synthesis and analysis, generalization, testing beliefs, and ultimately and most important, new action encourages the development of new or deeper values as one cognitively and affectively attends to and focuses on what is important. Valuing diversity requires right intention, effort, and caring so as to be compassionate in one's actions toward others.

Peter Frost

With this foundation on teaching issues involving diversity, we now proceed to the articles in this section. In her article, Joan Gallos alerts us to an overlooked aspect of diversity: developmental differences. She refers here to people's readiness to notice, understand, and deal with diversity based on where they are in their cognitive development. It is a hierarchical model that presumes greater understanding of and competence in matters such as diversity the further an individual is along the path of cognitive and ethical development. Gallos argues strongly that as educators, we must take into account the considerable limits to effectiveness that arise in the use of teaching techniques when the level of development of students is taken into account.

In her article, Ella Bell defines diversity as "a multicultural workplace where men and women from different racial and ethnic backgrounds have equal participation, respect and an opportunity to achieve in organizations." She points out the volatility of racism and the pervasiveness of sexism throughout the ages. Bell discusses the importance of teaching race and ethnicity to future managers given the pervasiveness of organizations and their microcosmic representation of society, and concludes with a presentation of ideas for overcoming these roadblocks.

Joan Gallos gave us an awareness of the interaction between intellectual factors of individuals and the effectiveness of diversity education. Ella Bell mapped some of the terrain of race and gender. Kate Kirkham, in her article, draws our attention to the way emotions are triggered when the topic of diversity is taught. Kirkham argues very cogently that recognizing the existence of often considerably intense emotional undercurrents around discussions of race and gender, and working to chart them as they unfold, significantly increases the likelihood that the educator can learn when and how to surface them. She suggests that bigoted or chauvinistic individuals in a group may not respond emotionally to discussions of gender or race, because they are so entrenched in their positions that they are unable to personalize and therefore feel the impact of the discussion and the critiques that take place. Kirkham ends her paper with a discussion of several classroom interventions designed to help surface the legitimacy of issues and the emotions that they trigger.

Following the suggested readings is a list of films, movies, and television series that discuss stereotypes, intergroup relations, within group relations, and the historic context of such issues. Marx, Jick, and Frost (1990) discuss some of these films as well as others.

References

Cox, T. H., & Blake, S. (1991). Managing cultural diversity: implications for organizational competitiveness. *Academy of Management Executive, 5*(3), 45-56.

Marx, R., Jick, T., & Frost, P. (1990). *Management live: The videobook.* Englewood Cliffs, NJ: Prentice-Hall.

Suggested Readings

Anson, R. S. (1987). *Best intentions: The education and killing of Edmund Perry*. New York: Random House. (Autobiographical)

Baldwin, J. (1963). *The fire next time*. New York: Dial Press. (Nonfiction)

Bell, D. (1979). *And we are not saved*. New York: Basic (Nonfiction)

Carter, S. (1991). *Reflections of an affirmative action baby*. New York: Basic. (Nonfiction)

Fefer, M. (1991, December 16). Gay in corporate America. *Fortune*.

Finder, J. (1987, February 22). A male secretary. *New York Times Magazine*.

Hacker, A. (1992). *Two nations: Black and white, separate, hostile, unequal*. New York: Macmillan. (Nonfiction)

Jacobs, H. (1987). *Life of a slave girl*. Cambridge, MA: Harvard University Press. (Nonfiction)

Jennings, D., Egri, C. P., Langton, N., & Frost, P. J. (in press). Teaching gender issues in introductory OB: Theory and exercises. *Journal of Management Education*.

Johnson, C. (1990). *Middle passage*. New York: Atheneum. (Fiction)

Malan, R. (1990). *My traitor's heart*. London, Vintage. (Nonfiction)

Moraga, C., & Anzaldua, G. (1981). *This bridge called my back*. New York: Kitchen Table. (Nonfiction)

Morrison, T. (1987). *Beloved*. New York: Knopf. (Fiction)

Murray, P. (1987). *Song in a weary throat*. New York: Harper & Row. (Fiction)

Page, C. (1986). *A foot in each world*. Evanston, IL: Northwestern University Press. (Nonfiction)

Schrenk, R. (1977, May-June). Two women, three men on a raft. *Harvard Business Review*, pp. 100-108.

Steele, S. (1990). *The content of our character*. New York: St. Martin's (Nonfiction).

Sut, J. & Lewis, J. (1992). *Enlightened racism: The Cosby Show, audiences, and the myth of the American dream*. Boulder: Westview Press. (Nonfiction)

Suggested Films and Movies

A Dry White Season

Affirmative Action: "The Oprah Winfrey Show"

A World Apart

Daughters of the Dust

Do the Right Thing (by Spike Lee)

Glory

Guess Who's Coming to Dinner

Gung Ho

The Long Walk Home

The Mommy Track (video)

"Roots" (television miniseries)

School Daze (by Spike Lee)

Shirley Valentine

Twenty-Two

Developmental Diversity and the Management Classroom
Implications for Teaching and Learning

JOAN V. GALLOS
Radcliffe College/Harvard University

Diversity is a reality in the management world. The organizations that we teach about are no longer guaranteed a homogeneous work force—a taken for granted certainty a decade ago. On a microlevel, management student populations are also more diverse, as educational opportunities are available to previously excluded groups, expanded life-style choices offer diverse career options, and higher education is promoted as a lifelong possibility. Differences in age, race, ethnicity, gender, national origin, and life experiences are now part of everyday organizational life. As management and organization teachers and theory builders, we need to deal with the implications of this diversity for the content of our discipline, the design and management of our classroom, and for learning.

When thinking about diversity, it is easy to overlook one very significant form—developmental differences. Managing diversity in the organization and management literature almost exclusively refers to gender, cultural, racial, and age differences (e.g., Johnson & Packer, 1987; Kellogg, Spelman, & Crary, 1984-1985; Lawrence, 1988; Loden & Rosener, 1991; Mai-Dalton, 1984-1985; Porter & McKibbin, 1988), ignoring powerful

This chapter originally appeared in *The Organizational Behavior Teaching Review*, Volume 13, Issue 4.

developmental distinctions that cut across race, gender, age, and ethnicity. How do people see and make sense out of their world? What commonly held psychological constructs do they use to interpret what goes on around them, establish their expectations for self and other, and guide their behavioral choices? How do these lenses differ among people? among the students in our organizational behavior classes? How can we better teach students to recognize, appreciate, and manage the implications of developmental diversity in their dealings with others?

This article explores the issue of developmental diversity and its implications for teaching. It is divided into three parts. Part one is a brief introduction to developmental stage theory. Part two illustrates what developmental differences look like in the classrooms and what they imply for choice of teaching methods and for attempts to introduce the topic of diversity into courses. Part three addresses what can be done—next steps for incorporating an understanding of developmental differences into the teaching of management courses and into teaching about diversity.

Developmental Stage Theory: A Simple Introduction

DEVELOPMENTAL STAGES: WHAT ARE THEY?

Individual development can be explored by examining typical patterns of psychological organization at different points in an individual's growth.[1] Developmental theorists such as Belenky, Clinchy, Goldberg, and Tarule (1986); Gilligan (1982); Kohlberg (1976); Loevinger (1976); and Perry (1968) have outlined a number of specific stages along a developmental continuum and provided descriptions of how one experiences the world at each of these junctures. The stages are arranged in hierarchical sequence and map a basic progression in ways of thinking, feeling, and responding.

Age alone is no guarantee of movement to higher or more sophisticated ways of making sense out of reality. Developmental stages, therefore, are abstract concepts—labels to describe the frame of reference used to structure one's world and from within which one perceives the world. Different capabilities for introspection, relative thinking, abstract conceptualization, acceptance of personal causality, and tolerance for ambiguity are essential dimensions for assessing developmental stages. Development implies increasing capabilities for understanding self, other, interpersonal relationships, and broad social issues; dealing with cognitive complexities; and applying more complicated (Weick, 1979) intellectual and ethical reasoning—capabilities called into play when students are asked to explore the issue of managing diversity in organizations. In that sense, development also implies greater capacities to acknowledge the legitimacy and importance of individual differences and to move beyond viewing diversity as an annoying impediment to learning, personal empowerment, and effective action.

DEVELOPMENTAL STAGES: CRITICAL ISSUES

Despite variations in language and focus, central developmental frameworks—the classic theories of Perry (1968), Loevinger (1976), and Kohlberg (1976), and an influential feminist update (Belenky et al., 1986)—agree on one main line of intellectual and ethical development that is illustrated by the continuum below.

right-wrong dualism	simple pluralism	realizing relativism	multiplicity of perspectives: tolerance for complexity

Main Line of Development

The continuum maps an individual development progression from an absolute "it's right or it's wrong" outlook and a search for "The One Truth," through simple pluralism—"Different views and beliefs exist but they are procedural impediments, something you need to sort through to find The Right Answer."—to an appreciation of contextual relativism— "Everyone is entitled to his or her own opinion." The end point of this developmental journey is a respect for multiple perspectives on the same event, a tolerance for ambiguity, a healthy appreciation of life's paradoxes, and a personal commitment to seek truth (with a small *t*).

Using this main line of development as a starting point, we can create four different developmental portraits by adding the central developmental concerns, the developmentally based expectations for education, the teacher and oneself as a student that individuals have at each of the four points along the continuum. Table 22.1 contains these four developmental portraits and illustrates four unique perspectives on self, others, and the world.

Developmental Diversity and the Classroom

Armed with this basic understanding of developmental theory, it is easy to see why students at various developmental stages respond differently to the classroom experience. Developmental stages suggest the possibility for radically different student views on the nature of truth, education, and

TABLE 22.1
Four Developmental Portraits

Stage	Central Developmental Concern	Nature of Education	Role of the Teacher	Self as Student
Right-wrong dualism	Self-protection	Structures, designed by authority, to convey The Truth Truth = authority Right = that which is approved, permitted, or condoned by authority	Demonstrator of Truth The enforcer	Sees the world as a dangerous place Has limited awareness of an internal world and few capacities for self-reflection Externalizes blame of failures or ineffectiveness Student role: protect self from powerful others
Simple pluralism	Conformity	Structures designed by legitimate authority to convey The Truth Truth is possessed by and comes from legitimate authority	A revealer or announcer of Truth An instructor The monitor of rules and requirements	Has strong desire of inclusion Feels guilt when breaking rules Sees students' views as impediments to finding Truth Limited capacity for introspection: ability to meet others' expectations Student role: follow the rules

Realizing relativism	Beginning recognition of conscience	Activities and structures, designed by knowledgeable authorities, that can help us learn and discover the truth	A role model A guide who shares acquired knowledge and shows the best ways for us to discover the truth	Interested in learning what others know and in learning about oneself Uses standards of excellence based on both authority's expectations and own budding self-evaluated ideals Acknowledges uncertainty as more than an impediment to truth Student role: learn what is out there but remember, in the end, everyone is entitled to his or her own opinion
Appreciating a multiplicity of perspectives	Autonomy	Events and activities, designed and facilitated by a knowledgeable source, to encourage personal insights about oneself and the world	A facilitator A designer of opportunities to foster personal insights An experienced fellow traveler who offers tips to the novices, support for the weary, and encouragement to all seekers on the road to truth	Has high toleration for ambiguity and life's paradoxes Sees autonomy and personal responsibility as critical to identity Assumes complexity as a rule Student role: one pilgrim, joining others travelers, on the same road to personally generated truth

learning; the appropriate role for a teacher; and the meaning of a mature and responsible student. In short, we need to expect and be prepared for developmentally diverse interpretations of and responses to all that we do in the classroom. How can we begin to understand what our teaching methods developmentally mean to students and use that information to predict their reactions and inform teaching choices? How do developmental differences affect student abilities to explore the topic of diversity and appreciate individual differences at work in our own classroom environment and beyond?

DIFFERENT STUDENT REACTIONS: IT'S MORE THAN CHANCE OR CHEMISTRY

If your experiences are like mine, there are painful memories about some teaching activity, case, or presentation that should have been a romping success and was not. It had worked beautifully with other groups and in other courses. It seemed appropriate for the present audience. It was done as well as it ever had been (maybe better because of age and seasoning). But the result was blank faces or, even worse, the chilling "you want us to do what?" stares.

We can write all this off as a lousy day, bad chemistry, or the luck of the audience draw. For me, a retrospective look at these instances from a developmental perspective sheds new light on how stage-related developmental comfort and preferences left me and members of the audience simultaneously experiencing completely different events. A closer look at what, for example, a case discussion might mean to students at different developmental stages illustrates this point.

Case discussions are opportunities for students to think through an organizational problem and devise appropriate strategies for responding. When things work well, students learn to appreciate multiple perspectives and recognize the subtle value differences that underpin alternative diagnoses. The result is learning about organizations, oneself, and others.

Imagine what an energized and free-wheeling case discussion looks like through the eyes of self-protective students. They enter a course expecting the instructor to provide The Right Answer, and to structure the learning environment to maximize the likelihood of having Truth recorded in their notebooks at the end of the term or program. Case discussions, in which the Keeper of Truth says very little and encourages students to speak to each other, seem confusing and foolish. Bombarded with all kinds of information and potential Right Answers, the self-protectors are left frantically searching for clues about what the instructor Really Wants. Our rhetorical questions, smiles, shoulder shrugs, and other case teaching theatrics, which encourage students to carry on enlivened debates, leave self-protectors deprived of even tacit ways of assessing what should be written down and feeling either manipulated or angry at the amount of time wasted before The Real Answer is revealed in the what-has-happened-since case.

It would not take too many of these classes before self-protectors, developmentally skilled at externalizing blame and limited in awareness of their own internal world, conclude that "this course is a lot of talking—no real answers here," and that the instructor is "a bad teacher, filling up the time when we already read the case the night before."

Life is somewhat easier for conformist students during case discussions, but the process can still be frustrating. Unlike their self-protective peers, conformists have budding recognitions of simple pluralism and are less baffled by the fact that others have views different from their own. From the conformist perspective, however, listening to others is an impediment: something that the instructor wants students to do before announcing the Truth. In that sense, conformists are like their self-protective peers, wondering why so much time needs to be spent when the answer is already known. Case discussions can look like a ploy to encourage participation for its own sake or a game to expose student naïveté or instructor know-how.

Conformists may hang in longer than their self-protective peers but perhaps at a cost to their sense of self. Conformist students are good soldiers. They enter courses willing to follow the rules. They answer the questions we ask and are concerned about meeting our expectations. Whereas self-protectors are more apt to get angry, conformists may feel a combination of guilt, confusion, and frustration. "If I think these case discussions are a waste of time, then maybe I'm not getting what my instructor obviously hoped and expected I would." Feelings of failure can accompany anger at the instructor for "not telling us what we need to know." Or, as an alternative, the conformists may continue along, dutifully participating in case discussions and silently hoping to catch on eventually, while missing the learnings we assume they are getting.

Large group case discussions better fit the expectations and capacities of conscientious and autonomous students. These people expect diversity and uncertainty as a general rule and relish opportunities to understand and articulate their own personal perspectives on a problem. Although these more developmentally sophisticated folks are interested in hearing about our experiences and reactions, they would be bored or infuriated by instructors who touted The Right Answer and stifled by courses that offered them opportunities to write down The Truth about organizational life and functioning.

The conscientious and autonomous students are the ones we have in mind when we design and teach large case courses. But we should not assume that all students are so developmentally sophisticated. In fact, those who teach undergraduates and young graduate students should realize that major studies of students during the college years—Perry's (1968) is the most well known—tell us they are not. And even with executives and seasoned managers, age and a plethora of organizational experiences are no guarantee of movement to higher or more sophisticated ways of reasoning and viewing the world.

Am I suggesting that cases be limited and reserved only for more developmentally sophisticated students? No, I am not. Rather I want to illustrate the implications of developmental diversity for our teaching choices and advocate the importance of working with any teaching materials and methods in ways that respond to the diverse developmental needs of students. I could take the same four developmental stages, for example, and look at how differently the four types of students would respond to experiential exercises or lectures with similar conclusions. If the management classroom world looks different to those at different developmental stages, what teaching approaches and learning vehicles are most apt to encourage learning across developmental stages?

BEYOND OUR METHODS: DEVELOPMENT AND TEACHING ABOUT DIVERSITY

Just as developmental differences affect teaching choices and methods, they also influence the capacities that students bring to understanding a topic as complex and emotionally laden as understanding and managing diversity itself. Developmental capabilities help to explain why students may question the legitimacy of studying diversity and what limits student abilities to work with the issues. Clearly, self-protective students, who see the world as "me-right/other-wrong" and feel compelled to protect themselves from powerful others, will have developmentally based questions about the need to study diversity and a very different definition of what diversity means from an autonomous counterpart, who relishes opportunities to explore the complexity of life and who enters the class with a deep appreciation of individual differences.

Working with diversity and its implications for management also requires a number of relatively sophisticated cognitive, social, and intrapsychic capacities that are beyond the developmental capabilities of many students. We need students intellectually to understand that equality and equity do not necessarily mean sameness—a cognitively complex distinction. We expect students to be able to comprehend and acknowledge that others may experience the world and organizations in ways different from themselves—a higher-level developmental skill. We ask for capacities to distinguish between a student's personal experiences and those of others with whom they share racial, gender, age, or ethnic similarities—an almost impossible task for self-protective students and a very difficult one for conformists. We call on student abilities to explore deep emotions, understand internal conflicts and identify the roots of one's personal beliefs—skills that only the best conscientious and autonomous students bring. At the most basic level, we assume introspection skills and the ability to stand back and reflect on experiences—an overgenerous assumption about those other than the more developmentally sophisticated students.

What Can We Do?
Implications for Management Education

Even these cursory explorations of developmental theory at work in the classroom suggest the powerful implications of developmental diversity for teaching and learning. What can we do? How can we begin to incorporate these insights into the design and management of classes? How can an understanding of developmental differences better inform teaching about the topic of managing diversity in organizations?

ACKNOWLEDGE DEVELOPMENTAL DIVERSITY

Acknowledging developmental differences as a legitimate form of diversity is an important first step. Age, gender, race, national origin, and ethnicity are the more visible forms of diversity: Developmental differences are hidden. We cannot look around the classroom and from the sea of student faces begin to speculate how different or similar students are developmentally to each other or to us. We cannot look at last names, birth dates, or majors and easily know our students' worldviews.

Acknowledging that developmental diversity contributes to the different responses we get from students allows us to move beyond personal preferences for certain types of student behavior to a more productive focus on the unique developmental messages that all students send. Even a basic understanding of what the world looks like through the developmental lenses of students provides new insights into the seeming power of quantitative colleagues who give students hard, bottom-line answers; the potential for students to take participative strategies less seriously; the reasons why some of the best students view heavy requirements and strict rules as nonpunitive and essential for their learning; and the difficulties students have in grappling with complex issues such as understanding and managing diversity in organizations.

LEARN ABOUT OUR STUDENTS

Once we have accepted the reality of developmental diversity, a logical next step is to begin gathering information about it. Who are our students developmentally? How similar are they to each other? To us? How can we begin to speculate about student developmental preferences and limitations?

A caution about assessing development is in order. Accurately determining developmental stage is a complex process. Developmental stages are inferred from what individuals say or how they respond to problems. Developmental theory is based on the premise that what a person says is not capricious or arbitrary but corresponds to the understanding of reality that a person has. Kohlberg (1976), for example, determined developmental stage by charting responses to the famous "would you steal the drug to save a dying spouse?" dilemma. Loevinger (1976), on the other hand, assesses development by asking people to respond to a series of sentence completions. Scoring the completions is complicated and done by trained scorers.

A complete and thorough assessment of each student's developmental stage is not possible for most of us—nor is it practical or necessary for incorporating developmental thinking into the design and management of courses. It is more essential to get the developmental flavor of the class and begin the process of gathering developmental data and forming developmental hunches that can be tested and refined over time. I view my instructor role as a developmental detective, looking and listening for clues that shine a developmental light on what may be happening for a particular student or group.

As a way of surfacing developmental diversity in the classroom, I have used some of Loevinger's (1976) sentence completions as the basis for discussing individual differences and their implications for working together. Sentence completions, for example, that deal with authority are useful during initial course contracting, mid-course evaluations, and classes on leadership and contingency theory. Completions that deal with personal responsibility and causality aid explorations of the impact of individual behavior on group outcomes. Completions that deal with the nature of education and learning are useful for individual goal setting and comparing different student expectations for the course.

After small and large group discussions of differences, I collect the sentence completions and look at their suggested developmental implications for my proposed course design, the structure of individual classes, and the ways in which I will approach particular topics. If there are project groups in the course, I will cluster the responses of group members to anticipate problems the groups may have as a result of strong developmental differences or similarities and to determine interventions that facilitate conversations across developmental stages and increase the likelihood of learning and success for all.

ENCOURAGING STUDENTS TO EXPLORE
AND MANAGE INDIVIDUAL DIFFERENCES

Working with an ongoing appreciation of developmental diversity in the classroom means encouraging students to take a problem-solving approach to individual differences. Rather than masking differences or seeing them as disruptive, I ask students to accept these differences as a reality and then think about how they can be managed to everyone's satisfaction and learning. This establishes a norm that in this class differences are okay and plants the seeds for later expanding definitions of diversity and individual differences beyond distinct expectations and points of view. Students need no understanding of developmental theory to do this.

In fact, I explicitly work the issue of developmental diversity while exploring other topics throughout the course: I do not set aside time when we read or review developmental theory or when students are asked to learn the development stages. Rather than getting lost in the lingo and labels or providing theory that might encourage students to rank responses or evaluate positions as more or less developmentally sophisticated, I want people focused on articulating their different views and perspectives, appreciating rather than fearing the differences, and thinking creatively about what they mean for working together. I teach about managing developmental diversity by explicitly managing it in the classroom and by providing students opportunities to recognize and manage it for themselves. This saves class instruction time for other issues or topics and avoids trivializing the issue of developmental diversity by relegating it to a class or two.

More specifically, I return all sentence completions and other difference-surfacing materials, for example, and refer students back to particular answers or items when I see them struggling with problems that look developmentally based. This is especially useful for long-term student project groups that need to understand and manage their group's process, choices, and alternatives.

There are developmental limitations to these conversions across stages that need to be remembered and that may require instructor interventions to reframe the meaning of statements and conversations in ways that students at both the lower and higher stages can understand. The reality of the hierarchical nature of developmental theory means that individuals at lower levels are limited to the perspective of their own stage, having few or no alternative vantage points from which to understand their own and others' behavior. Individuals at the higher stages can understand the lower ones, because each stage along the developmental continuum is broader in scope than the previous one, incorporating and transforming all preceding stages.

This instructor reframing of issues across stages is, therefore, critical. It encourages students in their own developmental growth, models patience for those less tolerant of their developmentally different peers and reinforces beliefs that with persistence, differences can eventually be bridged—an important and encouraging recognition for those newly introduced to the issues of managing diversity.

An additional benefit of having students work with issues of developmental diversity in the classroom is that their experiences can be used as a springboard for dealing with other forms of diversity such as race, gender, and ethnicity, which are more threatening and anxiety producing. The process of acknowledging disagreement with another or having different expectations does not evoke the strong cultural baggage and well-formed stereotypes that race, gender, and ethnicity can, providing an easier starting point for working on issues of diversity.

Developmental differences are masked for students in peer behaviors that they either like or dislike—"Gee, I really get along well with her." "Boy, I don't know where he's coming from."—in the same way that they are for instructors. If students have learned comfortably to acknowledge that they see things differently from their peers and can successfully manage the implications, then they have more confidence and a tested, problem-solving approach to face the more emotionally challenging forms of diversity. Being able to say with confidence "that's your opinion" and "I am different from you and that's okay" are important steps in differentiating self from other, strengthening one's sense of personal identity, and becoming clearer about the uniqueness of one's own experiences—prerequisites for meaningful discussions about race and gender differences.

EXPAND OUR UNDERSTANDINGS, BE FLEXIBLE IN OUR METHODS

As the developmentally different student responses to a case discussion and to the topic of diversity have shown, we need to be aware of what our methodological and content choices mean for students and be flexible in our ways of approaching topics and activities. We need to have options for how we teach and different ways of using methods or cases. An energetic large group case discussion—perhaps a perfect learning experience for more developmentally similar and sophisticated executives with organizational experience—may seem like avant-garde theater or blatant manipulation to young and inexperienced undergraduates without proper framing, masterful introductions, and detailed work to help students generalize and learn from this experience.

And let us not forget that there is developmental diversity both across the different kinds of groups that we teach—undergraduates, young graduate students, experienced MBAs, executive audiences, and so on—as well as within any of those groups. A well-seasoned, highly defensive, and cantankerous participant in an executive education program with years of organizational experience who claims that this classroom stuff is fun but a waste of learning time may be crying out for a more developmentally appropriate way of learning in the same way as disgruntled undergraduates do.

Conclusion

This article explores an often forgotten form of diversity—developmental differences. The developmental frameworks that students use to make sense out of course content, structures and roles are powerful influences on how well students respond to our offerings. When students developmentally understand our methods and teaching madness, they are better able to learn about organizations and about themselves. When they learn to accept and handle developmental differences in the classroom, they gain confidence and a problem-solving approach for managing other forms of diversity.

The article also advocates the importance of understanding and working with issues of developmental diversity in the classroom as a way of increasing our own success and satisfaction in the classroom. When we understand the developmental messages that students are sending through their behavior, we are less helpless and threatened when our usual and preferred approach does not work, more tolerant and respectful of individual differences, better prepared to respond to classroom conflict, and more able to appreciate and manage the challenge of the classroom experience or the difficulties of teaching about as complex an issue as understanding diversity.

Finally, this article points out a set of ideas about human developmental processes that need to become part of our evolving curriculum on managing diversity. Very little has been done to explore the implications of developmental diversity for classroom experiences (Andrews, 1981; Gallos,

1988; Weathersby, Bartunek, & Gordon, 1982;), despite the obvious power of the issues and the ease with which they can be incorporated into present course goals and topics. Developmental diversity has equally important implications for how well people are able to work together in organizations, and understand the behaviors and choices of their peers, bosses, and subordinates. We need to articulate better what developmental differences mean for organizational leaders and followers alike and ensure that developmental concerns are part of our budding approaches to the whole area of managing diversity in organizations.

Note

1. Development can also be explored by studying life phases—the age-specific achievements, transitions, and critical incidents faced over the course of a lifetime. Those interested in a more complete, historical introduction to developmental theory should see Cytrynbaum and Crites (1989). A detailed exploration of women's development is found in Gallos (1989).

References

Andrews, J. D. (1981). Student development and the goal of higher education: A conceptual framework for selecting teaching strategies. *Exchange: The Organizational Behavior Teaching Journal, 6*(2), 5-14.

Belenky, M., Clinchy, B., Goldberger, N., & Tarule, J. (1986). *Women's way of knowing: The development of self, voice, and mind.* New York: Basic.

Cytrynbaum, S., & Crites, J. (1989). A developmental model for career adjustment during adulthood. In M. Arthur, D. Hall, & B. Lawrence (Eds.), *Handbook of career theory: Perspectives and prospects for understanding and managing work experiences* (pp. 66-68). Cambridge, UK: Cambridge University Press.

Gallos, J. (1988). A need for reframing the gulag: A developmental perspective. *The Organizational Behavior Teaching Review, 12*(4), 74-76.

Gallos, J. (1989). Exploring women's development: Implications for career theory, practice, and research. In M. Arthur, D. Hall, & B. Lawrence (Eds.), *Handbook of career theory: Perspectives and prospects for understanding and managing work experiences* (pp. 110-132). Cambridge, UK: Cambridge University Press.

Gilligan, C. (1982). *In a different voice: Psychological theory and women's development.* Cambridge, MA: Harvard University Press.

Johnson, W. B., & Packer, A. E. (1987). *Workforce 2000: Work and workers for the twenty-first century.* Indianapolis: Hudson Institute.

Kellogg, D., Spelman, D., & Crary, M. (1984-1985). Introducing women in management issues in OB course. *The Organizational Behavior Teaching Review, 9*(3), 83-95.

Kohlberg, L. (1976). Moral stages and moralization: The cognitive-developmental approach. In T. Lickona (Ed.), *Moral development and behavior: Theory, research and social issues* (pp. 31-53). New York: Holt, Rinehart, & Winston.

Lawrence, B. (1988). New wrinkles in the theory of age: Demography, norms, and performance ratings. *Academy of Management Journal, 31*(2), 309-337.

Loden, M., & Rosener, J. B. (1991). *Workforce America! Managing employee diversity as a vital resource.* Homewood, IL: Irwin.

Loevinger, J. (1976). *Ego development.* San Francisco: Jossey-Bass.

Mai-Dalton, R. (1984-1985). Exposing business school students to cultural diversity: Becoming a minority. *The Organizational Behavior Teaching Review, 9*(3), 76-82.

Perry, W. (1968). *Forms of intellectual and ethical development in the college years.* New York: Holt, Rinehart, & Winston.

Porter, L. W., & McKibbin, L. E. (1988). *Management education and development: Drift or thrust into the twenty-first century?* New York: McGraw-Hill.

Weathersby, R., Bartunek, J., & Gordon, J. (1982). Teaching for "complicate understanding." *Exchange: The Organizational Behavior Teaching Journal, 7*(4) 7-15.

Weick, K. (1979). *The social psychology of organizing.* Reading, MA: Addison-Wesley.

Twenty-Three

Racial and Ethnic Diversity
The Void in
Management Education

ELLA LOUISE BELL
MIT Sloan School of Management

Diversity, particularly the significance of ethnicity, race, and race relations in the workplace are relatively neglected topics in management and organizational behavior courses. In this article, diversity refers to a multicultural workplace where men and women from different racial and ethnic backgrounds have equal participation, respect, and an opportunity to achieve in organizations. The relationships among racism, sexism, and diversity are tightly interwoven. Due to the sociopsychological history of race and its legacy of racial oppression, racism is one of the most volatile issues in this society. Sexism is one of the oldest forms of oppression and can be found on varying levels in all societies. Consequently, knowledge of both racism and sexism are pivotal for our understanding the value of diversity. Yet, a tremendous void exists in our courses, textbooks, and curricula regarding race and, to a smaller extent, gender.

We must begin to address with our students and colleagues and in organizations ways to explore diversity as it relates to race and gender. The goal of this article is to begin to fill in the void in our curriculum concerning diversity. Although the equal participation of women is extremely vital to organizations, this discussion focuses solely on diversity from the perspective of race and ethnicity. There are already a number of

This chapter originally appeared in *The Organizational Behavior Teaching Review,* Volume 13, Issue 4.

resources that address integrating women into the workplace (Hai, 1984; Harrigan, 1977; Hennig & Jardim, 1977; Josefowitz, 1980; Kanter, 1977; Morrison et al., 1987; Zeitz & Dusky, 1988).

This article is presented in three sections. First, the importance of teaching race and ethnicity is explored. Then the barriers that get in the way of teaching about such issues are addressed. The article concludes with several strategies for integrating race and ethnicity into the management education classroom.

The Importance of Teaching Race and Ethnicity

Recently, there have been a flurry of reports in the media and popular literature concerning racial problems. Even after the 1992 Los Angeles riots, the Rodney King beating incident has continued to spark forceful reactions, both verbal and physically violent, against pervasive police brutality and legal system injustice. Reports of racial incidents vary in severity from subtle (racial jokes, unexamined assumptions and stereotypes) to brutal assaults. For example, a growing number of incidents involving racial hostility was reported on college campuses across the country (Carmody, 1987; Simpson, 1987). Issues revealed in the reports included the high degree of isolation black students experience at predominately white universities, the lack of black faculty who can serve as role models and mentors, and the severe cutbacks in financial aid programs.

Besides the immense calamity surrounding the Rodney King incident in Los Angeles, there also have been racial incidents in many communities throughout the United States. Howard Beach, a predominately white neighborhood in the borough of Queens in New York City, has probably become synonymous with brutal racial violence. It was in this neighborhood that a racially motivated attack by a group of white youths occurred against three black men, leaving one black man dead and another severely beaten (Erlanger, 1987; Fried, 1987; Shipp, 1987). There have also been reports in Detroit, Los Angeles, Seattle, and Jersey City concerning anti-Asian racism, such as car-bashings, anti-Asian bumper stickers, and other cases of brutal violence (Narvaez, 1987; Wilkerson, 1987). In the past decade, we have witnessed a period of regressive race relations. This period is characterized by a general insensitivity toward people of color.[1] There have been severe cutbacks in affirmative action programs and a deemphasis on civil rights legislation. Such conditions have contributed to the ground swell of racial problems currently happening nationwide.

Incidents that occur in the external environment, such as racial tensions, can influence organizational life. Organizations, after all, are microcosms of society. Thus the current period of regressive race relations has spilled over into organizations. Media reports about blacks', Hispanics', Asians', and on rare occasions, native Americans' experiences in organizations are disturbing to read. Cases of blatant overt discrimination, inadequate career opportunities, lack of constructive feedback on job performance, and overcoming negative racial stereotypes are just a few of the many work-related concerns expressed by people of color (Mercer, 1988; Shenon, 1988).

What becomes apparent based on the accounts in the media is that organizations, in general, are slow to respond to internal racial problems. Too many organizations tend to mismanage issues related to race and ethnicity or, worse yet, simply ignore them (Dickens & Dickens, 1991; Fernandez, 1987). There is the prevailing expectation that people of color must fit into the organization's mainstream culture, rather than the organization finding creative ways to establish multicultural work environments where racial and ethnic harmony are actively sought. In fact, *The Wall Street Journal* speculated that more blacks are leaving corporate America preferring instead to join black-owned companies or to become entrepreneurs, rather than continue being subjected to discrimination (James, 1988).

Given the social and managerial implications, learning about race and ethnicity should be considered a vital component of a professional program in the business of educating managers. Educating managers on the importance of understanding race and ethnicity has even greater bottom-line ramifications. Jelinek and Adler (1988) reported that the business arena is becoming highly global where the focus is both multicultural and multinational. Beyond global competition and foreign markets and operations, there is also the trend that the American work force is becoming increasingly racially and ethnically diverse.

The recent report, titled *Workforce 2000*, stressed the urgent need to fully integrate people of color into the work force. The conclusions suggest a critical new direction for management education: that management must cross racial, cultural, and international boundaries to remain competitive in a steadily growing global economy (Nelton, 1988; Porter & McKibbin, 1988). Organizations will continue to lose vital human resources unless managers are educated to move beyond their own narrow ethnocentric frames. Thus managers must be groomed to develop interpersonal skills and conceptual frameworks to perform competently with people from a broad spectrum of racial and cultural backgrounds.

What Prevents Us From Teaching About Race and Ethnicity in Management Education

The global, social, and economic labor market trends concerning race and ethnicity described above merit a deeper exploration about why the void of these issues in management education persists. The *void* refers to the low level of awareness among many management education professionals about the importance of integrating this topic into courses in both the corporate and academic classroom settings. Beyond the lack of attention, I have observed both in my teaching and consulting a number of personal attitudes, sentiments, and tangible obstacles that get in the way of teaching about race and ethnicity. Such forces can be categorized into three specific areas: (1) political, (2) theoretical, and (3) pedagogical. Combined, these forces contribute to the racial void in management education, especially in understanding the dynamics of race relations in organizations.

The political force consists of the ideologies, sentiments, and theories that influence the ways we think about race and ethnicity in the managerial sciences. On the one hand, most management education professionals are probably convinced of the legitimacy of certain areas within the field, such as organizational theory, strategy, or organization development due to their own educational backgrounds. On the other hand, most management education professionals are probably unconvinced about the legitimacy of race and ethnicity in the field. There is a prevailing sentiment that issues concerning race and ethnicity have little impact on organizational life, in general. Consequently, the teaching of the topics seems more appropriate for schools of social work or education—professions dealing with societal ills.

The myth that racial problems have been eradicated in the workplace is another political sentiment that gets in the way of teaching race and ethnicity. Since the Civil Rights Amendment of 1964, people of color have only slowly progressed beyond many discriminatory barriers. In addition to overt racism, research indicates subtle discrimination, and covertly sophisticated forms of racism have arisen in organizations (Bielby, 1987; Braddock & McPartland, 1987; Pettigrew & Martin, 1987). The latter form of racism institutionalizes discriminatory practices within the organization's policies and structures (Faegin, 1987). Yet problems related to prejudice and discriminatory practices are frequently denied by members of the dominant white group. Such denial tends to be reinforced by the belief among whites that EEOC and Affirmative Action programs, legislative policies that have opened doors for minorities, have also erased discriminatory practices in organizations.

The question of legitimacy can adversely affect the way administrators, colleagues, and students perceive the teaching of race and ethnicity. They, too, may need convincing before offering any substantive support. Thus teachers may have to justify to administrators and colleagues why the topic is both appropriate and necessary in a business school. For instance, administrators can be doubtful that students, particularly white males, will show any interest in the topic. They often assume the topic is of interest only to students of color, and they are surprised to discover the number of white students (men and women) who wish to explore the topic. Strategies for managing the political force will be discussed further in this article.

A second obstacle that gets in the way of teaching about race and ethnicity is the near absence of well-developed conceptual models for understanding racial dynamics. Calas (1988) argues that there is a gap between organizational reality and conceptual material in this area. This gap is most evident in the managerial sciences literature. Thomas and Alderfer (1989) suggest that the behavioral sciences, in comparison to the managerial sciences, are far more advanced in investigating race and ethnicity. Theories explicit to understanding race and ethnicity are embedded in sociology, psychology, and anthropology. Much of the scholarly works represented in the behavioral sciences focuses on social stratification, oppression, black or minority psychological development, family dynamics and interpersonal relationships among minority men and women, and descriptions of subculture communities (Allport, 1954; Davis, 1978; Hill, 1980; Hill, 1981; Rothman, 1977; Turner, 1984). Thus a complexity of teaching about race and ethnicity is its interdisciplinary nature; management education professionals may feel challenged when they cross new scholarly boundaries, as discussed in the introduction to this series of articles.

There is a growing body of empirical research and paradigms in the managerial sciences about race and race relations, however (Alderfer, 1982; Denton, 1987; Herbert, 1986; Thomas, 1986). These scholarly works are critical because they begin to provide a bridge between theory and organizational reality. For example, the bicultural life structure concept describes the internal intrapsychic dynamics and external outer work relationships black men and black women adapt in response to living in an oppressive society (Bell, 1986). The bicultural concept is useful for understanding the tensions and difficulties black professionals experience in mainstream white organizations. The concept is also applicable to other racial and ethnic groups. Whenever one crosses into a new or different cultural context, one is likely to experience some bicultural tension due to their unfamiliarity with the behavioral and social systems. Teaching strategies incorporating theoretical models will be discussed further in this article.

Pedagogical considerations also represent a significant constraint when it comes to teaching race and ethnicity. The pedagogical problems inherent in teaching race and ethnicity are closely linked to the theoretical obstacles mentioned above. The former is how we teach, while the latter is what we teach. We don't know effective methods for instructing in this area. It is clear that we lack the pedagogical tools to teach race and ethnicity. Yet approaches to teaching this topic can be ambiguous because the subject matter is so complex. Teaching race and ethnicity demands more than merely presenting subject content. Innovative teaching strategies are needed to get students to understand cross-cultural dynamics. Because students have deeply internalized feelings and assumptions concerning racial issues, the emotional reactions of the students triggered by the content must be considered as equally important and taken into account when designing the instructional process. This is not a simple task by any means. As a black female, I have observed that people are rarely comfortable when the subject of race becomes the topic of conversation. This observation is most evident when I am in an integrated setting. Black and white people alike seem to freeze up in a dead silence if the issue of race becomes the topic. People don't know how to talk about racial issues because they are incredibly explosive. Cross-cultural conversations on race is a social taboo (Steele, 1988); race often triggers feelings of discomfort, confusion, guilt, and anger. Given the fact that racial issues are difficult to discuss socially, imagine the resistance one encounters when attempting to get students to explore such topics.

Despite the reluctance of people to discuss race, race relations between blacks and whites in American society have often been the focus of attention both in the popular literature and in the media. There is a tendency to overlook the experiences of other visible minorities (Asians, Latinos, and native Americans); these minority groups suffer from benign neglect in the literature and the media. Other groups also ignored are the so-called invisible minorities (Jews and regional white subgroups). All of the minority groups (visible and invisible) have different systems of learned behavior patterns, values, norms, and traditions.

In this context, the cultural experiences of white students are very relevant. Because whites are members of the dominant group, their awareness of what it means to be white is often low or even nonexistent. White people aren't forced to think about themselves as a racial group because of the power inherent in also being members of the dominant group. Thus white students find it difficult to get in touch with their own racial identity. When they do discuss race, it is usually framed as a problem experienced by blacks and nonwhites. It is easy for white students to become bystanders vicariously experiencing someone else's race, rather than exploring their own racial and cultural experience. Cross-cultural discussions of race and ethnicity can leave white students feeling vulnerable, confused, and inadequate.

Black students, on the other hand, have greater access to their racial identity: It is generally celebrated among black people. Unlike whites, race is a conscious life dimension for blacks, and it is a figural element of their core identity. Blacks experience less difficulty in denying their racial

identity because they have experienced racism and discrimination throughout their lives. As an oppressed group, they have been force to struggle for
equal opportunity, respect, and dignity. It is the struggle that reinforces the
bonds of the group. In comparison to white students, who often cannot
elaborate on their racial identity, black students can talk passionately about
the African-American experience. Yet, in integrated classroom settings,
black students are often reluctant to discuss their racial experiences. They
resent being the cultural experience for white students who they perceive
as denying racial identity. Consequently, in cross-cultural discussions,
black students can feel victimized and angry because they perceive themselves burdened by doing most of the work.

Students from other minority groups (Asian, Latino, native American,
and the invisible minority groups) can vacillate between being expressive
or feeling invisible when it comes to exploring race or ethnicity. Far too
often, they have to struggle to find their voice when it comes to sharing
their racial experiences. For example, Asian-American students have a
tendency to assimilate into the mainstream culture. As a group, they prefer
not to discuss openly racial stereotypes, assumptions, or expectations
attributed to Asian-Americans. Students responses to cross-cultural discussions vary, depending on their racial and ethnic group membership; a
student's behavior is strongly influenced by the socialization messages he
or she receives from the racial or ethnic identity groups in which one has
membership. Thus intragroup and intergroup dynamics are significant
factors when teaching race and ethnicity.

Beyond the group dynamics among the students, authority issues must also
be considered and managed throughout the learning process. In this context,
authority issues refer to the relationship between instructor and student. White
students often fear my judging them as prejudiced when they share their racial
experiences. The fear is reflected in their papers and in the way they cautiously
choose their words when telling their stories. White students are keenly aware
that I can't validate their experiences of what it means to be white because I
am black. Thus they can easily feel unsupported and misunderstood when it
comes to discussing racial or ethnic issues. Trust is a slow emerging process
between us. Students of color seem to have just the opposite experience in
relationship to my authority. They are highly visible and empowered in the
class sessions. I don't have to work as hard to build trust between us. Trust
from the students of color is given generously. I suspect the described situation
would quickly be reversed if the person in authority were a white male or
white female.

Given the range of cultural differences and authority dynamics described briefly above, it becomes necessary for students to have opportunities to explore their own cultural roots before learning about the cultures

of others. One innovative teaching strategy that facilitates cultural self-re-
flection is an enabling structure. It is a strategy that encourages the
exploration of delicate and sensitive issues. Enabling structures help
students to work through the encrusted barriers that get in the way of their
being able to appreciate racial diversity. As a pedagogical tool, enabling
structures are necessary to create a supportive learning environment so
students can safely explore their race and ethnicity and allow them eventually to engage in cross-cultural dialogues. Because of the supportive
class climate, trust develops between the teacher and students, and among
the students themselves. Enabling structures also prevent the teaching of
racial and ethnic diversity from being polarized as black or white.

One example of an enabling structure that I use in both my consulting
work and in my course, race and gender in organizations, is a relatively
simple experiential exercise. Students are asked to identify the various race
and ethnic groups represented in the class. I list the groups on the chalkboard. It is interesting to note that students and clients will often identify
geographic regions, such as the West Coast or Midwest rather than to
identify a racial or ethnic identity. Another example of this situation is
when a student states his or her ethnic membership as American. When
this occurs, I usually offer the definitions for racial group and ethnic group
to get the class back on track. Davis (1978) defines race as

> certain biological traits that enable mankind [and womankind] to be divided
> into rough, overlapping categories. Racial minorities usually are identifiable
> by shared culture or subcultural traits . . . as well as physical characteristics.

He defines ethnic group as a "group with a sense of identity based on
loyalty to a very distinctive cultural pattern" (p. 5). Still there may be times
when a person can't determine his or her racial or ethnic identity, so I allow
the person to choose the group that seems to fit the best.

When the racial and ethnic groups are identified, students are asked to
form the respective groups. Their task in the groups is to respond to the
following question:

What does it mean to be a member of your racial or ethnic group?

The groups are given 45 minutes to discuss the question and record their
key points on newsprint. Once the allocated time is over the groups come
together, and the responses are displayed so everyone can read the data and
compare notes. Table 23.1 shows the responses from one of my classes.

Five race and ethnic groups were represented in Table 23.1, including
(1) WASP, (2) German-American, (3) Italian-American, (4) Jewish-American,

TABLE 23.1
Feedback From Race and Ethnicity Exercise

WASP	German-American	Italian-American	Jewish-American	African-American
• Take racial majority for granted	• Focus on ethnic traditions	• Pride of heritage	• Education valued	• Identify being black first then being a woman
• Comfort with racial identity	• Work ethic	• Strong family unit	• Marriage to a Jewish man	• Strong sense of black history
• Little recognition of race in early life years	• Some racial awareness but little impact	• Holidays—special types of food	• Identify as being Jewish first then being a woman	• Value of education
• Fear and confusion about other racial groups			• Early awareness of anti-Semitism, i.e., white female college roommate asking if I have horns	• Growing up in predominately black communities
			• Being left out at Christmas	• Feeling ignored and neglected at integrated settings
				• Having to prove continually that you are just as good as whites

and (5) African-American. In this particular class there was one Puerto Rican woman who preferred not to work alone, and when given a choice she decided to join the Italian-American group with their consent. The group's responses to the exercise tend to underscore differences of racial and ethnic perceptions of membership across groups. For instance, based on Table 23.1, two groups (African-American and Jewish-American) mentioned incidents of discrimination and prejudice, whereas for the other groups (WASP, German-American, and Italian-American) racial discriminatory barriers weren't focal concerns.

As an enabling structure, the race and ethnicity exercise helps students to begin to explore their own cultural roots as well as gain insights into the experiences of other racial and ethnic groups. The exercise can be used to structure learning on three levels: (1) individual, (2) group, and (3) intergroup. Students on the individual level, have an opportunity not only to reflect on how it feels to be a member of a particular racial identity group but also to consider the price of membership. What does it mean to be a white male in comparison to being a black female? On the group level, students discover the cultural themes that bond a group together. What are the benefits from being a member of the group? Finally, on the intergroup level, students examine the commonalities between their group experience. In what ways do their cultural experiences differ? How do the varying experiences influence relationships between the groups?

The enabling structure exercise serves as a point of departure for students to engage in rich cross-cultural dialogues on issues related to power dynamics between groups, issues of exclusion and inclusion, discriminatory barriers, and varying social relationships between the groups. Through the dialogues, students gradually begin to understand their own racial assumptions and expectations and learn the ways in which such perceptions reduce their tolerance of people who are different from themselves. The exercise described above demonstrates teaching strategy that helps students to examine the racial and cultural barriers operating among them.

Strategies for Race and Ethnicity

Thus far, we have discussed the political, theoretical, and pedagogical forces that contribute significantly to the void in teaching race and ethnicity in management education. When combined, the forces are very complex and difficult to unravel. Strategies are necessary to pull apart and break down the forces, thereby making the teaching of race and ethnicity manageable. There are ways to integrate this important topic successfully into management courses. I have used the strategies offered below in my own teaching and consulting work. Categorized by each force that gets in the way of teaching race and ethnicity, the strategies are broad in scope and take into account the complexities of design, content, and facilitation.

Forces and Strategies for Change

POLITICAL

- Host an informal session, such as a brown bag lunch with colleagues and students to discuss the significance of cultural diversity as a way to generate awareness and stimulate interest in the topic.
- Identify and enlist the support of administrators, colleagues, and students who are interested in diversity issues.

THEORETICAL

- Integrate theories from sociology, psychology, anthropology, and ethnic-racial studies: Teaching cultural diversity must incorporate an interdisciplinary approach.
- Seek out and work with colleagues from the social sciences whose area of specialization is race and ethnicity to learn about theories of oppression and racial stratification.

PEDAGOGICAL

- Literature, because it mirrors life experiences, provides a rich source of learning about racial and cultural diversity. Have students read fiction and poetry written by people of color to get a broader understanding of racial and ethnic dynamics. James Baldwin's *The Fire Next Time,* Audry Lorde's *Sister Outsider,* and Cherrie Moraga's *This Bridge Called My Back* are excellent literary sources.
- Involve managers from different racial and cultural backgrounds in the class. Consider organizing a panel consisting of Asian-American, Hispanic, and black professionals who are in advanced managerial positions to talk about their organizational experiences. This type of learning experience gives students a chance to meet people of color in positions of authority and leadership, often a rare opportunity.

Conclusion

This article discussed the void regarding cultural diversity in many organizational behavior courses in both corporate and academic settings.

Embedded in the concept of cultural diversity are the racial and cultural dynamics that hamper the quality of organizational life. We cannot afford to overlook the relevance of cultural diversity in management education. The void in this area must be closed. We must recognize that issues related to race and ethnicity are not only legitimate but critical to address in our courses given both social and managerial transitions. And we must use creative teaching techniques, instructional materials, and other resources to facilitate the learning process. The forces working against teaching cultural diversity must be tackled effectively because cultural ignorance can no longer be accepted in the workplace or in society in general. Today's global society, where the nature of work is becoming increasingly cross-cultural and international, demands that managers become multiculturally astute. It is imperative that managers comprehend cultural dynamics beyond limiting ethnocentric perspectives. What this means is that they must understand the subtly attitudinal behaviors and institutional barriers that prevent organizations from becoming dynamic multicultural and multinational environments. As a result, management education classrooms must become cross-cultural laboratories so students can learn to engage in constructive dialogues and ultimately come to accept and manage cultural diversity.

Note

1. I use the term *people of color* to refer to African-Americans, Asian-Americans, Latino-Americans, and native Americans. The term will be used interchangeably with *minority* throughout this article.

References

Alderfer, C. P. (1982). Problems of changing white males' behavior and beliefs concerning race relations. In P. Goodman (Ed.), *Change organizations: New perspectives on theory, research, and practive* (pp. 122-165). San Francisco: Jossey-Bass.

Allport, G. (1954). *The nature of prejudice.* Reading, MA: Addison-Wesley.

Baldwin, J. (1963). *The fire next time.* New York: Dial Press. (Nonfiction)

Bell, E. L. (1986). *The power within: Bicultural life structures and stress among black professional women.* Unpublished doctoral dissertation.

Bielby, W. (1987). Modern prejudice and institutional barriers to equal employment opportunity for minorities. *Journal of Social Issues, 43*(1), 79-84.

Braddock, J. H., & McPartland, J. M. (1987). How minorities continue to be excluded from equal employment opportunities. *Journal of Social Issues, 43*(1), 5-33.

Calas, M. B. (1988). *Who is a manager?: An experiential exercise of race, ethnic and gender stereotyping.* Paper presented at the 1988 Eastern Academy of Management meeting Experiential Learning Association.

Carmody, D. (1987, April 23). Columbia report cites racial unrest. *New York Times*, p. B2.

Davis, G., & Watson, G. (1982). *Black life in corporate America.* New York: Random House.

Davis, J. (1978). *Minority and dominant relations.* Arlington Heights, IL: AHM.

Denton, T. (1987). *Bonding and supportive relationships among black professional women.* Unpublished doctoral dissertation, Case Western Reserve University.

Dickens, F., & Dickens, L. (1991). *The black manager: Making it in the corporate world,* rev. ed. New York: American Management Association Amacom Publishing.

Erlanger, S. (1987, December 27). After Howard Beach: A new militancy? *New York Times,* p. E3.

Faegin, J. R. (1987). Changing black Americans to fit a racist system? *Journal of Social Issues, 43*(1), 85-90.

Fernandez, J. (1987). *Survival in the corporate fishbowl.* Lexington, MA: Lexington Books.

Fried, J. (1987, December 11). Howard Beach jury gets case and asks to visit attack scene. *New York Times,* p. 54.

Hai, D. (1984). *Women and men in organizations: Teaching strategies.* Washington, DC: George Washington University, Organizational Behavior Teaching Society.

Harragan, B. (1977). *Games mother never taught you: Corporate gamesmanship for women.* New York: Rawson, Wade.

Hennig, M., & Jardim, A. (1977). *The managerial woman.* Garden City, NY: Doubleday.

Herbert, J. (1986). *An adult development study of black male entrepreneurs.* Unpublished doctoral dissertation, Yale School of Management.

Hill, R. (1980). Black families in the 1970s. In J. D. Williams (Ed.), *The state of black America,* (pp. 29-58). New York: National Urban League.

Hill, R. (1981). The economic status of black Americans. In J. D. Williams (Ed.), *The state of black America,* (pp. 1-59). New York: National Urban League.

James, F. (1988, June 7). More blacks quitting white-run firms. *The Wall Street Journal,* p. 37.

Jelinek, M., & Adler, N. J. (1988). Women: World class managers for global competition. *The Academy of Management Executive, 2*(1), 11-19.

Josefowitz, N. (1980). *Paths to power.* Reading, MA: Addison-Wesley.

Kanter, R. (1977). *Men and women of the corporation.* New York: Basic.

Lorde, A. (1984). *Sister outsider: Essays and speeches.* Freedom, CA: Crossing.

Mercer, J. (1988, February 7). Experience in business vary among blacks. *New Haven Register,* p. B8.

Moraga, C., & Anzaldua, G. (1981). *This bridge called my back.* New York: Kitchen Table. (Nonfiction)

Narvaez, A. (1987, October 8). Jersey city Indian community protests rash of racial attacks. *New York Times,* p. B3.

Nelton, S. (1988, July). Meet your new work force. *Nation's Business,* pp. 14-21.

Pettigrew, T., & Martin, J. (1987). Shaping the organizational context for black American inclusion. *Journal of Special Issues, 43*(19), 41-77.

Porter, L. W., & McKibbin, L. E. (1988). *Management education and development: Drift or thrust into the 21st century?* New York: McGraw-Hill.

Rothman, J. (1977). *Issues in race and ethnic relations.* Ann Arbor: University of Michigan, Peacock.

Shenon, P. (1988, January 25). Black F.B.I. agent's ordeal: Meanness that never let up. *New York Times,* pp. A1, A18.

Shenon, P. (1988, September 11). Hispanic F.B.I. agent's suit reflects a sense of betrayal. *New York Times,* p. 26.

Shipp, E. R. (1987, December 11). No more jury wooing: Lawyers await verdict. *New York Times*, p. B4.

Simpson, J. (1987, April 1). Black college students are viewed as victims of subtle racism. *New York Times*, p. A19.

Steele, S. (1988). I'm black, you're white, who's innocent? Race and power in an era of blame. *Harpers, 276*(1657), 45-53.

Thomas, D. A. (1986). *An intra-organizational analysis of black and white patterns of sponsorship and the dynamics of cross- racial mentoring.* Unpublished doctoral dissertation.

Thomas, D. A., & Alderfer, C. P. (1989). The influence of race and career dynamics: Theory and research on minority career experiences. In M. Arthur, D. T. Hall, & B. Lawrence (Eds.), *Handbook of career theory* (pp. 133-158). London: Cambridge University Press.

Turner, J. (1984). *Oppression: A socio-history of black white relations in America.* Chicago: Nelson-Hall.

Wilkerson, I. (1987, May 6). Asian-Americans outraged over acquittal in civil rights case. *New York Times*, p. A20.

Zeitz, B., & Dusky, L. (1988). *The best companies for women.* New York: Simon & Schuster.

Suggested Readings

Johnston, W., & Packer, A. (1987). *Workforce 2000.* Indianapolis: Hudson Institute.

Morrison, A., White, R., & Ven Velso, E. (1987). *Breaking the glass ceiling.* Reading, MA: Addison-Wesley.

Staff. (1988, June 10). When racism goes to college (Editorial Notebook). *New York Times*, p. A30.

Twenty-Four

Teaching About Diversity
Navigating the Emotional Undercurrents

KATE KIRKHAM
Brigham Young University

Different topics in management and organizational studies—power, motivation, the utility of small groups—generate different but reasonably predictable reactions in class discussions. However, nothing has proven more predictable than the reactions created by introducing race and gender topics into the curriculum. Any aspect (racism, sex role stereotyping, child care) produces emotionally charged statements that seem to ricochet in the discussion.

From my teaching, research, and consulting practice, I have learned that these emotional undercurrents in race and gender related discussions can be charted. Knowing more about the underlying emotions doesn't prevent them from being a part of the classroom but increases the likelihood of learning when and how to surface them in a discussion. This article identifies a source of the emotional intensity and explores diagnostic questions useful in understanding the emotional dimensions of race and gender topics.

Sources of Emotions

Emotional intensity is a part of teaching about race and gender topics in *any learning situation* whether it is the traditional graduate or undergraduate

This chapter originally appeared in *The Organizational Behavior Teaching Review*, Volume 13, Issue 4.

classroom, a corporate training session, or community workshop. In my experience, age, occupation, and education of those present *are not* consistent predictors of how emotional the discussion will be. Neither does the numerical distribution of men, women, and/or racially different individuals in a discussion totally explain the emotions. Although emotional intensity is often associated with a recent racist-sexist incident in the community or organizational lives of the participants, such incidents determine how the emotions will surface and not the underlying presence or absence of emotional tensions in race and gender discussions.

What are the sources of emotions? My colleagues and classroom participants can quickly identify the emotions that come from two clear sources: comments that are perceived as either *advocating* or *resisting* certain core beliefs or experiences. Wanting someone else to change and not wanting to be someone's "change target" do contribute to the ebb and flow of emotions. And my awareness of how those advocating and resisting certain views affects a group discussion has provided some help in effectively navigating race and gender topics. However, more recently, *advocate* and *resistor* have proven to be insufficient labels for the complexity of issues surrounding race and gender.

My work with both student and other groups indicates that the best predictor of emotions underlying a race and/or gender discussion is the criteria participants are using to determine the legitimacy of the topic. Individuals have implicit assumptions as criteria for their view of the legitimacy of race and gender issues in today's society and, therefore, for what is fair for them and others in a discussion. For example, the contributions of an individual who thinks that he or she or the topic are being treated unfairly are predictably going to be emotionally charged. The criteria individuals use for assessing legitimacy are not easily summarized as advocating or resisting change. Ferreting out the core assumptions about legitimacy enables the emotional intensity to be more richly explored for all involved in a discussion.

A brief comparison to other management and organizational topics helps illustrate this relationship between legitimacy and emotional intensity. I find a wide range of student emotional responses to the *dynamics* of political behavior in organizations but universal agreement that it is a legitimate area of study. Leadership is seen as a critical area of legitimate concern for all organizational members, even those who won't be CEOs. However, in many discussions the criteria governing *baseline* legitimacy of a race and gender topic are often not shared by participants in a discussion. What one person thinks is a discussion of how to address a specific racial incident in a company may be for someone else additional evidence that others don't understand the real problems. Having access to this undercurrent of assumptions and strong feelings about the legitimacy of race and gender issues is essential.

Diagnostic Guides

Three basic diagnostic questions enable individuals to surface their underlying assumptions about the legitimacy of race and gender topics and provides us, as instructors, with access to the core emotions that may be present in a discussion.

1. Who really is racist or sexist?
2. What constitutes *tangible* proof of race and gender issues?
3. What is the real problem and how big a problem is it?

Before discussing each of these questions, there are two observations important for the use of the diagnostic questions themselves.

1. Because two students are equally emotionally demonstrative doesn't mean that the *source* of their emotions is similar. And whether a student is relatively quiet or talkative in a classroom isn't the best indicator of his or her ability to articulate either the criteria they are using or emotions associated with it. Both the quiet person who really can clearly articulate issues and the very verbal one who isn't clarifying much are as present in race and gender discussions as in others. But we may make different assumptions about participation when the topic is race and gender.

2. The race and gender of individuals often does make a difference both in how they respond to issues and how they are seen by others. In teaching about diversity, this has meant I must watch for *similarities* for members of a group that accumulate without resorting to stereotypes about individuals because they are a member of a racial or gender group. My experience is that majority group members in the United States, whites and males, frequently have different assumptions underlying their emotional exploration of these three questions than do most members of other groups. I do not expect all racially alike or gender alike individuals to think alike. But there are similarities in the underlying assumptions that members of a racial or gender group bring to a discussion.

One such similarity is that many majority group members do not move quickly or comfortably back and forth between their individual identity and their identity as a member of a racial or gender group in this society. If they do think of themselves as a member of a group, it is often associated with negative emotions: feeling stereotyped or threatened, and so on.

Therefore, majority group members may enter a discussion less prepared to sort out what is being said about the behavior of numbers of whites (or men) as experienced by others and the impact of their own individual behavior. When I am working with minorities and white women they report more familiarity in examining the experiences of the many as well as their own unique and individually based experiences. Most can also articulate both the positive and negative emotions associated with their racial and or gender identity. Assumptions about individual and group identity invoke very different emotions in race and gender discussions.

Who Is Racist or Sexist?

The three questions listed above are linked and will not surface in a neat, orderly way in a discussion, but they can be identified. Surfacing assumptions about who *really* is racist or sexist (in an organization or in society) is of fundamental importance in teaching about diversity. Often student emotions surrounding this question are the touchstone for the other two questions.

When asked to respond to the question of who really is racist and/or sexist, many majority group individuals, in my research and teaching experience, assume, "If I didn't intend something as racist or sexist then it is not racist or sexist." In other words, the general criteria they use in testing for racism or sexism is an overpersonalized one. They believe that personal motive determines the presence of racism or sexism in interactions.

An example of this assumption is present in the pattern of reactions of a majority group member in a graduate organizational behavior course during a discussion of racism and sexism in the workplace. Every comment made by a woman or minority student in the class was responded to by him (as soon as he had a chance) as if they had been directing their comments to him personally, therefore indicting his intentions. He resented this and kept saying so with increasing emotional intensity. With some assistance, he identified the core reason for his reactions. He became aware that he was using what he thought was intended as the only legitimate criteria. If the point someone was making did not fit what he thought was intended in an example, then it was not an example of racism or sexism. Because he was emotionally defending what he thought were personal and unfair accusations, he could not broaden his understanding of racism and sexism. Once he realized that others were using criteria that included intended *and* unintended outcome of behavior, he could better understand their examples.

An additional insight came from the above class discussion and indicates the usefulness of surfacing underlying assumptions that trigger emotions in a discussion. Many of the majority group members, who had been quick to label a minority group member as oversensitive, became more aware of how their own version of oversensitivity was showing up with just as much emotional conviction behind it.

Ironically, the most bigoted or chauvinistic majority group member is sometimes the least likely to overpersonalize in the way I have just described. The class member whose opinions are very entrenched may not be affected at all by a discussion. The more moderate or naive or frustrated students who are more vocal in a discussion can buffer attention to the most opinionated person. In a recent class, one usually talkative student, whose prior comments outside of the class had indicated to some that he had strong stereotypes about women, had not been participating and was finally asked for his reactions to the current discussion of gender issues. He indicated that it had not bothered him at all because he thought it was a waste of time to be discussing these issues in the course anyway. Perhaps this majority group member represents those with the most tenacious personal criteria: I do not intend to examine my views.

The societal context of race and gender issues in this country affects our ability to navigate these underlying emotions in classroom discussions, especially exploring the different assumptions about who really is racist or sexist. In fact, the accessibility of the assumptions is a good barometer of the legitimacy generated by the larger political and economic climate outside the classroom. A decade ago, the most bigoted persons spoke out. Often in defending their views they claimed an absent but interested constituency through expressions such as "lots of us believe" or "this is the way things are supposed to be, we have always . . ." Later, the messages from society conveyed by political and legal means suggested to many that stereotypic views were no longer appropriate. My experience during this time was that majority group members who became more involved with race and gender issues reported in their discussions that the messages had generated either a reluctant awareness that the issues represented changes they would have to learn to live with or a genuine interest but lack of experience or awareness with either racism or sexism.

Teaching about race and gender issues is still affected by the larger societal context. Students of diversity now describe messages from society that support the core assumption by many majority group members that individual intention is a sufficient criteria in determining who or what is racist or sexist. These include (1) statements that represent the view "we've dealt with the civil rights issues"; (2) discrimination cases that require proof of intention and personal discrimination, rather than exist- ence of certain conditions for affected groups; and (3) a decreasing atten- tion in the dominant media to the severity of race and gender group issues, while highlighting the success of individuals. These messages and their role in legitimizing certain assumptions must be explored in a discussion of race and gender issues and the emotional implications surfaced.

What Constitutes Proof?

Majority and minority participants in a discussion also have different assumptions about what constitutes sufficient proof of the existence of discrimination, racism, or sexism. Once participants in a discussion realize that intention is not the only criteria, they can better discern that men and women working in the same organization may experience the *outcome* of company practices differently because of their gender. Also, white and black coworkers may have different perceptions of the affect of behaviors in a meeting. A man may focus on the outcome of one example and fail to find sufficient evidence of sexism, whereas the woman experiences the one example as symptomatic of the experience of being different in a sexist organization.

Individual majority group members do not hear or see in their day-to-day interactions the very examples the minority person offers as proof of the existence of racism or sexism. Certainly majority group members do not pass on stories to each other about what they did to contribute to sexism in their organization. The research on sexual harassment, for example, has recorded that it is a few of the men who do most of the harassing. The problem is that the behaviors of many of the men may not make it obvious who is the one who will later harass. Several men may "enjoy" a sexist joke but only one may continue his enjoyment of sexism by harassing women he works with in the organization. However, the men that allow the joke, all look like potential harassers. The men may individually (i.e., personally) dismiss or tolerate the joking without seeing how it fuels the one or two men who will continue to bring inappropriate sexual conduct into the workplace. The women who hear or hear about the joking may be weary of all those who allowed it. The men who allow joking, language, or inappropriate discussion of women's appearance to occur at one point in time will not be present later when the behavior of other men becomes even more severely sexist.

Participants in race and gender discussions might also assume that only the most severe examples constitute real proof of a problem. So if someone can't produce the "Archie Bunker incident," then those suggesting that racism exists are discounted or accused of exaggerating the issues for today's work force. But it is the accumulated impact of subtle expressions of racism and sexism that is often the most severe "incident."

Majority group members are faced with some additional problems in both generating or hearing several examples that would provide more proof. If a majority group member isn't convinced yet of the existence of a problem of discrimination or managing diversity and more data are offered, those additional data can be experienced as complaining. This is especially true if the person offering the examples is a minority or a woman. The person offering the example ends up getting the attention rather than the example itself: A man says, "I just don't understand" when asked about discrimination in his department; a woman then offers an example or two and he responds, "Is that it?" She offers a few more examples before he says in essence, "If you're so bothered by all this why are you working here?" Even though her response is that she is not personally complaining but attempting to inform him about the ever-present experience of being different, the discussion now shifts to her oversensitivity rather than a discussion of his ability to explore these examples or discuss differences in general.

Not only are these additional data seen as complaining but it is difficult for a majority group member to listen to a series of examples without beginning to feel implicated and, therefore, more emotionally defensive as indicated in the earlier example of how certain assumptions can result in overpersonalizing a discussion of the issues. However, if the majority group members have been prepared for this interaction, they then can hear any number of examples and think, "I don't want to be identified with racism [or sexism], so it is in my self-interest to learn more about it so that my behavior is more nonracist [nonsexist]." This posture invites more dialogue than the retorts such as, "Hey, you can't say that about all whites [or men]" or "You haven't seen me do that." It is important to examine assumptions about what constitutes proof of a problem and differences that may exist for majority and minority group members.

All this is not to say that every example of racism or sexism offered in a discussion is always racist or sexist. Poor communication skills can be perceived as racist, for example, or a man questioning a women's ability to do a job may have nothing to do with her gender. What is evident is that the legitimacy of some of the examples offered as proof are more easily challenged than the behaviors of majority group members as they react to or discuss the examples.

What Really Is the Problem and How Big a Problem Is It?

In addition to the emotion generated by assumptions about one's personal intentions and the proof required, there are often fundamental differences in how the problem is defined. Some people assume that the real problem is the presence or absence of women and minorities. Others may believe that the real problem is the behavior of the different person: not aggressive enough or qualified. Still others assume it is the policies of an organization or its practices that favor one group at the expense of another.

Perhaps the most emotional aspect of defining the problem is in examining the perceptions held by racially different women and men about the magnitude of the problem for today's work force. If the assumptions operating about the definition and magnitude of the problem are not explored, then talking about solutions will deteriorate because suggestions made by some based on one definition will not be viewed as legitimate by someone else. Problem and solution simply will not match.

In some discussions about the definition of the problem, the fundamental assumption will center on who really has the right to define the problem. Defining a problem is a form of power. Difference, diversity, and discrimination are all embedded in power relationships in most organizations. In fact, the core assumptions discussed earlier are often emotionally anchored in one's view of who is in charge and why. Surfacing the criteria individuals are using to define the problem is essential in planning for change.

Classroom Interventions

In teaching about diversity there are many ways to generate examining assumptions of both majority and minority group members—within and between groups. Each of the following ways can make a contribution to the challenge of exploring diversity and navigating the underlying emotions.

Present Agree-Disagree Statements. Give students agree-disagree statements that have a range of ambiguity in them, then provide small group discussion time. Examples of statements that can help surface the legitimacy of issues and the emotions involved are

1. Women are as capable and able as men in organizations to hold upper level management positions.
2. One's race or gender is a part of the first impressions a person makes in an organization.
3. I can identify prejudicial behaviors in others.
4. Current practices in organizations limit advancement for minority women and men.

Assign Student Interviews. Assign students to interview other students who are racially different from and racially similar to the interviewer.

Provide suggestions for questions such as: "What is it like to be X on this campus?" (Change the X to either a race, culture, or gender identity) or "Do you think your race [gender] affects how others interact with you?"

Assist Students in Getting an Historical Perspective. To help students with an historical perspective, first, use readings from different decades, especially those that convey personal experiences from another period. Second, assign or prepare an historical survey of major business journals for illustrations or articles with race or gender implications. It would also be possible to interview individuals from a different generation than those in the class.

Creatively Use the Resources in Different Materials. Present students with a diversity of materials, such as video, news programs, talk shows, and films.

Create Visions of Integrated Society or Organizations. Explore perceptions of how problems are defined, what constitutes proof and perceptions of how committed racially different women and men are to achieving the vision.

Appendix

The following is a bibliography of very useful articles from past volumes of the journal of the Organizational Behavior Teaching Society. As you can see, the articles reach far beyond what may be considered as the traditional field or curriculum of organizational behavior. This list is organized into three sections: key methods and approaches in management education, general course management, and major disciplines in management education. If your local library does not have particular articles listed here that are of interest to you, send for them through the interlibrary loan and copy service that most libraries provide.[1] If your institution's library does not currently subscribe to *The Journal of Management Education* through Sage Publications, see what you can do to encourage its adoption, for this journal will be one of the most valuable acquisitions that your library can make for you and your institution.

A. Key Methods and Approaches in Management Education

COMPETENCY AND SKILL BASED APPROACH

Albanese, R. (1988-1989). Competency-based management education: Three operative and normative issues. *The Organizational Behavior Teaching Review, 14*(1), 16-28.

Bigelow, J. (1983). Teaching action skills: A report from the classroom. *Exchange: The Organizational Behavior Teaching Journal, 8*(2), 28-34.

Bradford, D. L. (1983). Some potential problems with the teaching of managerial competencies. *Exchange: The Organizational Behavior Teaching Journal, 8*(2), 45-49.

Fleming, R. K. (1992). An integrated behavioral approach to transfer of interpersonal leadership skills. *Journal of Management Education, 16*(3), 341-353.

Knippen, J. T. (1988-1989). Teaching management skills. *The Organizational Behavior Teaching Review, 13*(2), 39-46.

EXPERIENTIAL METHOD

Berg, D. N. (1984). Authority and experiential methods. *The Organizational Behavior Teaching Review, 9*(1), 36-41.

House, R. J. (1979). Experiential learning: A sad passing fad? *Exchange: The Organizational Behavior Teaching Journal, 4*(3), 8-12.

Litt, B. (1982). Silent learning . . . four axioms for teaching via experiential methods. *Exchange: The Organizational Behavior Teaching Journal, 7*(1), 5-12.

Molstad, C., & Levy, S. (1987-1988). Developing experiential analogs to cases. *The Organizational Behavior Teaching Review, 12*(2), 28-32.

Sanders, P. (1986-1987). Enthusiasm awareness in experiential learning. *The Organizational Behavior Teaching Review, 11*(4), 21-30.

SIMULATION

Barry, D. (1988-1989). Twincorp: Extensions of the classroom-as-organization model. *The Organizational Behavior Teaching Review, 14*(1), 1-15.

Clawson, J. E., & Pfeifer, P. E. (1989-1990). Global markets. *The Organizational Behavior Teaching Review, 14*(2), 70-82.

Ettinger, J. S. (1982). Courtroom simulation as an approach to teaching organizational behavior. *Exchange: The Organizational Behavior Teaching Journal, 7*(3), 33-36.

Frost, P. J., Barnowe, J. T., & Mitchell, V. F. (1976). Using sequential simulations to teach introductory organizational behavior. *Exchange: The Organizational Behavior Teaching Journal, 2*(2), 15-20.

Greenhalgh, L. (1979). Simulating an on-going organization. *Exchange: The Organizational Behavior Teaching Journal, 4*(3), 23-27.

Oddou, G. R. (1988-1989). Managing organizational realities: An evaluation of a semester-long experiential simulation. *The Organizational Behavior Teaching Review, 13*(2), 47-54.

CASE METHOD

Brown, D., Schermerhorn, J. R. Jr., & Gardner, W. L. (1986-1987). "Planned fading," as a technique for introducing case analysis methods in large lecture classes. *The Organizational Behavior Teaching Review, 11*(4), 31-41.

DuBrin, A. J. (1992). Computer-assisted scenario analysis (CASA): Using word processing to enhance case analysis. *Journal of Management Education, 16*(3), 385-390.

Kellogg, D. M. (1991). Assigning business writing to increase the learning potential of case course. *Journal of Management Education, 15*(1), 19-34.

Klein, N. (1981). The case discussion method revisited: Some questions about student skills. *Exchange: The Organizational Behavior Teaching Journal, 6*(4), 30-32.

Miner, F. C., Jr. (1978). An approach for increasing participation in case discussions. *Exchange: The Organizational Behavior Teaching Journal, 3*(3), 41-42.

Zierden, W. E. (1981). Some thoughts on the case method. *Exchange: The Organizational Behavior Teaching Journal, 6*(4), 19-24.

MEDIA AND COMPUTER APPLICATIONS

Szewczak, E. J., & Sekaran, U. (1987-1988). Introducing personal computer technology in the teaching of organizational behavior courses. *The Organizational Behavior Teaching Review, 12*(1), 74-83.

Weber, R. J. (1976). Using videotape to teach organizational behavior. *Exchange: The Organizational Behavior Teaching Journal, 2*(1), 37-42.

THE USE OF ACADEMIC
AND POPULAR LITERATURE

Bluedorn, A. C. (1979). Winning the race: A report on the use of science fiction in the organizational theory classroom. *Exchange: The Organizational Behavior Teaching Journal, 4*(1), 7-11.

Cowden, A. C. (1989-1990). Mystery novels as organizational context. *The Organizational Behavior Teaching Review, 14*(2), 93-101.

Frost, P. J., & Moore, L. F. (1976). Obtaining organizational reality through the business novel. *Exchange: The Organizational Behavior Teaching Journal, 2*(2), 11-14.

Weick, K. E., & Orton, J. D. (1986-1987). Academic journals in the classroom. *The Organizational Behavior Teaching Review, 11*(2), 27-42. Executive Education

Jelinek, M. (1979). Executives and MBAs in the classroom. *Exchange: The Organizational Behavior Teaching Journal, 4*(4), 26-29.

Jenks, S., & Haskell, J. (1979). Managing Executive Development Programs. *Exchange: The Organizational Behavior Teaching Journal, 4*(4), 30-33.

Lewicki, R. J., & Gabarro, J. J. (1979). Organizational behavior for executives. *Exchange: The Organizational Behavior Teaching Journal, 4*(4), 34-39.

Neilsen, E. H. (1986-1987). Two roles, four realities in the executive classroom. *The Organizational Behavior Teaching Review, 11*(3), 1-15.

Schein, E. H., Beckhard, R., & Driscoll, J. W. (1980). Teaching organizational psychology to middle managers. *Exchange: The Organizational Behavior Teaching Journal, 5*(1), 19-26.

MISCELLANEOUS TECHNIQUES AND APPROACHES

Boje, D. M. (1991). Learning storytelling: Storytelling to learn management skills. *Journal of Management Education, 15*(3), 279-294.

Greenberg, E., & Miller, P. (1991). The player and the professor: Theatrical techniques in teaching. *Journal of Management Education, 15*(4), 428-446.

Koller, M. R. (1988-1989). Humor and education: Are they compatible? *The Organizational Behavior Teaching Review, 13*(2), 1-9.

Lindsay, C. (1992). Learning through emotion: An approach for integrating student and teacher emotions into the classroom. *Journal of Management Education, 16*(1), 25-38.

Odiorne, G. S. (1976). The use of the lecture in management education. *Exchange: The Organizational Behavior Teaching Journal, 2*(3), 7-14.

Posner, B. Z., & Randolph, W. A. (1978). A decision tree approach to decide when to use different pedagogical techniques. *Exchange: The Organizational Behavior Teaching Journal, 3*(2), 6-19.

Sankowsky, D., & Ornstein, S. (1989-1990). A process model of humor: Bringing spam to the classroom. *The Organizational Behavior Teaching Review, 14*(2), 83-92.

Vance, C. M. (1986-1987). Extending academic impact: Teaching students how to teach interpersonal skills to their future subordinates. *The Organizational Behavior Teaching Review, 11*(3), 86-94.

B. General Course Management

GROUP MANAGEMENT

Bowen, D. D. & Jackson, C. N. (1985-1986). Curing those ol' "omigod-not-another-group-class" blues. *The Organizational Behavior Teaching Review, 10*(4), 21-31.

Boyer, E. G., Weiner, J. L., & Diamond, M. P. (1984-1985). Why groups? *The Organizational Behavior Teaching Review,*(4), 3-7.

Lundberg, C. C., & Lundberg, J. (1992). Student team analysis: An experiential task. *Journal of Management Education, 16*(3), 371-373.

Michaelsen, L. K., Watson, W. Cragin, J. P., & Fink, L. D. (1982). Team learning: A potential solution to the problems of large classes. *Exchange: The Organizational Behavior Teaching Journal, 7*(1), 13-22.

Neilsen, E. H. (1977). Applying a group development model to managing a class. *Exchange: The Organizational Behavior Teaching Journal, 2*(4), 9-16.

SELF-MANAGED LEARNING

Akin, G. (1991). Self-directed learning in introductory management. *Journal of Management Education, 15*(3), 295-312.

Allen, B., & Enz, C. A. (1986-1987). Journal writing: Exercises in creative thought and expression. *The Organizational Behavior Teaching Review, 11*(4), 1-14.

Porras, J. I. (1975). Using personal journals in cognitive and experiential courses. *Exchange: The Organizational Behavior Teaching Journal, 1*(2), 30-33.

Woodworth, W. (1979). A self-structured approach to organizational behavior: Toward de-institutionalizing the classroom. *Exchange: The Organizational Behavior Teaching Journal, 4*(3), 13-17.

TESTING, GRADING, AND FEEDBACK

Cullen, T. P. (1988-1989). Improving inter-grader reliability in large classes with multiple sections. *The Organizational Behavior Teaching Review, 13*(1), 32-37.

DiStefano, J. J., & Howell, J. M. (1989-1990). Multiple methods for evaluating management skill development. *The Organizational Behavior Teaching Review, 14*(2), 1-14.

Enz, C. A., Ornstein, S., & Allen, B. (1987-1988). Improving the teaching evalutation process: A report from the classroom. *The Organizational Behavior Teaching Review, 12*(4), 114-123.

Ferris, W. P., & Hess, P. W. (1984-1985). Peer evaluation of student interaction in organizational behavior and other courses. *The Organizational Behavior Teaching Review, 9*(4), 74-82.

Michaelsen, L. K., Cragin, J. P., & Watson, W. E. (1981). Grading and anxiety: A strategy for coping. *Exchange: The Organizational Behavior Teaching Journal, 6*(1), 32-36.

Sleeth, R. G. (1979). Involving students in test construction and correction: Making positive use of true/false ambiguity. *Exchange: The Organizational Behavior Teaching Journal, 4*(3), 44-45.

Waters, J. A., Adler, N. J., Poupart, R., & Hartwick, J. (1983). Assessing managerial skills through a behavioral exam. *Exchange: The Organizational Behavior Teaching Journal, 8*(2), 38-44.

GENDER AND DIVERSITY ISSUES

Betters-Reed, B. L., & Moore, L. L. (1988-1989). Managing diversity in organizations: Professional and curricular issues. *The Organizational Behavior Teaching Review, 13*(4), 25-32.

Burke, R. J., & Weir, T. (1977). Experiences and needs of female college students in administration. *Exchange: The Organizational Behavior Teaching Journal, 2*(4), 33-35.

Clutts, A. M. (1975). Women in organizations: Implications for organizational behavior. *Exchange: The Organizational Behavior Teaching Journal1*(3), 33-37.

Mai-Dalton, R. (1984-1985). Exposing business school students to cultural diversity: Becoming a minority. *The Organizational Behavior Teaching Review, 9*(3), 76-82.

Rizzo, A.-M. (1979). How to succeed without selling out: Teaching career strategies for women in management. *Exchange: The Organizational Behavior Teaching Journal, 4*(1), 16-20.

Rosener, J. B., & Pearce, C. L. (1988-1989). Men and women in organizations: Are future managers exposed to the issues? *The Organizational Behavior Teaching Review, 13*(2), 55-67.

Seashore, E. W. (1976). The new role for white male managers. *Exchange: The Organizational Behavior Teaching Journal, 2*(1), 43-45.

Shallenberger, D. (1991). Invisible minorities: Coming out of the classroom closet. *Journal of Management Education, 15*(3), 325-334.

Sullivan, S. E., & Buttner, E. H. (1992). Changing more than the plumbing: Integrating women and gender differences into management and organizational behavior courses. *Journal of Management Education, 16*(1), 76-89.

Waters, H., Jr. (1988-1989). Making the organizational behavior course relevant to black students. *The Organizational Behavior Teaching Review, 13*(3).

Waters, H., Jr. (1991). Introducing race into the undergraduate organizational behavior course. *Journal of Management Education, 15*(4), 447-464.

GENERAL ISSUES IN COURSE DESIGN AND MANAGEMENT

Harvey, J. B. (1979). Learning not to teach. *Exchange: The Organizational Behavior Teaching Journal, 4*(2), 19-21.

Miner, R. (1992). Reflections on teaching a large class. *Journal of Management Education, 16*(3), 290-302.

Rasmussen, R. V. (1982). Exampling strategies in teaching organizational behavior. *Exchange: The Organizational Behavior Teaching Journal, 7*(4), 26-32.

C. Major Disciplines in Management Education

BUSINESS POLICY AND STRATEGIC MANAGEMENT

Balke, W. M. (1981). The policy learning co-op: Treating the classroom as an organization. *Exchange: The Organizational Behavior Teaching Journal, 6*(2), 27-32.

Jemison, D. B., & Lenz, R. T. (1980). Reframing the business policy course: Alternatives and implications. *Exchange: The Organizational Behavior Teaching Journal, 5*(4), 20-26.

Kraft, K. L., Snodgrass, C. R., & Jauch, L. R. (1986-1987). Teaching strategy from teaching strategy: Lessons for large required courses. *The Organizational Behavior Teaching Review, 11*(1), 50-67.

Learned, K. E. (1991). The use of living cases in teaching business policy. *Journal of Management Education, 15*(1), 113-120.

LeBreton, P. P., & Beard, D. W. (1980). Contributions of organizational behavior to the teaching of business policy and planning. *Exchange: The Organizational Behavior Teaching Journal, 5*(4), 11-19.

Molz, R. (1988-1989). A research simulation for business policy courses. *The Organizational Behavior Teaching Review, 13*(4), 89-102.

Morris, R. J., & Johnson, B. R. Computerization in the strategic management course: Current status and future directions. *Journal of Management Education, 16*(4), 461-478.

Pearce, J. A. II, & Randolph, W. A. (1980). Improving strategy formulation pedagogies by recognizing behavioral aspects. *Exchange: The Organizational Behavior Teaching Journal, 5*(4), 7-10.

Shirley, R. C. (1981). Integrating organizational behavior concepts into the teaching of strategic management. *Exchange: The Organizational Behavior Teaching Journal, 6*(1), 12-16.

Wheatley, W. J. Anthony, W. P., & Maddox, E. N. (1988-1989). Imagery in the business policy course: An experiential pedagogy. *The Organizational Behavior Teaching Review, 13*(2), 28-38.

HUMAN RESOURCE MANAGEMENT AND LABOR RELATIONS

Brown, D. R. (1988-1989). Learning about performance appraisal the experiential way. *The Organizational Behavior Teaching Review, 13*(4), 138-141.

Gardner, W. L., & Larson, L. L. (1987-1988). Practicing management in the classroom: Experience *is* the best teacher. *The Organizational Behavior Teaching Review, 12*(3), 12-23.

Harris, C., & Brown, W. (1989-1990). Careers in context: Multiple perspectives on working lives. *The Organizational Behavior Teaching Review, 14*(2), 15-27.

Huber, V. L., & Lee, T. S. (1987-1988). Job design: The airplane assembly exercise. *The Organizational Behavior Teaching Review, 12*(3), 80-90.

Kotter, J. P., Faux, V. (1975). Self-assessment and career development: A course in the selection and management of a career. *Exchange: The Organizational Behavior Teaching Journal, 1*(3), 19-21.

Linowes, R. G. (1989-1990). Assuming a management perspective: A job interviewing exercise. *The Organizational Behavior Teaching Review, 14*(2), 129-137.

Strauss, G., & Driscoll, J. W. (1980). Collective bargaining games. *Exchange: The Organizational Behavior Teaching Journal, 5*(2), 12-20.

Twomey, D. F. (1987-1988). The evaluation/development dichotomy: Experiencing the dual role of performance appraisal. *The Organizational Behavior Teaching Review, 12*(3), 24-38.

ORGANIZATION DEVELOPMENT

Bartee, E. (1978). Using the school as a laboratory for teaching organization development. *Exchange: The Organizational Behavior Teaching Journal, 3*(4), 26-30.

Lundberg, C. C. (1980). On teaching organization development: Some core instructional issues. *Exchange: The Organizational Behavior Teaching Journal, 5*(2), 21-24.

Neilsen, E. H. (1978). A developmental approach to teaching OD. *Exchange: The Organizational Behavior Teaching Journal, 3*(4), 18-25.

Plovnick, M. S., & Burke, W. W. (1978). Perspectives on teaching OD in an MBA program. *Exchange: The Organizational Behavior Teaching Journal, 3*(4), 8-12.

NEGOTIATION AND BARGAINING

Dworkin, J. B. (1986-1987). The basics of negotiations: A pedagogical note. *The Organizational Behavior Teaching Review, 11*(1), 9-17.

Lewicki, R. L. (1981). Bargaining and negotiation. *Exchange: The Organizational Behavior Teaching Journal, 6*(2), 33-42.

Neale, M. A., Northcraft, G. B., Magliozzi, T., & Bazerman, M. H. (1985-1986). The buyer-seller transaction: A simulation of integrative bargaining in a competitive market. *The Organizational Behavior Teaching Review, 10*(2), 28-38.

INTERNATIONAL MANAGEMENT

Andre, R. (1985-1986). Designing a course in international OB/HRM. *The Organizational Behavior Teaching Review, 10*(2), 48-59.

Balfour, A.(1988-1989). A beginning focus for teaching international human resources administration. *The Organizational Behavior Teaching Review, 13*(2), 79-89.

Easterby-Smith, M. & Boot, R. (1986-1987). Between cultures: Issues in transferring Western management education methods to China. *The Organizational Behavior Teaching Review, 11*(3), 95-103.

Harris, C. (1988-1989). Using short stories to teach international management. *Journal of Management Education, 15*(3), 373-378.

Mendenhall, M. (1988-1989). A painless approach to integrating "international" into OB, HRM, and management courses. The Organizational Behavior Teaching Review, 13(3), 23-37.

Mendenhall, M., & Gale, J. (1987-1988). Teaching about Japanese management practices: A while-feathered arrow. *The Organizational Behavior Teaching Review, 12*(4), 1-11.

Van Buskirk, B. (1991). Five classroom exercises for sensitizing students to aspects of Japanese culture and business practice. *Journal of Management Education, 15*(1), 96-112.

COMMUNICATION SKILLS

Axley, S. R. (1985-1986). Case presentations: Better student performance through bad advice. *The Organizational Behavior Teaching Review, 10*(4), 111-113.

Axley, S. R. (1989-1990). Improving written and oral communication skills through reaction papers. *The Organizational Behavior Teaching Review, 14*(2), 124-128.

Clement, R. W. (1987-1988). Teaching management presentation: A behavior modeling approach. *The Organizational Behavior Teaching Review, 12*(1), 49-59.

Finan, M. C. (1992). Manager and staff: A business communication course goes live! *Journal of Management Education, 16*(4), 479-493.

Golen, S., Lynch, D., Smeltzer, L., Lord, W. J., Jr, Penrose, J. M., & Waltman, J. (1988-1989). An empirically tested communication skills core module for MBA students, with implications for the AACSB. *The Organizational Behavior Teaching Review, 13*(3), 45-58.

Michaelsen, L. K., & Schultheiss, E. E. (1988-1989). Making feedback helpful. The Organizational Behavior Teaching Review, 13(1), 109-113.

Parker, B. (1985-1986). Exercises to improve students' oral presentations. *The Organizational Behavior Teaching Review, 10*(4), 105-107.

Powell, G. N., & Graves, L. M. (1988-1989). Behaving on paper: An exercise on communicating effectively in writing. *The Organizational Behavior Teaching Review, 13*(3), 126-132.

Stewart, L. P., & Lederman, L. C. (1988-1989). The Marble Company: A simulation game for organizational communication and information management. *The Organizational Behavior Teaching Review, 13*(1), 96-105.

BUSINESS ETHICS

Flemming, J. E. (1983). On business ethics. *Exchange: The Organizational Behavior Teaching Journal, 8*(1), 3-9.

Harris, C., & Brown, W. (1988-1989). Teaching business ethics using fiction: A case that failed. *The Organizational Behavior Teaching Review, 13*(1), 38-47.

Jones, T. M. (1988-1989). Ethics education in business: Theoretical considerations. *The Organizational Behavior Teaching Review, 13*(4), 1-18.

King, J. B. (1983). Teaching business ethics. *Exchange: The Organizational Behavior Teaching Journal, 8*(3), 25-32.

Liedtka, J. (1992). Wounded but wiser: Reflections on teaching ethics to MBA students. *Journal of Management Education, 16*(4), 405-416.

Payne, S. L., & Pettingill, B. F., Jr. (1986-1987). Management and values/ethics eduction. *The Organizational Behavior Teaching Review, 11*(1), 18-27.

Note

1. You can also receive a copy of any of the articles listed in this Appendix by writing to the Organizational Behavior Teaching Society Business Office, College of Business Administration, 307 West Brooks, Room 4, University of Oklahoma, Norman, OK 73019-0450.

At the same address you can also obtain a copy of a more comprehensive annotated bibliography of past articles from the journal, which has been compiled by James G. Clawson of the University of Virginia.

About the Editor

Charles M. Vance (Ph.D., Syracuse University) teaches undergraduate and MBA students at Loyola Marymount University in the areas of human resource management and training and development.

As a consultant in training and organization development, he has worked with several companies and nonprofit organizations, including ARCO, the Archdiocese of Los Angeles, American Management Association, U.S. Department of Labor, Arthur Andersen & Company, Borg-Warner Corporation, and the *Los Angeles Times*. He has focused his consulting and research in the United States and abroad on the design and management of human resources and learning systems to enhance organizational performance.

Vance has published widely in such journals as *Training and Development Journal, Human Relations, Management International Review, Journal of Management Education, Management Development Journal, Human Resource Development Quarterly, Journal of Management Inquiry,* and *Journal of Organization Change Management.*

Established in 1974, the Organizational Behavior Teaching Society (OBTS) is an international association of teachers, consultants, trainers, facilitators, and administrators concerned with improving the teaching and learning of management and organizational behavior.

In addition to a newsletter, quarterly updates, and information on management education conferences (including the annual Organizational Behavior Teaching Conference), OBTS members receive the *Journal of Management Education* as part of their membership package.

To receive the *Journal of Management Education* you may either subscribe through Sage Publications or join the Organizational Behavior Teaching Society.

For information on Society membership or to obtain copies of past journal articles, please contact:

OBTS Business Office
College of Business Administration
307 West Brooks, Room 4
University of Oklahoma
Norman, OK 73019-0450
(405) 325-2931

For journal subscription information only, please contact:

Sage Publications, Inc.
Journals Marketing Department
2455 Teller Road
Newbury Park, CA 91320
(805) 499-0721